MANATEE WINTER

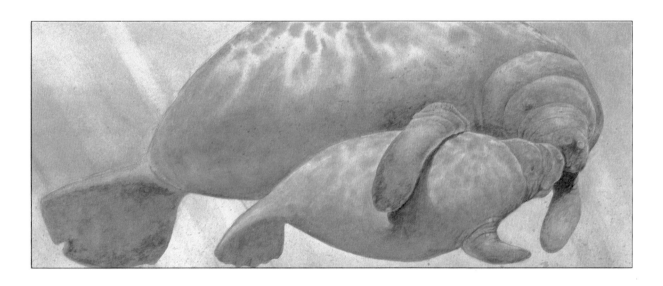

by Kathleen Weidner Zoehfeld   Illustrated by Steven James Petruccio

Soundprints
Where Children Discover Nature

For Geoffrey
—K.Z.

For Marie and Albert Petruccio,
my mom and dad, with my love for theirs
—S.P.

Text copyright © 1994 Kathleen Weidner Zoehfeld.
Illustration copyright © 1994 Steven James Petruccio.
Book copyright © 1994 Trudy Corporation and the Smithsonian Institution.
Reprinted by permission of Soundprints, A Division of Trudy Corporation. All rights reserved.

Soundprints is a Division of Trudy Management Corporation, Norwalk, Connecticut.

Book Design: Shields & Partners, Westport, CT

First Edition
10 9 8 7 6 5 4 3
Printed in the U.S.A.

Acknowledgements:
 Our very special thanks to Dr. Charles Handley of the department of vertebrate zoology at the
Smithsonian's National Museum of Natural History for his curatorial review.

Library of Congress Cataloging-in-Publication Data

Zoehfeld, Kathleen Weidner.

Manatee winter / by Kathleen Weidner Zoehfeld; illustrated by Steven James Petruccio.
        p.   cm.
Summary: A mother manatee and her little calf travel from the Gulf of Mexico through
dangerous water full of speeding boats.
1. Manatees—Juvenile fiction. [1. Manatees—Fiction.]
I. Petruccio, Steven, ill. II. Title.
        PZ10.3.Z695Man 1994   94-158
        [E]—dc20   CIP
                                                               AC

Prologue

There are only about 1800 West Indian manatees left in North America, and they are listed as an endangered species. Living mainly around the coast of Florida in estuaries and bays and in Florida rivers, these curious and gentle creatures have no natural enemies. Once hunted for their meat and hides, today manatees are protected by law from human hunters and poachers. However, many manatees are killed accidentally every year in collisions with speeding boats, in spite of boating regulations in some areas where manatees gather. Also, as new houses and businesses are built along the coastline and near the riverbanks, the seagrasses the manatees feed on are often destroyed.

As more and more people come to live and play along the Florida coast, manatee lives are threatened. Now only the care and concern of people can save the manatee from extinction.

This book is about one West Indian manatee and her little calf.

A cold November wind blows, chilling the north-west coast of Florida and stirring up the waters of the Gulf of Mexico.

Underwater, a huge gray manatee paddles lazily. Her six-month-old calf swims by her side.

Below them, a tuft of seagrass sways invitingly, and Mother manatee stops to browse. Little Calf nibbles and waits.

Mother rises to the surface, and Little Calf follows. They reach their noses up above the choppy waves to take a breath.

Mother is alarmed by the cold air on her nose. Soon the water will be getting colder, too. She must get her calf to warmer waters. No manatee can endure the winter chill of the Gulf. For a calf, the cold is especially dangerous.

Mother follows the coastline south for several miles.
She and Little Calf swim steadily until they approach
the mouth of a river Mother knows well. She has spent
many winters basking in the waters there —
near the warm spring that wells up from the
riverbottom, at the place where the
river begins.

As they turn up the river, Little Calf nuzzles Mother and squeaks with hunger. She relaxes and lets him nurse and rest. The safety of warm spring water is not far away now.

Then, as Mother dozes, Little Calf wanders off. He begins to nibble at some water-weeds near the riverbank.

Suddenly — BROOOOM! — he hears a sharp roar overhead. A dark shadow darts past. He screams in fear.

Mother squeals for him to come to her side — down on the riverbottom.

Just a little way up the river, the dark form slows and then stops. It is a boat, dropping anchor. All is quiet.

Slowly and carefully, they swim over to investigate — nuzzling and rubbing the boat with their muzzles.

Tap, tap, tap — thump, thump — the boat makes a strange noise. Startled, Mother stops their exploration. She leads Little Calf away, as fast as their big tails can take them. Besides, now even the river-water feels chilly. Mother must get her calf to the warm spring.

But the river is busy with boats, zooming here and there. She leads Little Calf through the maze of activity.

BROOOOOM! A boat comes up behind them. Mother screams to Little Calf, and they dive, thrashing their tails and churning the water into foam.

Mother reaches the bottom, safe from the cutting blades of the boat's propellers. Mud clouds the water around her. She peers through the murk.

Little Calf has disappeared!

She squeaks for him frantically. But the roar of the motorboat drowns out her call.

Lost and confused, Little Calf looks for a place to hide. He spots a dense clump of water-weeds and plunges in, head first.

But he cannot hide in the weeds for long. He must get to the surface for a breath of air. As he works his way up through the weeds, thick stems wind around his flippers and hold him fast.

Squeak, squeak! He calls for his mother.

Mother hears his squeak in the distance and follows his call.

She can barely see him, struggling in the knot of weeds. She swims closer and nudges him. Encouraged, he wiggles harder, pulling himself through the tangle of stems.

She guides him to the surface for a breath. They press on upriver, Little Calf clinging close by Mother's side.

When they finally arrive at the spring, the sun is setting, and the air is growing colder. Mother lets herself sink down to the warm, sandy bottom. Little Calf settles comfortably on her tail. They close their tiny eyes and snooze for a while, basking in the spring's warmth.

Every few minutes, they bob up to the surface to breathe. They are tired from their long swim, and the air feels so cold that they huddle near the warm spring all night.

Early next morning, bright rays of sunshine shimmer through the clear blue-green waters. One by one, other manatees have come from far and wide to warm themselves in the waters of the spring.

Little Calf follows Mother through the small crowd, as she walks with her flippers along the bottom.

Soon he notices some other calves who have just arrived. Living alone with his mother all summer in the vast Gulf-coast waters, he has never seen another young manatee before.

He bumps a year-old calf with his nose, curious to see what the little manatee will do. They nibble each others' backs in a friendly way. Then they tumble and play.

While Little Calf glides upside down near the bottom, an old bull wakes up and stretches. His big tail swings up and thumps Little Calf by accident.

Little Calf squeals in surprise. Mother swims over and gently nudges Little Calf away from the sleepy bull.

Little Calf and his mother kiss and hug. Together they cruise away, exploring every corner of their winter home, always looking for more good plants to eat.

Throughout the cold winter, Mother and Little Calf will remain near the spring. On sunny days, they may venture downriver in search of seagrasses. But they never stay away long from the warmth and safety of the spring.

About the Manatee

Manatees are mammals that spend all their lives in water. They are quite unusual in that they thrive in both fresh and salt water. Like all mammals, manatees are warm-blooded and breathe air. They are among the world's larger mammals, some growing to be as big as 13 feet long and weighing about 1300 pounds. Individual manatees may live as long as 30 years.

In the warm summer months, some manatees travel as far north as Virginia or as far west as Louisiana, but, wherever they go, the water they swim in must be warm for them to survive. As winter comes, the manatees return south and swim up many of Florida's shallow rivers and waterways in search of warmer waters, where they congregate in small groups.

For more information about manatees or manatee adoptions, please contact the Save the Manatee Club, 500 North Maitland Avenue, Maitland, Florida, 32751, or call 1-800-432-5646.

Glossary

bull: An adult male manatee.

coastline: The boundary line that is formed where the land meets the sea.

gulf: A large area of ocean surrounded on three sides by land.

river: A large natural stream of fresh water.

seagrass: Any of a variety of grasses, such as turtle grass, manatee grass and star grass, that grow underwater.

spring: A source of water coming from underground. Spring water can be warmed by the natural heat deep within the earth's crust.

water-weeds: Any of a variety of aquatic plants.

Points of Interest in this Book

pp. 4-5, 18-19, 20-21, 24-25 seagrass.

pp. 6-7, 10-11, 20-21, 24-25 striped mullet.

pp. 12-13, 20-21 red mangrove roots.

pp. 20-21 bay scallops.

pp. 22-23 egret, red mangrove trees.

A BANNER YEAR AT INDIANA

By BOB HAMMEL

The Herald-Times · Indiana University Press

**Other publications by Bob Hammel
and The Herald-Times:**

Books:
NCAA All the Way
The Champs
Beyond the Brink with Indiana

Magazines:
Bob Hammel's Indiana Basketball

For more information on these publications or daily editions of The
Herald-Times newspaper call 800-422-0070 or write to:

The Herald-Times, Inc.
c/o Basketball Publications Dept.
P.O. Box 909
Bloomington, IN 47402-0909

Manufactured in the United States of America

ISBN 0-253-32687-7

A BANNER YEAR AT INDIANA

By BOB HAMMEL

Acknowledgments

Editor John Harrell

Art Director Steve Snyder

Art Assistance Stewart Moon

Photography Editor David Snodgress

Photography Staff Kent Phillips, Sam Riche, Tom Weis, John Terhune

Editorial Assistance Allan Murphy

Production John Matson

Graphic Arts Dan Wagoner, Glen Workman

Project Director Michael L. Hartman

General Manager Michael Hefron

'We spanked them pretty good'

Bob Knight, with a 1989 recruiting class touted as the best in the nation, saw his problem early. 'There are a lot of talented players here . . . We have to get them to understand that there is a tremendous difference between playing in high school and playing here . . . We're trying to get these guys to play in a zone beyond what they're used to playing in.'

Whether this group is any good or not will not be decided in 1990. It will be decided in 1993. Then we'll know.

— Bob Knight, 1989

Oct. 15, 1989, was a Sunday, the day that seven teenagers in Bloomington, Ind., had awaited for . . .

For how long indeed?

When *did* the tension, the excitement, the aura and the unrealistic expectations start to build among and around the players designated to carry Indiana University's basketball hopes for the next four years?

More than a year before, it certainly was under way. On July 6, 1988, Greg Graham remembers, he announced that he would go to Indiana, his senior year at Warren Central still ahead of him. "I was the second one to commit," he said. "Chris (Lawson) was the first."

Those were two tasty tidbits to whet the insatiable appetites of Indiana basketball's recruiting freaks. All the college basketball world has them: the devoted fans who would never admit it but fret more over who might be coming to play at IU some day than over the ones who are playing at that moment. This was a dream recruiting year for IU's version of those, because after home boy Lawson of Bloomington South announced his commitment just after his junior season ended (March 25), Graham followed in three months, and . . .

"I went away for a while," Graham said, "and I came back and found somebody else had committed. Then it was like a chain reaction." It was Pat Graham on July 19, Calbert Cheaney Sept. 1, Chris Reynolds Oct. 20.

"It was a nice feeling – like, *Wow!* What a team we're going to have,' " Greg Graham said. "To commit to somebody and then to find out you're getting the top players in the state – plus Chris (Reynolds, of Peoria, Ill.) and Lawrence (Funderburke, of Columbus, Ohio)."

Funderburke announced just after New Year's but toyed with the signing right up through the April signing period. In the meantime, sophomore Jay Edwards had been named Big Ten Player of the Year for leading Indiana to a surprise conference championship, and Edwards dropped his own surprise by entering the NBA draft. That opened a scholarship that closed quickly: Hoosier coach Bob Knight offered it to Todd Leary, who snapped it up.

When Funderburke announced, the buzz started: best recruiting class ever.

Knight was never hype-notized. In this fall of 1989, he told his team, "The magazines that have been talking about what a great group of freshmen we have will push another group next year . . . and they're already pushing groups that have been signed this year." By that time, North Carolina was putting together its group that replaced Indiana as "the

His freshman year was one long coming-out party for Calbert Cheaney.

'As a little kid, I just dreamed of playing college basketball. I never knew what offers I might get. But I always liked Indiana, and to sign with them and play with them – it's a good feeling.'

Pat Graham

best recruiting class ever." And the year after that, Michigan's recruits retired the trophy – for a while.

But this was Oct. 15, 1989, and the seven were about to participate in their first college basketball practice.

They had met and played with and against their older teammates, of course. "I was surprised," Leary admitted at the time. "I thought with everyone talking about the class so much, they might resent us. But they've been nice."

The rookies weren't yet widely known on campus. "There's a few (students) who know you," Greg Graham said. "You know they have the feeling you're some kind of athlete. You get that look."

Graham is a face-reader. A good one. He knew those older players were waiting for this day, too, curious to see these highly touted kids with the pressure on. "Sometimes you can see little gleams of it," Graham said. " 'They're going to come in here and try to take our positions.' "

Pat Graham tried to keep things in perspective.

"They started talking about us being the best ever – silly things like us winning three national championships," he said. "It's a great feeling, but with the pressures, sometimes it might not be worth it. I'd rather go in with the best than not have the best.

"I don't think anyone has been overrated. Some of us may not have the greatest athletic ability, but everything written about us always says that. And Calbert and Chris are just great athletes, and quick.

"Most of us, being from Indiana, have dreamed of going to Indiana. We all have the same thing in our heads: we want to work hard and try to win a national championship.

"As a little kid, I just dreamed of playing college basketball. I never knew what offers I might get. But I always liked Indiana, and to sign with them and play with them – it's a good feeling."

Cheaney had come in less touted than most of his classmates, because he had lost the critical weeks of his senior year – from mid-February on – to a broken foot. He admitted to a tiny self-doubt or two, but mainly he had come in wondering about his new teammates. "I really hadn't played against some of them. I was a little curious about how good they are.

"It's fun playing with them. They're good guys to be around – down-to-earth, like I am. They don't think much about themselves."

The key reason all of them were together, Cheaney said, "was Coach Knight – the best coach in the country, in my opinion. And this is a good school academically. That's the reason I came. I didn't come because a lot of good players were coming. I came for my own benefit.

"But it's great that I'm playing with them."

That Sunday morning, even the best of them were having some doubts. Greg Graham admitted his had started in the euphoria of all those announcements the year before. "There's a little bit of fear, wondering how you compare with them and how they play and actually where you fit in," he said. "But once you get out on the floor with them, it's not about proving yourself, it's going out and playing your game."

Greg Graham had a poet's feel for the life he was entering.

Those pick-up games had been on the same court, in the same spacious arena, where this first practice would be. He had even played there before. The previous spring, most of the recruits – all but Cheaney, still out with the foot injury, and augmented by some underclassmen: juniors Damon Bailey of Bedford North Lawrence and Eric Montross, Leary's teammate on the state champion Lawrence North team, and a good-looking young colt of a player, sophomore Alan Henderson of Brebeuf in Indianapolis – had played together on an AAU team that swamped the national junior team from the Soviet Union before a huge Assembly Hall crowd. "That was just a little mini-basketball game, compared to when you're wearing an Indiana uniform," Pat Graham had said. "It was a big thing, just to look at all the fans and see the support we do have in the state and know it will even be bigger. It was real loud. And playing the Russians isn't anything like playing Purdue or Kentucky."

Sure, Greg Graham remembered the roar of that night well. But he also remembered a day when he slipped into Assembly Hall when it was dark, and there wasn't another soul around.

"The place is empty," he said, recreating the scene. "You walk in there . . . and it's like you can actually hear the hysteria.

"It's still *there*. You can hear the fans hollering . . . "

And your eyes go to those banners that celebrate the best of Indiana's basketball years. "Oh, they do," Graham said.

"I'd like to add a couple more."

Chris Reynolds (left) and Calbert Cheaney (right) had barely turned 18 and Matt Nover 19, and their frames show their youth as they close in on Wichita State center Lance Kroll in a 75-54 Hoosier Classic victory for the Hoosiers. The Indianapolis tournament brought rookie Cheaney his first collegiate MVP award.

For freshman Greg Graham, taking a pounding from Notre Dame's Keith Robinson, Assembly Hall's fabled banners were among the daily reminders of Indiana's basketball tradition. "I'd like to add a couple more," he said.

And at last it was afternoon and time to go to practice.

The rookies always get duly warned from upperclassmen about what to expect on opening day. You'll learn a whole new level of concentration, they're warned. You'll be dead tired when that first practice is halfway over – partly because you're so nervous and partly because you really never worked quite like that: so intensely, so focused, so hard. You'll . . .

Truth doesn't always constrain those advance horror stories. Part of the fun of being an Indiana basketball upperclassman is telling tales to the newcomers about what to expect.

Reynolds had been there Oct. 15, 1988, when he was making his final visit: to Duke, to Michigan, and now to Indiana. He saw that Hoosier team put in an afternoon of emphasis on fundamentals: one-on-one, two-on-two, three-on-three; created situations, focusing the instruction on one tiny, basic element of the Knight game, of The Game. If there was any five-on-five that first day, it was incidental to the emphasis on learning the way things should be done, starting with the most basic of teachings.

That opening day a year before hadn't properly prepared Reynolds for *his* opening day. It was unlike any before or since in the Knight era.

It began with a game. Game-opening tap, officials, scoreboard and clock, everything.

And the matchup wasn't happenstance. Six against seven. The six holdovers on one side, the touted seven freshmen on the other.

The freshmen from Indiana knew those holdovers well. They knew sophomore Eric Anderson had been Big Ten Freshman of the Year for that championship team the year before. They knew Lyndon Jones had been the leader of three straight state champions at Marion, and that at Indiana Jones had worked his way into a three-guard lineup that had had late-season success, both his freshman and sophomore years.

Down deep, though, they hadn't been overly impressed with the other four: Mark Robinson, Jeff Oliphant, Jamal Meeks and

Matt Nover. But the rookies already had learned some things in pick-up games.

"They're so much better than you thought when you saw them on TV)," Greg Graham said. "You play with these guys, and they're a *lot* better."

Knight gave the rookies their chance. He played them together against the returnees. It was a blowout.

Veterans 84, Freshmen 65.

Knight hadn't had to say one word to get the rookies' attention. They saw, they felt, how the Indiana system works. *They* were the ones suddenly having to find their way through screens, to get a shot when their original move got them past their defender but suddenly that guy had a helper. Every time. "We got the message," Cheaney said.

For a few early moments, it had seemed Knight might have gambled and lost. The freshmen made some plays, hit some shots, and led much of the first half. They were down 39-33 at halftime. Opening the second half, the veterans executed that offense like it was mid-February. They ran off 12 points in a row and kept the rookies buried the rest of the way. "We spanked them pretty good," said Nover, whose red-shirt year put him with the upperclassmen. "I think we really surprised them. It was a splash of cold water in their face."

The next day, practice *really* began.

Knight went through those next few weeks as curious as anyone outside Assembly Hall's walls. He had a far more realistic idea about what to expect, and shared it in some pre-season speaking appearances.

"We have a collection of kids that have been able to drive around people, shoot over people, jump above people, knock people out of the way," he said.

"That's all stopped now. There's a distinct equality physically from this point on, with the players that they're going to be playing against.

"There are a lot of talented players here, most of whom have never played college basketball, and all of whom think that they are here to singularly raise the standard of Indiana basketball. Little do they know that there have been some pretty good players precede them and some teams that have been pretty good, going back decades.

"We have to get them to understand that there is a tremendous difference between playing in high school and playing here. Each knows how to play basketball, at his speed.

"In athletics, in any sport, among the coach's primary objectives has to be getting kids to reach a plateau beyond their comfort zones.

"The difference in expended effort can then make up for a lot of things: experience, size, strength – a lot of things. We're trying to get these guys to play in a zone beyond what they're used to playing in."

It didn't happen immediately.

Two of the rookies, Cheaney and Funderburke, started in the season opener, the first left-handed players of the Knight era at IU. Cheaney gave a quick glimpse of what was to come: he took 11 shots and hit nine, leading both teams with 20 points in a 77-66 victory over Miami of Ohio.

Three nights later, the opposition was Kent State, and Greg Graham scored 24 points in a 79-68 victory. Then it was the Hoosier Dome and a matchup with Kentucky, under a new coach: Rick Pitino. Pat Graham was the freshman *du jour*, coming off the bench to drill three 3s and rally the Hoosiers to a 71-69 victory.

'There are a lot of talented players here, most of whom have never played college basketball, and all of whom think that they are here to singularly raise the standard of Indiana basketball. Little do they know that there have been some pretty good players precede them and some teams that have been pretty good, going back decades.'

Bob Knight

Chris Reynolds got his first start against Notre Dame and scored 14 points in an 81-72 Hoosier victory. An interesting combination opened the game that night: Cheaney, Funderburke and Reynolds 18, Anderson and Greg Graham 19. The starters' average age that night was 18.8. No doubt there were high school teams older.

The Hoosiers moved into the Indiana Classic and clouted South Alabama, 96-67, and Long Beach State, 92-75.

Funderburke didn't start either night, but he came off the bench in the championship game to score 26 points and make all-tournament. Six days later, on his 19th birthday, the Hoosiers flew to El Paso, Tex. – without him. Upbraided for his play in practice the day before, Funderburke – his first-semester finals over that day – had quit the team.

The Hoosiers passed their toughest pre-conference test that weekend. Texas-El Paso, well schooled as always under coach Don Haskins and backed by a full house, came at the young Hoosiers hard. Down the stretch, Indiana met the Cheaney it was to ride the next four years. Cheaney slashed down the baseline for repeated baskets, scored 22 points, and Indiana won, 69-66. The rumblings over the Funderburke departure had just begun – a messy transfer that delayed everything for a year and kept popping into the headlines intermittently throughout that period before he landed back at home and resumed his career at Ohio State. But the Hoosiers kept winning, big: 115-66 over Iowa State, 75-54 over Wichita State and 94-66 over Texas A&M to win the Hoosier Classic at Indianapolis and finish their pre-Big Ten "season" 10-0, which only three previous Knight teams had done. Each – in 1974-75, 1975-76 and 1982-83 – had gone on to win the Big Ten championship.

This group (1) lost its league opener at Ohio State, 69-67; (2) stumbled to an 8-10 league finish but became the only Big Ten team so far to get an NCAA tournament invitation with a sub-.500 league record – thanks to that 10-0 takeoff, and (3) departed the NCAA in minimum time, beaten 65-63 by California in the opening round at Hartford.

Cheaney, Nover, Anderson, Greg Graham and Meeks started that tournament game – two sophomores, a redshirt freshman, and two freshmen, their average age on the last night of their season 18.97. The five Michigan freshmen when they stepped on the court for the 1992 national championship game averaged 19.00.

And now it's 1993. As Knight said way back up the trail for those freshmen of 1989-90, it has been decided whether they were any good.

They were.

Nine banners hang from on high at Assembly Hall. Five at one end each mark a national championship (won in 1940, 1953, 1976, 1981 and 1987. At the opposite end of the court, four banners (red, with white printing) celebrate something special in a non-championship season: 1973, when the first Indiana team that used Assembly Hall as its base made it to the NCAA Final Four; 1975, when perhaps the best of Knight's 22 Indiana teams finished its schedule undefeated and No. 1-ranked (the

In 1993, the Bob Knight verdict on his once-touted freshmen came in: 'They were kids who played themselves into a spot that really will be a great thing in the history of Indiana basketball.'

feats noted on the banner) but – hampered by an injury to its best player – lost out in the tournament quarterfinals; 1979, when the Hoosiers won the school's only National Invitation Tournament championship, and 1983, when Indiana won the Big Ten championship.

The 1983 championship is just one of 19 Big Ten titles won by Indiana teams, one of now 11 won by Knight's teams. That one 1983 title has banner recognition because of its emotional finish: another injury to a star, a three-game finish at home against three teams contending for the championship. Minus the star (Ted Kitchel) but spurred by impassioned home-arena support, Indiana won all three games and swept to the championship. On the night the championship was won, Knight promised that title would get its banner, as a tribute to that special fan support.

In '93, it all happened again. The Hoosiers, as in 1975, finished the season No. 1-ranked nationally. As in both '75 and '83, they took a major hit down the homestretch – a knee injury took out leading rebounder and No. 3 scorer Alan Henderson. They continued to win and finished with a 17-1 record that was the best by a Big Ten team in 17 years. They lost at the same point the '75 team did, on the doorstep to the Final Four, and like the '75 team never lost their coach's admiration.

In the minutes after their season ended with a loss to Kansas, Knight said, "I'm incredibly pleased to have had a chance to have coached these kids. I think they have left a real impression on Indiana basketball. We really did about everything that was available to us in this season but get on to the next step (the Final Four).

"I'd give anything for these four seniors if I could have figured out a little better plan to get us there. We just weren't able to make it.

"But they were kids I think who played themselves into a spot that really will be a great thing in the history of Indiana basketball."

Their spot will be *the* spot at Assembly Hall: representation in the array of banners. It was that special a year at Indiana.

Actually, theirs will be the 11th banner at The Hall. Ordered along with it was one marking the 1992 march to the Final Four. Both will be up when the 1993-94 Hoosiers begin play.

Fulfilled – in not quite the way envisioned but as a significant honor, nonetheless – is the wish freshman Greg Graham made out loud, before his first practice or game in Assembly Hall, when he thought of those hallowed banners and said:

"I'd like to add a couple more."

The muscles and the records came later, but even as a freshman, Calbert Cheaney jumped out.

CHAPTER 1

If you can make it there...

If Calbert Cheaney was a little apprehensive entering his final collegiate season, who could blame him? Cheaney's basketball history was a teaser. Great things seemed out there in front of him as he approached his senior year, but they had been there before. There was his senior year four years earlier at Evansville Harrison High ...

Young Calbert Cheaney hadn't grown up with basketball grandeur as a dream. Very early, he recalls, "My dad got me started. I took to the game as soon as I started playing it." But that was true of all games for little Calbert. As a boy, he was a sprinter and a long jumper in track, then in high school, city high hurdles champion as a junior, qualifying for the state meet in both the high and low hurdles. In Little League baseball, "I played first base, pitcher – just about every position." At the same age, he was a running back on his Optimist League football team. "That was fun. I used to score a lot." He didn't play any more football, though in high school, "The coach wanted me to be quarterback. The only time I had ever thrown a football was in touch football.

"I liked baseball best. I was all right in basketball. When we'd go play street ball, I definitely never stood out. There were always some players who were better than me in the neighborhood."

Dirkk Searles, from that neighborhood, wound up being the leader of the George Washington team that gave Michigan a fierce battle in the Sweet 16 this year. Andy Elkins of Evansville's Midwestern Collegiate Conference champions was there, too. "We went to the same middle school," Cheaney said. "Then we separated – they went to Bosse and I went to Harrison. I was two or three houses away from the Bosse district." Washington Middle School in Evansville remembered and honored the three at a special gym-dedication ceremony this year.

For Calbert Cheaney, celebrating with teammate Todd Leary, the drive to College Player of the Year began with a performance the basketball-watching nation saw as Indiana won the Pre-Season NIT in Madison Square Garden.

As a freshman, Cheaney "just played freshman ball. I got up to the reserve team at the end of the year but I didn't play much." Jerrill Vandeventer came in as the new coach the next season. As the freshman coach at Boonville, Vandeventer had seen the lean left-handed Cheaney in action. "He called me in his office one day and said, 'Cal, you have a chance to be a Division I basketball player. You have the talent and skill.'

"It kinda shocked me. I just thought I was going to play high school ball and that was it. I started working on my game right then.

"I was second-team or third-team all-city that year. My junior year was better, but not that good."

It was good enough that the colleges started to check him out. In February of Cheaney's junior season, Bob Knight flew to Evansville, met with former assistant Jim Crews, who had his own program going well at the University of Evansville by then, and the two went to see Harrison play Jasper.

Against Seton Hall, Bob Knight called Calbert Cheaney's play 'great . . . and I use that word great sparingly'

"I didn't know Coach was coming until just before the game," Cheaney said. "The reserve game went into quadruple overtime. While we were waiting for it to get over, I saw him standing in the hallway."

Cheaney and Harrison had a horrid night. Knight left in the third quarter, Harrison already hopelessly down to a mediocre Jasper team, and Harrison was having a better night than its junior star. "That was one of the worst shooting nights I ever had," Cheaney said. "Coach says I shot 6-for-31. I've seen the stat sheet. It was 8-for-25.

"It wasn't very good."

The same season, Knight checked out junior Pat Graham at Floyd Central, and Graham had an awful shooting night. Yes, Graham admitted later, knowing Knight was watching did have an effect. The more shots he missed, the tinier the basket seemed to get. Cheaney understood. "It got *really* small," he laughed.

But he insisted that he really didn't feel Knight's presence affected him in the Jasper game. "The shots that I put up were pretty good. It would be different if I was putting up a shot and the thing went – boink! Brick, brick, brick. They just didn't go in."

The word filtered back to Evansville that Indiana probably wouldn't be recruiting Cheaney.

Still, Cheaney said, Hoosier assistant coach Ron Felling "kept in touch. We went to Lexington for an AAU tournament that summer and I played pretty well down there."

It was after that tourney that Knight, in a staff meeting, asked a routine question about who his aides had seen. "I know you weren't very impressed with him," Felling said, "but the best player out there is Calbert Cheaney."

"Well, then," Knight said, "let's get *on* him." In October, Cheaney announced he was going to Indiana.

That cleared the way for focusing on a big senior season.

Harrison, one of Evansville's consistent powers of the '60s, '70s and '80s, had never won a sectional tournament, the first round of the four-week state tournament. The pieces were in place to change that drastically. "Oh, yeah, definitely," Cheaney said. "We had a legitimate shot to win the state championship." Harrison was 15-0, No. 3-ranked in the state, and Cheaney was averaging just under 23 points a game when the Warriors played a big game at No. 1 Terre Haute South – which had a great athlete of its own: robust 6-6 Tony McGee, a 1993 Rose Bowl star for Michigan and a third-round NFL draftee as a tight end. Cheaney and Harrison exploded out of the gate that night. After a quarter, Harrison had 14 points and most of them were Cheaney's.

"At the end of the quarter, I put up a shot from the left side, and I just came down wrong on my foot," Cheaney said. "It turned over and snapped. I fell to the floor. I said, 'It's not really broken.' I tried to get up and walk, and I couldn't, it was that bad. I knew something was really wrong.

"I was stupid. I tried to come back and play. I went up and down the floor and just couldn't."

Postgame x-rays confirmed a fractured fifth metatarsal, requiring surgery that meant his high school career was over. Harrison didn't win its sectional. "Other people have forgotten that year," Vandeventer said. "I still think about it every day and every night."

Cheaney also was knocked out of the summer all-star series between Indiana and Kentucky and most of the summer AAU play. That made him the least visible of the seven freshmen who came in together that fall in Bloomington.

It started a string of near-misses for Cheaney.

His freshman year at Indiana, the team struggled but Cheaney was outstanding.

Jimmy Jackson of Ohio State was graded just a little better and beat him out as Big Ten Freshman of the Year.

As a sophomore, Cheaney became one of the Big Ten's top stars. He was having a brilliant day on national television at Columbus, Ohio, in February, leading Indiana's young team toward an apparent victory over Jackson and Ohio State. With less than a minute to go and Indiana leading by 3, Cheaney held the ball near center court, running the 45-second shot clock down. When he started a one-on-one move to try to add to the margin with a basket or free throws, he had the ball stripped away – and in instinctive reaction reached out to reclaim it and fouled: his fifth. Ohio State came back to tie, then win in the second overtime to complete a season sweep over the Hoosiers. The teams wound up as league co-champions, but Jackson, who had a career-high 31 points in that double-overtime classic widely hailed as the year's best college game, beat out Cheaney as the Big Ten MVP.

Cheaney's junior season wasn't as good as his sophomore year. It began with a national TV game against UCLA, in the pre-season Tipoff Classic at Springfield, Mass., benefiting the Basketball Hall of Fame. Shut down by Gerald Madkins of UCLA, Cheaney scored eight points, his collegiate low, and UCLA won easily, 87-72.

That started a rocky pre-Big Ten stretch for Cheaney which included the only two times in his 132-game Indiana career when he didn't start. Cheaney did more watching than playing as Indiana overwhelmed Vanderbilt, 88-51, and Boston University, 88-47. He understood the message being imparted.

"They were coming at me on defense, and I wasn't ready for it mentally," Cheaney said. "I started playing a little better when the Big Ten season started . . . "

Starting with the opener against Murray State, senior Calbert Cheaney showed he was 'ready for it mentally,' when opponents came after him.

The Hoosiers swept both games that year from Ohio State, Cheaney outscoring Jackson 28-24 in another nationally televised Sunday-in-February game at Columbus. The 86-80 Indiana victory moved the Hoosiers two full games ahead in the league race, but the last two weeks of the season, a team that shot .518 for the rest of the year unaccountably went cold – .377 over a four-game stretch that included losses at Michigan and Purdue and handed the clear-cut championship to Ohio State.

Cheaney hit 13 of 17 shots in a 29-point performance at Iowa as Indiana – despite 12-for-42 (.286) from everybody else – squeezed through, 64-60. Four days later at Michigan, Cheaney was 3-for-13 and the Wolverine freshmen took advantage to win, 68-60, and start their remarkable run to the NCAA championship game.

Cheaney had awakened that morning with 103-degree temperature. The fever abated and he was approved to play, but it was the start of a virus attack that "affected me for several days. Basically, you get weak and lose a little weight." He came back 1-for-10 in a 66-41 victory over Wisconsin. At Purdue, he scored 15 points in the first half, 17 while the Hoosiers were opening a 42-32 lead with just over 12 minutes to go. He had little left, and no one stepped up to fill in for him. Purdue's victory was an uproarious hit in Mackey Arena. "It's the highlight of my career," Purdue senior Woody Austin said. "To beat them in the final game . . . we busted their hope for a No. 1 seed and the Big Ten title."

Knight, an inveterate walker, extended his range that night. He walked home from Bloomington airport, more than six miles. It was a time to mull over something that never had happened in his 21 years at Indiana: a team, a good Indiana team, with the Big Ten championship in its hands, had blown it down the stretch.

His solution was to start the new season immediately. Knight told his team to pick new leadership for the tournament and extending into the year to come. The squad ultimately sent back three names as captains: juniors Cheaney and Chris Reynolds and sophomore Damon Bailey.

For senior Calbert Cheaney, a whole new dimension of leadership.

Even before Knight's sort-it-out stroll was over, the Hoosiers had their own meeting. "We knew we were a much better team than Purdue," Greg Graham said, "and then to go out and *lose* to them . . . If we had lost to Purdue playing as well as we could, we could accept that, but we didn't play well at all. I think it was us just getting wrapped up in thinking teams were going to lie down and die for us, instead of going out and knocking them down."

For Cheaney, leadership took on a whole new dimension – for the first time, a vocal one. "We got together at my apartment and said, 'We lost the Big Ten. Let's make up for it in the tournament.' "

The shooting slump vanished. The Hoosiers played at their very best and reached the Final Four before Duke turned them back, 81-78. Jackson again was Big Ten MVP and a consensus all-America pick who turned pro a year early and ultimately signed for more than $3 million a year.

Cheaney, third-team all-America, said he never thought seriously about leaving early. "I said my freshman year my intentions were to get my degree. That's what you go to college for – to get your degree, and worry about basketball second." Getting the degree meant something else to Cheaney: "Paying my mother back for what she has done for me over the years. She did an excellent job raising me. She put me on the right path and told me what's necessary to do in life to be a better person." One of the reasons she insisted that Calbert keep an open mind about Indiana – when at one point prior to Indiana's re-entrance into the recruiting game he had told Crews he'd like to go to Evansville – was Knight's widely known emphasis on his players' coming out of their IU years with a degree. In May, Calbert Cheaney got his.

In November, though, Cheaney was back in a position familiar to him: hopeful that things would go wonderfully, not at all sure that they would.

He had received a minor slap the previous summer. Despite his brilliant tournament play in leading Indiana to the Final Four, Cheaney was not invited when a group of collegiate underclassmen was put together to help train the U.S. Olympic "Dream Team." Invited were Grant Hill and Bobby Hurley of Duke, Chris Webber (Michigan), Eric Montross (North Carolina), Jamal Mashburn (Kentucky), Rodney Rogers (Wake Forest), Anfernee Hardaway (Memphis State) and Allen Houston (Tennessee). "It would be nice to go, but it's no big deal – not to me it isn't," Cheaney said after his snub. But it amounted to a pointed reminder that, a la all those times when Jackson was rated better, he hadn't truly reached college basketball's top echelon. The pre-season all-America team picked by Associated Press from national sportswriter balloting reflected that. All five came from the Olympic opposition team: Webber, Mashburn, Hurley, Hardaway and Hill.

Whatever proving was left for both Cheaney and his team to do began before most teams had achieved good practice form. This was the year when the NCAA's basketball cutbacks – fewer scholarships (14, down from 15, headed for 13 in 1993-94), fewer games, a limit on practice hours per week – had included a two-week shortening of the pre-season practice period. The first day was moved from Oct. 15 to Nov. 1.

For 16 teams with berths in the Pre-Season National Invitation Tournament, the season opener was just two weeks beyond that start – where college teams customarily had had five or six weeks of lead-up time before.

Knight wanted his veteran-stocked team – with all five starters back from its Final Four run – to begin practice in high gear. To achieve that, he departed radically from his norm. Staid, no-glitz Indiana joined the "Midnight Madness" set and had its first practice at 12:01 a.m. Sunday, Nov. 1. He didn't go all the way; there was no show biz to it, just a practice. But he did one other thing different from his norm: he opened the practice to the public.

And the public came. Assembly Hall's balconies were closed, and every other seat was filled. Knight was delighted. "It had never even crossed my mind (to have a midnight practice)," he said. "Because of things we're trying to accomplish with this team, I decided to do it. Opening it to the public was really an afterthought. But it was so well received and the support for our players was so good I will seriously consider doing it again."

It amounted to a sneakily effective way to get an extra practice in. The Hoosiers came back for another session later Sunday morning, then another Sunday evening.

Associated Press	
PRE-SEASON, NOV. 17	
1. Michigan (23)	1,536
2. Kansas (19)	1,513
3. Duke (15)	1,504
4. Indiana (6)	1,489
5. Kentucky	1,341
6. Seton Hall (2)	1,300
7. North Carolina	1,171
8. Memphis State	1,158
9. Florida State	1,089
10. Arizona	1,053
11. Iowa	738
20. Michigan State	326

MURRAY STATE 80

No.	Min	3FG	AFG	FT	R	A	BS	St	TO	PF	Pts
20 Hoard, f	15		2- 3	0- 0	2	1	0	0	6	1	4
24 Cannon, f	28	1- 5	4-10	2- 2	3	1	0	2	2	4	11
44 James, c	18		4- 6	0- 0	3	0	1	0	2	4	8
5 Brown, g	26	0- 1	4- 6	3- 4	1	0	1	1	2	5	11
33 Allen, g	36	3- 4	6-13	4- 4	4	4	0	0	3	5	19
10 Taylor	20	1- 1	2- 5	1- 2	5	1	0	2	4	3	6
3 Teague	11		1- 4	1- 2	1	0	1	0	0	3	3
14 Wilson	9		1- 2	0- 1	1	0	0	0	1	1	2
23 Bailey	18		3- 6	3- 4	2	0	0	1	4	3	9
25 Bussell	10		1- 3	0- 0	4	0	0	0	2	1	2
43 Sivills	5		0- 0	1- 2	0	0	0	0	0	1	1
4 Gumm	4		2- 3	0- 0	0	0	0	0	0	0	4
Team					2						
Totals		5-11	30-61	15-21	28	7	3	6	26	31	80

INDIANA 103

No.	Min	3FG	AFG	FT	R	A	BS	St	TO	PF	Pts
40 Cheaney, f	26	1- 3	5-12	2- 2	5	2	0	0	3	1	13
44 Henderson, f	24		6- 8	1- 2	9	1	2	2	3	3	13
24 Nover, c	26		3- 4	3- 6	3	1	0	0	2	2	9
20 G.Graham, g	31	0- 1	5-13	12-13	7	1	0	0	1	1	22
21 Reynolds, g	23		2- 2	8- 8	2	4	0	2	4	3	12
22 Bailey	15		5- 6	2- 2	2	2	0	0	2	3	12
33 P.Graham	8	0- 2	1- 4	2- 2	0	1	0	0	2	0	4
30 Leary	13	0- 1	2- 3	3- 3	1	3	0	0	0	2	7
34 Evans	18	1- 2	3- 6	2- 2	4	0	0	0	1	1	9
11 Sims	9		0- 1	2- 2	0	0	0	0	1	1	2
25 Knight	7		0- 1	0- 0	0	2	0	0	1	0	0
Team					5						
Totals		2- 9	32-60	37-42	38	17	2	4	20	17	103

SCORE BY HALVES			3FG	AFG	FT
Murray State (0-1)	36	44— 80	.455	.492	.714
Indiana (1-0)	53	50—103	.222	.533	.886

Officials—Mike Panco, J.C. Liembach, Gene Millentree.
Attendance—13,619.

Even on a 28-point night, Alan Henderson knew some humbling moments against scrappy Tulane.

They looked ready 15 days later when they previewed their season with a 115-108 victory over Athletes in Action. Sophomore Henderson had 27 points and 13 rebounds in 21 minutes; Greg Graham 23 points (8-for-10 shooting) in 19 minutes; Cheaney 20 points in 19 minutes – and Pat Graham, in his first competitive basketball in 20 months, 9 points in 15 minutes, on 4-for-5 shooting that included a swish on his only 3-point try.

Two nights later, the season and the Preseason NIT began.

Murray State, which had won the Ohio Valley Conference regular-season title five straight years, was the opening opponent at Assembly Hall. Indiana led at halftime, 53-36, and sailed in, 103-80, though Cheaney had just a 12-point night. Greg Graham's 22 points, including 12-for-13 on free throws, led the way.

Two nights later, the opposition was stiffer. Tulane spent most of the season in the Top 25 and closed it in the NCAA tournament. The Green Wave took a horrid jolt in the opening minutes at Assembly Hall when pre-season all-Metro Conference pick Kim Lewis tangled legs with Chris Reynolds and came down awkwardly. Lewis left the game with a knee injury that ended his season – torn anterior cruciate ligament, an injury with which Indiana was to become painfully familiar.

Indiana was merciless. The Hoosiers shot out 54-28 by halftime, 79-43 seven minutes into the second half. "You get to a point where even with considerable time left on the clock, you just have to substitute," Knight said. "I've always operated under the theory that when we get to a point in the game where everybody should play, then everybody is going to play." A lot of Knight's theories date to personal playing experiences. For all the coaching wisdom he picked up from his Ohio State years under Fred Taylor, for all the respect and near-reverence he holds for Hall of Famer Taylor, Knight never has forgotten sitting on the Buckeye bench, the unused sixth man, while Ohio State starters stayed in to the last minute and scored every point in a 100-65 get-even game for Ohio State against Indiana and the late Branch McCracken in Knight's junior year, 1960-61. That game was 45-23 by halftime. The feeling he carried from that experience had nothing to do with sympathy for Indiana, solely for how the backup troops feel when their time comes and they don't get a call.

This day, Hoosier backups got that call in the debris of what had figured to be a good

Preseason NIT, second round
Nov. 20, Assembly Hall

TULANE 92

No.	Min	3FG	AFG	FT	R	A	BS	St	TO	PF	Pts
44 Popp, f	7		1- 1	0- 0	0	1	0	0	0	2	2
55 Reed, f	37	3- 3	7-17	1- 2	3	0	1	0	2	2	18
34 Perry, c	18		1- 4	3- 4	5	2	0	0	1	5	5
4 Williams, g	26	1- 3	5-10	2- 4	1	6	0	2	4	3	13
23 Lewis, g	5	1- 1	1- 1	0- 0	1	0	0	0	1	0	3
5 Hunter	28	2- 3	4- 9	2- 2	0	2	0	4	2	4	12
30 Greene	32		6-13	3- 6	8	2	0	1	1	3	15
32 Hartman	19		6- 8	3- 3	6	1	0	0	2	5	15
3 Simmons	20	1- 3	4- 8	0- 0	3	3	0	0	4	3	9
54 Rasche	8		0- 2	0- 0	3	0	0	0	0	1	0
Team					6						
Totals		8-13	35-73	14-21	36	17	1	7	17	28	92

INDIANA 102

No.	Min	3FG	AFG	FT	R	A	BS	St	TO	PF	Pts
40 Cheaney, f	26	1- 2	9-14	2- 2	7	4	1	0	3	2	21
44 Henderson, f	27		10-12	8-11	9	2	1	2	1	1	28
24 Nover, c	18		3- 4	1- 4	5	0	0	0	4	3	7
20 G.Graham, g	32	0- 1	6-10	2- 4	4	2	0	2	0	0	14
21 Reynolds, g	28		2- 4	1- 4	5	5	0	0	1	1	5
22 Bailey	19	2- 3	3- 6	0- 0	0	4	0	0	1	4	8
30 Leary	10	1- 2	2- 3	2- 2	0	0	0	1	2	1	7
33 P.Graham	14	0- 1	2- 5	2- 2	0	0	0	1	0	1	6
34 Evans	13	0- 1	0- 1	2- 2	0	0	0	0	1	2	2
11 Sims	8		0- 1	3- 4	0	0	0	1	1	2	3
25 Knight	5		0- 0	1- 2	1	0	0	0	0	0	1
Team					2						
Totals		4-10	37-60	24-37	33	17	2	7	14	17	102

SCORE BY HALVES			3FG	AFG	FT
Tulane (1-1)	28	64— 92	.615	.479	.667
Indiana (2-0)	54	48—102	.400	.616	.649

Officials—Ed Schumer, Paul Kastor, Bill Westbrook.
Attendance—14,008.

Todd Leary made finding a passing target tough for Tulane's G.J. Hunter.

early-season matchup of national powers.

Darned if they didn't turn it into one.

On court for Indiana were players who, individually and collectively, had many excellent minutes before the year was over. This time, they had none of them. With 4:09 left and the 36-point lead down to 94-78, Knight reluctantly put his starters back in. "I'm not sure that I might not have just left those guys in the game, if it wasn't a tournament game," he said.

"I'm not positive I *would* have, either."

Tulane hit the returned starters with an 8-0 greeting that cut the lead to 94-86 with 2:25 still to go – barely five minutes after the Hoosiers had been up 92-61, a 25-2 turnaround.

Damon Bailey stopped the Green Wave's charge with two key plays: penetration for a drop-off pass to Henderson, who hit a two-shot foul, and a block from behind on an attempted Tulane shot, regaining possession for the Hoosiers, Indiana went on to win, 102-92.

Knight pardoned the starters' poor beginning after their sudden recall to duty. "What could be harder than thinking the game's over and then coming back in the game? They came back in cold as hell but they got the thing straightened out pretty quickly and got it going back our way."

Overall, he said, "I'd be happy to take that kind of performance the rest of the season.

On a career-best 34-point night, Calbert Cheaney, in Bob Knight's appraising eye, 'didn't play basketball very well.'

If we play as well as we played tonight, that's all we can ask." As for the reserves: "Guys who had played well in the first half came in and played like crap. That's all I'm going to say about that part of it because the rest of it was too good for us."

Cheaney, who had 21 points, said, "I take my hat off to Tulane – they did a great job. Gosh, they just swarmed. They didn't give up. But . . . I'm not putting the guys on our team down, but they have to come in and work a little harder. We can't have that happen, where we're up 35 and in the blink of an eye it's 17."

This was the Cheaney, always inclined toward soft speaking, who had given basketball leadership at Indiana a definition: "The key to being a leader here is just being on each other's butt all the time . . . not to make that person mad but help them in a way that makes them do better." Cheaney was leading.

The Hoosiers went to New York and Madison Square Garden as part of a distinguished Final Four in the eighth Preseason NIT.

Indiana-Florida State and Seton Hall-UCLA were the matchups, Nos. 3, 7, 8 and 13 in the freshest AP poll – "25 percent of the teams that played in the (1992) NCAA regionals," Knight pointed out.

It was the third straight year with a tournament collision for Indiana and Florida State. Indiana came from behind with a withering second half and shot the Seminoles out of the 1991 NCAA tournament in the second round at Louisville, then played from on top most of the way – and played very well – in hurdling them again in the third round of the '92 tournament at Albuquerque.

This time, Cheaney had nine points and Greg Graham seven in a 22-7 Indiana breakout. Over the next 20 minutes, Florida State hammered the Hoosiers by an unimaginable 49-22 score to go into the last 12 minutes up 56-44. "A good team can't allow that," Knight said of the midgame Seminole blitz, "which would indicate to me we're a long way from being a good team."

"I think we were lucky to win," Chris Reynolds said. More than luck was involved. Pat Graham came off the bench to score 10 points in five minutes, capped by a 3-point play that pulled Indiana even, 62-62. For Hoosiers, Graham's performance was spectacular news. He had missed the whole 1991-92 season after breaking a bone in his left foot – twice. This night, he was back. He delivered another 3-point play that put the Hoosiers up 69-67 with 1:00 to go, and he had the basketball, protecting it and trying to draw a foul, when the Seminoles punched it loose and – with six seconds left – got the basket from star forward Doug Edwards that forced overtime.

Indiana won, 81-78, but in the last minute of the overtime, Graham crumpled to the floor, with new pain and old recognition. He lay there in a combination of pain, anger and frustration, aware he had rebroken his foot. "It wasn't like I stepped on anyone's foot," Graham said. "It wasn't like I came down on it wrong. I just went to take off and run and it broke."

Cheaney set a career record with 34 points, seven in the last 86 seconds of overtime, but Knight noticed other things. "Cheaney scored," he said, "but do you want me to talk about the blockouts he missed and the screens he didn't set? Cheaney scored a lot of points and didn't play basketball very well."

A good portion of the New York press brigade went away wondering about the Indiana coach: What does he *want* from this kid?

Two nights later, they saw.

Indiana vs. Seton Hall was probably as good a college basketball game as ever has been played in November. It turned out to be the champion of the Big Ten vs. the champion of the Big East, in what Charlie McCarthy of the New York *Post* called "March Madness-like atmosphere" . . . in New York, in Madison Square Garden, on a night when the air waves were uncluttered by the usual multitude of college basketball offerings.

It probably was the night Calbert Cheaney became College Basket-

Preseason NIT, semifinals
Nov. 25, Madison Square Garden, New York

FLORIDA STATE 78

No.	Min	3FG	AFG	FT	R	A	BS	St	TO	PF	Pts
34 Dobard, f	39		4-10	2- 2	5	0	2	3	2	3	10
32 Edwards, f	41		7-17	2- 6	12	2	0	1	4	5	16
44 Reid, c	23		0- 3	2- 4	6	0	1	0	1	4	2
10 Cassell, g	40	1- 7	7-20	3- 3	5	2	0	2	4	5	18
3 Sura, g	41	2-11	5-24	5- 8	10	4	0	1	2	3	17
33 Wells	28	1- 1	4- 5	0- 0	10	3	0	0	1	3	9
11 Hands	4	0- 1	2- 4	0- 0	1	0	0	0	1	1	4
15 Shepherd	5		1- 1	0- 0	0	0	0	0	1	0	2
21 Carroll	4		0- 0	0- 0	0	0	0	0	0	1	0
Team					7				1		
Totals		4-20	30-84	14-23	56	11	3	7	17	25	78

INDIANA 81

No.	Min	3FG	AFG	FT	R	A	BS	St	TO	PF	Pts
40 Cheaney, f	42	1- 3	12-22	9-10	8	1	0	2	5	3	34
44 Henderson, f	40		5-11	2- 5	12	0	3	1	1	4	12
24 Nover, c	25		1- 3	1- 2	7	0	2	2	1	2	3
20 G.Graham, g	37	1- 3	4-14	3- 4	7	3	0	1	5	1	12
21 Reynolds, g	22		1- 3	0- 0	2	5	0	0	0	2	2
22 Bailey	24	0- 2	1- 5	0- 2	4	6	0	0	0	2	2
34 Evans	8	0- 1	0- 1	0- 0	1	0	0	0	0	0	0
33 P.Graham	21	1- 2	5- 6	3- 5	1	2	0	2	2	1	14
30 Leary	5		0- 1	2- 2	0	0	0	0	0	1	2
11 Sims	1		0- 0	0- 0	0	0	0	0	0	0	0
Team					1				1		
Totals		3-11	29-66	20-30	43	17	5	8	15	16	81

SCORE BY HALVES				3FG	AFG	FT
Florida State (2-1)	37	32	9— 78	.200	.357	.609
Indiana (3-0)	39	30	12— 81	.273	.439	.667

Officials—Mark DiStaola, Joe Mingle, Sean Corbin.
Attendance—12,641.

Officials Tom Lopes (left) and Tim Higgins share a high five and a laugh with Bob Knight before final game.

The Pre-Season NIT's MVP award was the start of a seasonful of honors for Calbert Cheaney.

ball Player of the Year. With the national spotlight riveted on this one active college basketball stage, Cheaney was brilliant.

Seton Hall, from coach P.J. Carlesimo down, was city-tough – metropolitan New Yorkers in the main, defending basketball turf. The only previous time the two programs had met predated any of the participants in this game, except for the coaches. Seton Hall muscled aside Indiana's 1989 Big Ten champions in the third round of the NCAA tournament and went on to do the same thing to Nevada-Las Vegas, a year ahead of that Vegas group's two-year run as the game's dominant team; and to Duke, when the names were Christian Laettner and Bobby Hurley and a three-year run of greatness was set to happen. Michigan beat those Pirates in overtime in the championship game.

The Garden was almost Carlesimo's romper room. His father, Peter Carlesimo, was prominent in Metropolitan New York and Madison Square Garden basketball when P.J. was born – and still is. Along the way, that made the Carlesimos, father and son, special friends to the young coach who started at Army and made his name a national one primarily through his Cadets' unparalleled, before or since, success at The Garden. Bob Knight was, if not an adopted basketball son and brother of the Carlesimos, certainly a favorite adopted nephew and cousin.

The Preseason NIT's champion takes home the Peter Carlesimo Trophy. Because of that, Carlesimo told Billy Reed of *Sports Illustrated* just before the championship game, for P.J. to win it "would be my greatest thrill. Nothing would mean more to me." But when he wound up handing the trophy to Knight, who gave him an appreciative hug, Carlesimo the Elder said, "I'm disappointed that P.J. and Seton Hall didn't win, but if you have to lose, there's nobody I would rather lose to than Bobby Knight."

P.J. and his team didn't settle easily into their runner-up role.

Cheaney started spectacularly. He hit his first three shots for seven points as Indiana jumped out 15-3. When Indiana led 29-16, Cheaney personally had matched Seton Hall's 16. But, with 12:25 left, almost the precise point where Florida State had topped out a round before, Seton Hall led 54-48.

From there on in, Cheaney scored 16 points. His 3-point basket with 10:20 left moved Indiana ahead, 55-54. Seton Hall was within 75-72 when Cheaney moved the Hoosiers out of reach with two free throws at 0:20.8 – his 35th and 36th points of his career-best night. Greg Graham added his 14th point with 10.5 seconds left in a 78-74 Indiana victory.

There was no doubt about the tournament MVP. Cheaney that night, P.J. Carlesimo said, was "a true all-American. They needed a super effort from him and they got it."

Cheaney hasn't forgotten, may not ever forget, just how that evening felt.

"When you get in something like that," he said, "you're playing well, not just scoring but playing well at both ends of the floor . . . you feel like it's hard to stop you. You really can't *be* stopped.

"It's a great feeling."

Cheaney had signaled for a break when he had helped boost Indiana's lead to 29-16.

Out less than two minutes, he watched the lead shrink to 31-23. He didn't come out the rest of the game. "I was tired then," he said. "I didn't get tired in the second half. Everything just felt good."

Knight recalled his cool reception of Cheaney's 34-point performance two nights before. "I didn't think he played well. I really think tonight he played a great basketball game, and I use that word great sparingly."

Seton Hall's TerryDehere, who was to finish the season as the all-time leading Big East scorer (beyond Patrick Ewing and Chris Mullin, to drop a couple of names), said, "Cheaney was just too tough."

Carlesimo, who had coached Cheaney (and another former Hoosier, New York Knicks forward Eric Anderson) on the gold-medal U.S. team at the 1991 World University Games, teased:

"We told our kids, 'Hey, guys, no one can guard Calbert.'

"That may be reality, because they do a lot of good things. But we had to make him work a little harder than we did. We didn't 'give' him 36, but he was a little too comfortable most of the game.

"I think he's a fabulous player. He shoots 3s, he's very quick, he's a leaper, he has good size, he can put the ball on the floor – and he can do it all when it matters.

"He's a great, great talent."

It was a game for the Knicks to note. It was Cheaney's third game at Madison Square Garden. He had 25 as a junior when Indiana and St. John's played there on the 100th anniversary of basketball and the Hoosiers won. Those points, plus the 70 in the Florida State and St. John's games, gave him 95, a 31.7 average, and a 3-0 career record there.

"I like this place," he said.

It probably was the night Calbert Cheaney became College Basketball Player of the Year.

Assistant coach Ron Felling and Calbert Cheaney – a New York minute.

Preseason NIT, championship game
Nov. 27, Madison Square Garden, New York

INDIANA 78

No.	Min	3FG	AFG	FT	R	A	BS	St	TO	PF	Pts
40 Cheaney, f	39	2- 4	14-27	6-10	4	3	0	1	3	2	36
44 Henderson, f	30	0- 1	4- 8	3- 6	7	1	1	1	4	4	11
24 Nover, c	22		2- 6	2- 2	5	2	0	1	0	2	6
20 G.Graham, g	33	1- 1	4- 8	5- 8	4	4	0	0	1	3	14
21 Reynolds, g	29		0- 2	3- 4	3	5	0	2	1	1	3
22 Bailey	16	0- 1	0- 1	1- 2	4	3	0	0	0	3	1
30 Leary	6	0- 1	0- 1	0- 0	0	0	0	0	1	1	0
34 Evans	22	1- 3	3- 9	0- 0	8	1	0	1	1	1	7
25 Knight	1		0- 0	0- 0	0	1	0	0	0	0	0
11 Sims	2		0- 0	0- 0	0	0	0	0	1	1	0
Team					6						
Totals		4-11	27-62	20-32	41	20	1	5	12	18	78

SETON HALL 74

No.	Min	3FG	AFG	FT	R	A	BS	St	TO	PF	Pts
55 Karnishovas, f	30	3- 5	8-11	5- 6	8	2	1	0	0	5	24
21 Walker, f	35		1- 4	2- 2	2	2	0	0	4	4	4
50 Wright, c	26		2- 9	2- 5	11	0	1	0	1	2	6
10 Caver, g	23	1- 3	3- 6	1- 2	3	5	0	1	3	5	8
24 Dehere, g	36	3- 6	6-14	2- 2	1	4	0	1	4	5	17
15 Hurley	21	1- 2	3- 6	2- 4	0	1	0	0	1	1	9
30 Leahy	21	2- 4	2- 5	0- 0	2	0	0	0	2	2	6
4 Griffin	5		0- 0	0- 1	1	1	0	0	0	2	0
32 Shipp	2		0- 0	0- 0	0	0	0	0	0	0	0
22 Duerksen	1		0- 0	0- 0	0	0	0	0	0	0	0
Team					6						
Totals		10-20	25-55	14-22	34	15	2	2	15	26	74

SCORE BY HALVES				3FG	AFG	FT
Indiana (4-0)		37	41— 78	.364	.435	.625
Seton Hall (3-1)		33	41— 74	.500	.455	.636

Officials—Jody Silvester, Tim Higgins, Tom Lopes.
Attendance—14,338.

CHAPTER 2

Some home runs, and two Ks

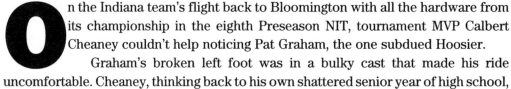

No one knew better than Bob Knight the impact to the Hoosiers of the foot fracture that put Pat Graham (below) out for 11 weeks. 'He provides us a way to score, and a way to get on the (free-throw) line,' Knight said.

On the Indiana team's flight back to Bloomington with all the hardware from its championship in the eighth Preseason NIT, tournament MVP Calbert Cheaney couldn't help noticing Pat Graham, the one subdued Hoosier.

Graham's broken left foot was in a bulky cast that made his ride uncomfortable. Cheaney, thinking back to his own shattered senior year of high school, empathized. Once the Hoosier plane was on the ground and the team was on its way back to Assembly Hall by bus, Cheaney quietly pulled out of his own bags the all-tournament plaque that he had received along with the MVP trophy. He gave it to Graham with the comment, "Here, Pat, we wouldn't have won this championship – we wouldn't have even been in the final game – without you."

That's the Cheaney Matt Nover was to describe later in terms as warm as that plaque-presenting gesture. "Not only did he have outstanding talent – a lot of players have outstanding talent but they don't work with it," Nover said. "He worked with it so *hard*. I could see right away his freshman year he had a determination that he was going to be a great player. He doesn't only work hard to get shots and try to score, he works hard on defense, to stop a guy from driving, to block a guy out.

"What gets me, too… I think he really cares about everybody on the team a lot. He's a really huggy kind of person at times, which is great. We all love that and appreciate that. That's the kind of bond this team has, the togetherness that helps us win."

The success against Seton Hall notwithstanding, Bob Knight knew the Hoosiers had taken a major hit when Pat Graham went out – for 10 to 12 weeks, the guessing was, maybe for the year.

Only a few days before the injury, at a Floyd County speaking appearance that drew more than 700 fans and raised more than $30,000 for the IU Library Fund, Knight had told an audience that included Graham's parents:

"He provides us a way to score and a way to get on the (free-throw) line, and some real important things, whether he's starting or coming off the bench. Not having him was a big loss to this team, maybe more than even I thought at the beginning."

Knight wants a team with everybody contributing, and every player getting as much as possible back from the season. The return of Graham was a key to another major personnel decision that had been made before the Athletes in Action game: to red-shirt sophomore center Todd Lindeman.

That left the Hoosiers with just an 11-man team, but Knight had

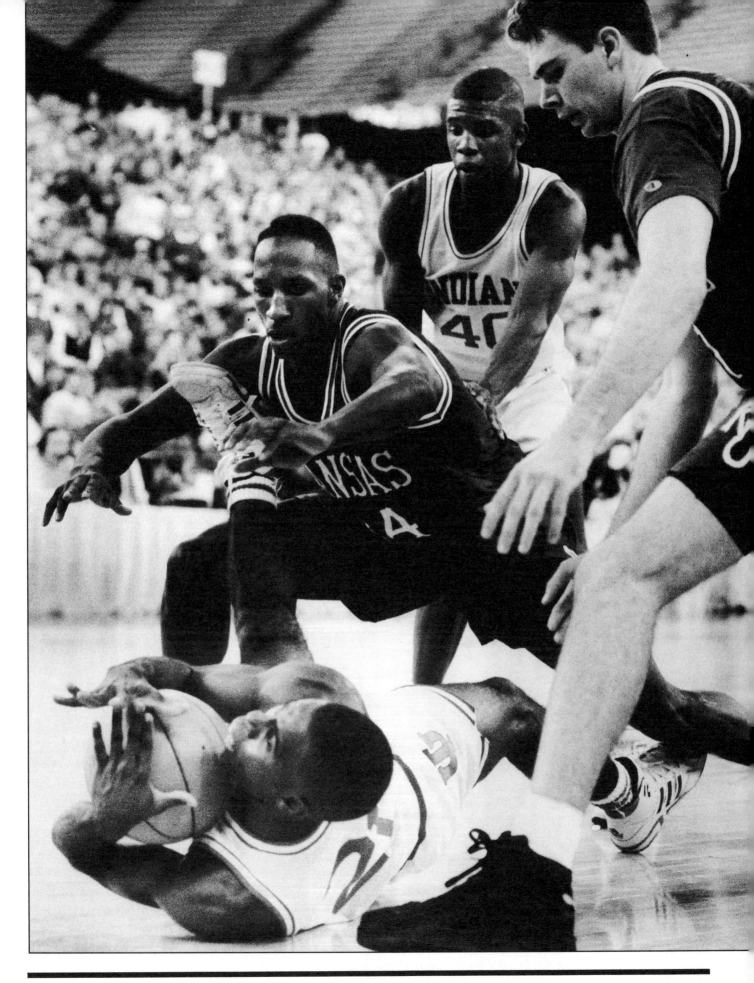

Before pouncing Jayhawks Richard Scott and Eric Pauley can strike, quick-thinking Chris Reynolds calls a timeout.

mulled over all the likelihoods and decided that Lindeman – much as he liked the way the 7-foot youngster from Michigan's sparsely populated Upper Peninsula had developed – probably wouldn't be playing any more than he had as a freshman in 1991-92 (140 chiefly mop-up minutes spread over 20 games, with 64 points, 39 rebounds and six blocked shots). Lindeman had gone that full season without ever really having to be used at a critical time. Eric Anderson was on that team, but the present one had added red-shirt freshman Brian Evans to the front-court corps – plus Pat Graham.

"We've got two or three kids who can play either guard or forward – the Graham 'twins' (Greg and Pat) and (Damon) Bailey," Knight had said that November night in Floyd County. "We could play with two of them at forward. If we have to, we can back up (center Matt) Nover with (forward Alan) Henderson.

"We really need another big kid. Lindeman would be perfect, had I red-shirted him last year, which was my error. But now . . .

"I think that Lindeman with another year (of weight work and development) would be our starting center. The question then becomes, 'Do we want Lindeman as a starting center for two years, or for three years?' "

Factoring into the decision was the fact that Lindeman had undergone left elbow surgery early in the summer. The operation was successful, in correcting a problem that traced to an eighth-grade fracture and kept him from more than about 65 percent extension of his left arm when he reached for a rebound. However, while recovering from the surgery, he had been unable to do any of the lifting exercises crucial to the upper body strength development that Knight saw as crucial to Lindeman's overall effectiveness in the muscular inside areas of Big Ten basketball. From a body-building standpoint, Lindeman's summer was lost.

The decision was to red-shirt him, let him work nightly in practice against Nover and Henderson, and give him a full year of weightlifting – through the season, then into and through the summer. It was a decision that had major ramifications later, when Henderson went down, but Knight's only second-guessing of the entire matter, ever, involved his own decision to play him the year before. This year, he felt strongly, he owed to Lindeman, for his own long-range benefit. In October, when it was time for a go or no-go decision, Knight had listened to all the arguments for playing Lindeman, including the ultimate one: you teach a team game, and as much as the year off obviously would benefit this one player, he might really help this team. The likelihood of a second wasted year for Lindeman swung the decision. A coach frequently accused of a lack of consideration for his players made that choice without a waver.

The Hoosiers checked out their revised playing rotation with a 97-79 exhibition victory over the Cuba National team. Center certainly wasn't an evident problem that night. Nover, who had never scored more than 17 points in a college game, topped that in each half and totaled 37. He was the only senior who had played in the game – Cheaney, Greg Graham and Chris Reynolds, as well as sophomore Alan Henderson, were given the night off.

Dead ahead was another major collision: against Kansas, before a

Dec. 5, Hoosier Dome, Indianapolis

KANSAS 74

No.	Min	3FG	AFG	FT	R	A	BS	St	TO	PF	Pts
32 Hancock, f	22	0- 1	1- 5	1- 2	3	1	0	0	1	1	3
34 Scott, f	14		6-11	1- 3	3	0	0	1	3	5	13
51 Pauley, c	27		1- 8	0- 0	6	2	1	0	1	3	2
23 Walters, g	27	2-11	6-15	2- 3	4	3	0	0	2	4	16
30 Jordan, g	34	2- 4	4- 6	6- 6	2	3	0	1	0	0	16
12 Richey	23	0- 1	0- 1	1- 2	4	1	0	1	0	1	1
20 Woodberry	29	1- 3	4-12	4- 4	7	1	1	0	0	0	13
00 Ostertag	13		1- 2	0- 0	5	0	2	0	2	1	2
21 Pearson	7	1- 2	2- 3	0- 0	1	0	0	0	1	2	5
10 Rayford	4	1- 1	1- 1	0- 0	0	1	0	0	0	0	3
Team					4						
Totals		7-23	26-64	15-20	39	12	4	3	10	17	74

INDIANA 69

No.	Min	3FG	AFG	FT	R	A	BS	St	TO	PF	Pts
40 Cheaney, f	35	2- 3	11-19	2- 4	9	0	0	0	4	4	26
44 Henderson, f	23		3- 6	0- 0	9	0	2	1	0	4	6
24 Nover, c	35		8-16	2- 7	10	1	1	1	2	2	18
21 Reynolds, g	24	0- 1	0- 2	0- 0	5	4	0	0	2	2	0
22 Bailey, g	35	1- 5	5-11	0- 2	3	4	1	0	1	4	11
20 G.Graham	29	2- 5	3-11	0- 0	1	3	0	0	1	2	8
34 Evans	14		0- 1	0- 0	2	1	0	0	1	0	0
30 Leary	3		0- 0	0- 0	1	0	0	0	1	0	0
25 Knight	1		0- 0	0- 0	0	0	0	0	0	0	0
11 Sims	1		0- 0	0- 0	0	0	0	0	1	1	0
Team					3						
Totals		5-14	30-66	4-13	43	13	4	2	13	19	69

SCORE BY HALVES			3FG	AFG	FT
Kansas (2-0)	38	36— 74	.304	.406	.750
Indiana (4-1)	40	29— 69	.357	.455	.308

Officials—Stan Reynolds, Paul Caster, Scott Thornley.
Attendance—31,197.

23

national TV audience and a live crowd of 31,197 at the Hoosier Dome.

Only a few Jayhawks – starters Adonis Jordan and Richard Scott and sixth-man Steve Woodberry – were back from the Kansas team that coach Roy Williams had led to a surprising 83-65 NCAA tournament blowout of Indiana's co-Big Ten champions in 1991. Like the Seton Hall game, this one, too, turned out to be an early meeting of major conference champions. Kansas won its third straight Big Eight title.

This time, Indiana led 52-47, Kansas 64-58, then Indiana 69-66, with 3:30 left. The Hoosiers didn't score again, and Kansas was a 74-69 winner – the game key 45 points from perimeter players Walters (16), Jordan (16) and Woodberry (13). There was another key: Indiana hit just four of 13 free throws, to 15-for-20 for Kansas.

On his Sunday TV show, Knight pinpointed the backcourt points in the game. "Kansas gets 45 points from its three guards and we get 19," he said (Damon Bailey 11, Greg Graham 8 and Chris Reynolds none). "That is a big deficit to make up. We've got to have more scoring from our guards. An answer for us, and we'll definitely go in this direction in our game with Notre Dame Tuesday night, is Todd Leary."

Leary gained special status in Indiana fans' eyes when he sank three 3-point baskets in 27 seconds to raise the Hoosiers from the dead and give them a last-gasp chance against Duke in the 1992 Final Four semifinals at Minneapolis. Leary was the outside threat to complement 7-foot Eric Montross on Lawrence North's 1989 state championship team. Then he wore Steve Alford's No. 12, combed his hair like him, and shot like him. He was an unabashed Alford fan. The year he and the six other 1989-90 freshmen checked in at Indiana, Leary had said, "I met him when we played some exhibition games this summer. I guarded him – held him to 43 points."

At Indiana, knee problems cost Leary the whole 1990-91 season and dropped him back a class in eligibility. The injury flared up anew a few times after that, but he never lost his zest for putting the ball up. Long before the Duke game, Leary had eye-popping stretches in practice against the Hoosier starters.

Notre Dame, though, was not for Leary a game that departed from his playing-time norm. He came off the bench to play just four minutes, hitting one of two 3-point shots.

The Hoosier led 35-18, then 43-33 at halftime, and Cheaney by then had taken just three shots but dealt off five assists, one short of his career high. Notre Dame, in a subpar

A victory in the Hoosier Dome over Indiana meant celebration time for Jayhawks Greg Ostertag (00) and Darren Hancock.

Damon Bailey (top) gets a step on Notre Dame's David Justice, but for Alan·Henderson, defense against Monty Williams was heady stuff.

season, didn't didn't play like that the second half. Going into the last three minutes, the Irish led, 69-67.

Cheaney, with 15 second-half points that lifted him to a game-high 19, scored all the Indiana points as the Hoosiers went up 73-70 and got the ball back with 1:02 left on an exceptional defensive play by Alan Henderson.

Indiana ran the 45-second shot clock down, but when it came time to pop Cheaney free, or Damon Bailey, or someone, it didn't happen. Matt Nover, mystifyingly and uncharacteristically ineffective from the 15-foot free-throw line up to then in his senior season, had the ball as the shot clock reached 4, and 3. In semi-desperation, he went straight up – from 15 feet – and hit, for the 75-70 lead that stood up to the finish. "We were going to have 10 to 15 seconds to get a shot to tie," Notre Dame coach John MacLeod said. "(Nover's shot) looked awful good going up there. I thought, 'Oh, my God, *no*.'

Dec. 8, Joyce Athletic and Convocation Center, South Bend

INDIANA 75

No.	Min	3FG	AFG	FT	R	A	BS	St	TO	PF	Pts
40 Cheaney, f	36	2- 4	6-10	5- 8	3	6	0	2	4	3	19
44 Henderson, f	33		4-10	1- 2	13	0	2	1	4	2	9
24 Nover, c	30		5- 9	6-12	8	1	0	0	5	3	16
20 G.Graham, g	34	2- 3	5-10	3- 4	2	2	1	2	2	5	15
22 Bailey, g	27		2- 3	0- 0	2	3	1	0	1	2	4
21 Reynolds	22		1- 1	0- 0	0	3	0	0	2	2	2
34 Evans	10	1- 2	1- 3	4- 4	3	0	0	0	0	2	7
30 Leary	4	1- 2	1- 2	0- 0	0	0	0	0	0	0	3
25 Knight	3		0- 0	0- 0	0	0	0	0	0	0	0
11 Sims	1		0- 0	0- 0	0	0	0	0	0	0	0
Team					3						
Totals		6-11	25-48	19-30	34	15	4	5	18	19	75

NOTRE DAME 70

No.	Min	3FG	AFG	FT	R	A	BS	St	TO	PF	Pts
3 MWilliams, f	21	2- 2	5-12	3- 4	12	1	1	1	4	5	15
21 Russell, f	35		3- 8	0- 0	3	4	1	1	5	4	6
53 JoeRoss, c	14		0- 1	2- 4	4	0	1	0	0	2	2
5 Hoover, g	16	2- 5	2- 6	0- 0	1	1	0	0	3	1	6
30 Taylor, g	39	1- 3	3-14	2- 5	2	2	0	2	1	3	9
54 JonRoss	27		2- 5	3- 4	3	0	0	0	0	4	7
24 Justice	24	2- 2	4- 4	2- 2	2	6	0	2	4	1	12
50 Cozen	18	3- 5	3- 6	2- 2	4	0	0	0	0	4	11
15 Boyer	5		1- 1	0- 0	0	0	0	1	1	0	2
23 JWilliams	1		0- 0	0- 0	0	0	0	0	0	0	0
Team					5						
Totals		10-17	23-57	14-21	36	14	3	7	18	24	70

SCORE BY HALVES			3FG	AFG	FT
Indiana (5-1)	43	32— 75	.545	.521	.613
Notre Dame (2-1)	33	37— 70	.588	.404	.667

Officials—Tom Rucker, Sid Rodeheffer, Tom Clark.
Attendance—11,418.

"That was a mortal blast. I wish I'd had a gun – I'd have dropped him right there."

It was much too close a call for Knight against a team that he respected as competitive, well prepared, inspired and all that, but obviously was not as talented as the competitive, well prepared, inspired Big Ten teams waiting for the Hoosiers. On the busride home from South Bend, Knight thoroughly digested the game box score, as is his habit, and his eye was caught by one number: shots taken by Cheaney, 10.

"He called me up to the front of the bus and said, 'Calbert, you've got to get 20 shots a game,'" Cheaney said.

"I love to score, but I thought, 'Dag-gone. That's a lot of shots.'

"I think he really meant not necessarily 20 shots a game, but *look* to shoot – 'Don't be bashful, shoot the ball. If you've got an open shot, take it. If you've got a drive, take it.' I'm the scorer and my job is to put the ball in the bucket – 'Put it up as many times as you can. Don't be bashful. Keep shooting.'"

It was the same message Knight had reached into the Hoosier past to impart to Cheaney last year, after he averaged just 11.3 shots per game during the first half the season. That time, Knight brought in two veterans of the role Cheaney was playing – the two who were the prototypes for all following after in the scoring forward spot in Knight's motion offense: Scott May and Mike Woodson.

"I wasn't being involved in the offense like I should be," Cheaney said. "That may have hurt us as a team last year, in some aspects. Coach asked them to talk to me about that – just put the ball up."

The message Cheaney got from the conversation with May and Woodson was, "When they played, some shots they put up were not good shots. But what's Coach going to do? You're the scorer. If you put up a bad shot every now and then, that's what happens. You can't put up a perfect shot every time."

Cheaney came back with 38 points in 48 minutes as Indiana swept to its 19th straight Indiana Classic championship with cruises past Austin Peay (107-61) and Western Michigan (97-58). He shared tournament MVP honors with Alan Henderson, who also had 38 points for the two games plus 22 rebounds, 14 in the Western Michigan game.

Indiana set a tournament record by shooting .654 against Western Michigan, coached by former IU aide Bob Donewald. Donewald was completing his postgame press remarks when Henderson and Cheaney came into the room. "Hey, you two," Donewald said to the surprised pair. "You're playing for the greatest. This year, don't screw it up. You've got a great basketball team."

Cheaney smiled in giving his reaction, after Donewald had left. "He was here for five years," Cheaney said, "so I guess you have to pay heed to that advice. Coach *is* one of the greatest... and I guess we can't screw it up."

With his 22 final-game points, Cheaney had become the fourth Hoosier and 18th Big Ten player to score 2,000 career points. That began a countdown: At 2,015, Cheaney had 424 points to go to top Steve Alford's IU record. He had a minimum of 23 games left: 18.5 a game

Calbert Cheaney jams against Western Michigan and Mike Mosely.

Indiana Classic, first round
Dec. 11, Assembly Hall
AUSTIN PEAY 61

No.	Min	3FG	AFG	FT	R	A	BS	St	TO	PF	Pts
25 Yudt, f	37	1- 3	12-23	0- 1	6	1	0	0	2	3	25
42 Jenkins, f	21		1- 2	1- 2	1	0	0	0	5	1	3
5 Dupree, c	16		2- 4	0- 0	2	0	1	0	1	3	4
20 Franklin, g	24		4- 6	0- 1	1	2	0	1	6	3	8
22 Meriwether, g	27	0- 1	0- 2	2- 2	3	4	0	0	6	4	2
44 Beck	23		2- 3	2- 2	8	1	1	1	3	2	6
3 Casbon	8		0- 2	0- 0	1	1	1	0	1	0	0
23 Savage	20	1- 2	2- 4	0- 0	1	0	0	1	2	0	5
31 McCormick	13		3- 5	2- 2	3	1	0	1	2	0	8
24 Bell	9		0- 3	0- 0	0	0	0	1	0	3	0
50 Heien	1		0- 0	0- 0	1	0	0	0	1	0	0
55 Key	1		0- 1	0- 0	0	0	0	0	0	1	0
Team					4						
Totals		**2- 6**	**26-55**	**7-10**	**30**	**10**	**3**	**5**	**29**	**20**	**61**

INDIANA 107

No.	Min	3FG	AFG	FT	R	A	BS	St	TO	PF	Pts
40 Cheaney, f	20	3- 4	6-11	1- 1	3	3	0	2	0	1	16
44 Henderson, f	22		10-15	5- 6	8	2	1	3	2	3	25
24 Nover, c	17		1- 4	5- 8	3	0	1	0	1	1	7
20 G.Graham, g	22	0- 1	4- 8	4- 5	4	3	0	1	1	2	12
30 Leary, g	18	1- 2	2- 5	0- 0	3	0	0	0	1	1	5
22 Bailey	26	1- 1	7-13	1- 1	5	6	0	1	0	4	16
21 Reynolds	22		7- 7	2- 4	0	1	0	3	1	1	16
25 Knight	21		3- 6	0- 0	4	1	0	0	0	1	6
34 Evans	17		0- 0	0- 0	2	1	0	1	2	2	0
11 Sims	15	0- 1	0- 2	4- 4	1	0	0	2	2	2	4
Team					4						
Totals		**5- 9**	**40-71**	**22-29**	**35**	**17**	**2**	**13**	**10**	**18**	**107**

SCORE BY HALVES			3FG	AFG	FT
Austin Peay (1-2)	28	33— 61	.333	.473	.700
Indiana (6-1)	46	61—107	.556	.563	.759

Officials—Randy Drury, Sam Lickliter, George Demos.
Attendance—16,482.

26

Indiana Classic, championship game
Dec. 12, Assembly Hall
WESTERN MICHIGAN 58

No.	Min	3FG	AFG	FT	R	A	BS	St	TO	PF	Pts
12 McGee, f	21	0- 2	5-11	0- 0	2	1	0	0	2	2	10
32 SeWightman, f	37	3- 7	5-13	3- 4	0	1	0	2	3	2	16
50 VanAbbema,c	23		2- 6	0- 1	3	0	0	1	3		4
4 ESanders, g	29	1- 3	3- 6	2- 4	0	2	0	1	4	2	9
23 Brooks, g	32	1- 6	5-14	0- 0	2	2	0	4	0	1	11
24 Jackson	5		0- 0	0- 0	0	1	0	1	3	3	0
35 Handlogten	6		1- 2	0- 0	4	0	0	1	1	5	2
11 JSanders	10		0- 0	0- 0	1	0	0	1	0	0	0
21 Johnson	11		2- 5	0- 0	1	0	0	1	0	0	4
34 ShWightman	2	0- 2	0- 0	0- 0	2	1	0	0	0	0	0
33 Mosely	13		1- 2	0- 0	3	0	0	0	1	0	2
30 Schaffer	2		0- 0	0- 0	0	0	0	0	0	0	0
10 Bennett	4		0- 0	0- 1	0	0	0	0	0	1	0
22 Pearson	5		0- 0	0- 0	1	0	0	0	0	1	0
Team					1						
Totals		5-20	24-63	5-10	20	8	0	11	16	20	58

INDIANA 97

No.	Min	3FG	AFG	FT	R	A	BS	St	TO	PF	Pts
40 Cheaney, f	28	2- 4	9-14	2- 2	7	3	0	2	3	4	22
44 Henderson, f	23	1- 1	4- 6	4- 7	14	0	1	1	4	3	13
24 Nover, c	23		8- 8	3- 4	6	2	1	0	1	0	19
20 G.Graham, g	35		3- 6	3- 4	2	6	0	2	2	4	9
30 Leary, g	21	1- 1	3- 5	0- 0	1	3	0	1	4	1	7
22 Bailey	19		3- 5	4- 4	2	3	0	1	2	1	10
21 Reynolds	23		2- 3	4- 4	1	1	0	0	3	1	8
34 Evans	15	0- 1	2- 3	3- 4	7	1	0	1	1	0	7
25 Knight	9		0- 2	0- 0	1	0	0	0	0	0	0
11 Sims	4		0- 0	2- 2	2	1	0	0	0	1	2
Team					1						
Totals		4- 7	34-52	25-31	44	20	2	8	20	15	97

SCORE BY HALVES			3FG	AFG	FT
Western Michigan (1-3)	37	21— 58	.250	.381	.500
Indiana (7-1)	48	49— 97	.571	.654	.806

Technical fouls—Indiana bench.
Officials—Sam Lickliter, Randy Drury, Rick Wulkow.
Attendance—16,528.

Indiana's Alan Henderson, co-MVP with Calbert Cheaney in the Indiana Classic, works inside 7-foot Matt Van Abbema of Western Michigan for rebounding room.

would do it, without any NCAA tournament games. He was averaging 23.4. Clearly, he was likely to make it, barring an injury.

At 7-1 and No. 4 in the land, the Hoosiers got a pre-Christmas surprise. Their only true freshman, guard Malcolm Sims of Shaker Heights, Ohio, had decided to transfer. "Malcolm said he did not feel he fit into our style of play," Knight said. "He said he would prefer more set plays and a chance to play his game." He enrolled at Cleveland State.

Sims, the Ohio coaches' choice as Class A (major schools) Player of the Year over Ohio State recruit Greg Simpson, had played 41 minutes in eight games. He hadn't hit a field goal (in four shots), but he was 11-for-12 on free throws. From the standpoint solely of 1992-93 value, it didn't seem to be a major loss for the Hoosiers.

But the numbers game came back into play. Now the Hoosiers were a nine-man active squad, 10 for practice with red-shirt Lindeman. Obviously, it was going to be that way for a while. Pat Graham's surgery had seemed to go well, but he was far from being ready to come back – a good two months from it.

Knight mulled over options. Activating Lindeman didn't get much of a thought: if it would have been unfair to Lindeman's future to play him in November, it would have been even more unfair to use him for three-fourths of a season. The name of Ross Hales kept popping up in staff discussions. Hales was a 6-7, 265-pound tight end on the Hoosier football team, an NFL prospect with good agility and exceptional hands. He had been a top basketball player as well at Elkhart Memorial High. There was one problem: he had a year of football eligibility left, and he already had lost one football season – to a knee injury, from summer basketball. Knight considered asking football coach Bill Mallory if he had an objection but ultimately decided not to put Mallory on the spot. "I know he was up against it," Mallory said later, "and I'm sure I'd have said OK. But it did bother me that he had had that basketball injury."

Knight and his nine moved on.

Indiana's pre-Big Ten schedule may have been the best a Hoosier team has played, and Knight always has tried to keep his pre-league schedule strong.

The Hoosiers already had played teams that in the latest AP poll were Nos. 2 (Kansas), 7 (Seton Hall), 10 (Florida State) and 18 (Tulane). Still ahead in pre-conference play were Nos. 3 (Kentucky) and 19 (Cincinnati), with seven games against ranked opponents coming up on the league schedule: two with Nos. 6 (Michigan), 8 (Iowa) and 16 (Purdue) and one with No. 23 (Michigan State).

Cincinnati came into Assembly Hall with a year-old grievance. The '91-92 Bearcats had almost a dream season under coach Bob Huggins, reigning in the strong Great Midwest Conference and driving all the way to the Final Four before losing to Michigan on the day when Indiana lost to Duke.

The only embarrassment in that superb season was an 81-60 home-court loss dealt out by Indiana. "I think everybody is pumped up for this one," Bearcat star Nick Van Exel said. "Last year, we went into halftime with the lead (36-30). They broke our pressure, and we never really knew when to get out of it. In our half-court defense, they just ripped us apart."

The team Indiana defeated in Assembly Hall, 79-64, wasn't the one that in March came within an overtime loss to future champion North Carolina of making it back to the Final Four. That team had added 6-foot-10 Corey Blount, who was under NCAA ineligibility when Cincinnati played at Bloomington. And, the Bearcats also were without their standup comedian and defensive ace, 6-6 Terry Nelson. Two hours before they were to leave their hotel to go to Assembly Hall, Nelson was hurried to Bloomington Hospital to treat an irregularly beating heart. He was back the next game and played the rest of the year.

Nelson would have been the deep man in the Cincinnati press. In man-to-man coverage, he probably would have guarded Cheaney. That sudden and scary loss of a teammate and key player "obviously has to be a very, very tough thing for a team to be confronted with," Knight said.

Yes, it was, Huggins said, "but that's not why we lost. They're a whole lot better than we are at this point in time."

Cashing in was easy for Damon Bailey (left), but Chris Reynolds had his hands full with Cincinnati star Nick Van Exel.

Indiana blitzed the Bearcats for a 38-18 halftime lead, the key figure Cincinnati's paltry 18. "I thought we probably played about as well defensively as we could play," Knight said.

Greg Graham sniped two 3s opening the second half and the lead reached 48-23. Things weren't pretty for the Hoosiers the rest of the way. Van Exel, confined until then, led Cincinnati back to within 56-43 with 8:30 left. A nine-point Indiana burst ended any developing suspense. "We'll get better," Huggins promised. "We're going to be a good basketball team."

Coming into Assembly Hall right behind Cincinnati was St. John's, which figured to have a long season. The Redmen, in their first year after Hall of Fame coach Lou Carnesecca's retirement and the promotion of his longtime aide, Brian Mahoney, were operating without first-round Indiana Pacer draftee Malik Sealy and other keys to the 19-11 Carnesecca team that had shared the Big East title. Indiana exploded to a 57-29 halftime lead and moved right on to a 105-80 victory – the first time a St. John's opponent had scored 100 points in 15 years, in 481 games.

As with Cincinnati, it was the first visit to Assembly Hall for St. John's. Huggins had joked that his team's loss had nothing to do with the arena. "It's not the building, it's those guys wearing those suits – they're pretty good," he said. But St. John's, which uses hallowed Madison Square Garden as its home arena in Big East play, wasn't so quick with such denials. In an amusing role reversal, the team that commonly over the years had seen out-of-town op-

Cincinnati's Tarrance Gibson finds Calbert Cheaney out of reach.

Dec. 19, Assembly Hall

CINCINNATI 64

No.	Min	3FG	AFG	FT	R	A	BS	St	TO	PF	Pts
21 Gregor, f	32	0- 1	0- 2	2- 2	3	3	0	0	3	5	2
43 Bostic, f	21		2- 5	0- 1	4	0	0	0	2	5	4
4 Martin, c	22		1- 7	3- 3	6	0	0	2	1	5	5
31 Van Exel, g	38	4-14	8-26	2- 4	1	3	0	2	3	0	22
52 Jackson, g	31	1- 3	5-11	2- 2	4	2	0	1	2	5	13
10 Gibson	19	1- 3	2- 4	0- 0	4	1	0	1	4	2	5
23 Durden	13	1- 3	1- 4	0- 0	0	0	0	0	1	3	3
32 Harris	22		4- 8	2- 5	10	0	0	0	0	4	10
54 Ford	2		0- 0	0- 0	0	0	0	0	0	0	0
Team					5						
Totals		7-24	23-67	11-17	37	9	0	6	16	29	64

INDIANA 79

No.	Min	3FG	AFG	FT	R	A	BS	St	TO	PF	Pts
40 Cheaney, f	37	0- 3	6-16	5- 6	10	4	0	1	1	1	17
44 Henderson, f	31		3- 7	5- 6	10	0	1	0	1	3	11
24 Nover, c	23		5- 7	4- 8	5	0	0	0	3	4	14
20 G.Graham, g	23	2- 2	5- 6	3- 5	4	3	0	0	4	4	15
22 Bailey, g	30	1- 2	4- 7	3- 5	5	3	0	0	2	4	12
21 Reynolds	24		1- 1	5- 8	1	2	0	1	0	2	7
34 Evans	13		0- 1	0- 0	3	1	0	1	1	1	0
30 Leary	9	0- 1	1- 3	1- 2	0	0	0	0	1	0	3
25 Knight	10		0- 0	0- 0	0	2	0	1	2	0	0
Team					4						
Totals		3- 8	25-48	26-40	42	15	1	4	15	19	79

SCORE BY HALVES					3FG	AFG	FT
Cincinnati (3-1)		18	46—	64	.292	.343	.647
Indiana (8-1)		38	41—	79	.375	.521	.650

Officials—Ed Hightower, Mac Chauvin, Ed Schumer.
Attendance—17,124.

ponents bitten by "Garden jitters" confessed to some Bloomington awe. "I was excited a little bit," the one holdover St. John's starter, Shawnelle Scott, said. "You see (Assembly Hall) all the time on TV and finally we got a chance to play there." Guard Derek Brown said, "We just had to relax. I think everybody was overwhelmed about coming here to play." Mahoney, who took a time out after the teams had made just 13 trips up and down the court, said, "The whole atmosphere we were a little taken aback by."

Cheaney continued to thrive under New York scrutiny. He had 21 first-half points, and Knight lifted him early in the second half – with 23 points, on 10-for-15 shooting. "Cheaney played extremely well," Knight said. "There wasn't much sense in him playing a lot in the second half. I don't think he was any more interested in going back in than I was in putting him in."

The St. John's team that left 4-3 and riddled added no personnel, a la Cincinnati, but made an even more dramatic turn-around. The Redmen led the Big East for much of the season and wound up second only to Seton Hall – and Mahoney was the league's Coach of the Year, his team bowing out of the NCAA tournament with the same record as Carnesecca's last one, 19-11.

Market Square Arena, where Indiana now is 30-0, never was Damon Bailey's favorite basketball spot. Twice at Bedford North Lawrence, he led teams into the Final Four there, and each time the Stars were sent home in their first game.

Greg Graham drives to a 20-point night against St. John's and David Cain.

Dec. 23, Assembly Hall
ST. JOHN'S 80

No.	Min	3FG	AFG	FT	R	A	BS	St	TO	PF	Pts
31 Middleton, f	21		3- 8	5- 5	3	0	0	0	2	3	11
44 Lyson, f	12	0- 1	1- 2	0- 0	1	0	0	0	0	2	2
42 Scott, c	29		6-11	0- 0	5	3	0	0	1	4	12
11 Cain, g	31	0- 1	1- 8	0- 2	3	2	0	3	5	2	2
23 D.Brown, g	28	4- 5	10-12	1- 2	2	2	0	2	3	0	25
34 Minlend	19		3- 6	3- 3	0	1	0	1	0	3	9
24 Barrett	8		0- 2	0- 0	2	1	0	0	2	1	0
15 Foster	11		0- 3	4- 4	4	0	0	0	0	4	4
5 M.Brown	9	0- 1	1- 3	0- 0	0	1	0	0	0	0	2
13 Green	12		2- 5	0- 0	2	0	0	2	1	1	4
3 Luyk	13	1- 3	3- 6	0- 2	1	0	0	0	2	1	7
30 Beckett	7		1- 1	0- 0	2	0	0	0	0	0	2
Team					4						
Totals		5-11	31-67	13-18	29	10	0	8	16	21	80

INDIANA 105

No.	Min	3FG	AFG	FT	R	A	BS	St	TO	PF	Pts
40 Cheaney, f	27	1- 2	10-15	2- 3	6	1	0	0	1	1	23
44 Henderson, f	32		7-15	6- 8	14	3	2	2	1	3	20
24 Nover, c	21		5-10	0- 3	5	2	0	1	2	4	10
20 G.Graham, g	26	4- 5	7-10	2- 3	3	3	0	2	1	2	20
22 Bailey, g	21	0- 1	5- 7	2- 2	3	6	0	0	2	1	12
21 Reynolds	21		1- 1	2- 2	2	6	0	0	2	4	4
34 Evans	17	1- 2	2- 3	2- 2	1	1	0	0	0	0	7
30 Leary	16		3- 5	1- 2	2	1	0	0	3	1	7
25 Knight	19		1- 2	0- 0	2	6	0	0	2	3	2
Team					4						
Totals		6-10	41-68	17-25	42	29	2	5	14	19	105

SCORE BY HALVES			3FG	AFG	FT
St. John's (4-3)	29	51— 80	.455	.463	.722
Indiana (9-1)	57	48—105	.600	.603	.680

Officials—Jody Silvester, Randy Drury, Steve Welmer.
Attendance—17,051.

For Damon Bailey (with Colorado's Pete Hefty), two 17-point nights at the Hoosier Classic meant his first MVP award at IU

He won there with the Indiana All-Stars against Kentucky, and with BNL against Bloomington North, but neither of those was a vintage Bailey game, either.

When the Hoosiers went back in there for their 11th straight Hoosier Classic championship, Bailey took home the first MVP trophy he had won as a Hoosier.

He had 17 points when the Hoosiers put all five starters in double figures for a third straight game in ripping Butler, 90-48. And when that string reached four in an 85-65 victory over Colorado, Bailey came back with 17 points, including four 3-point baskets, plus four rebounds, five assists, two blocked shots, a steal – "he just stuck it in our face," Colorado coach Joe Harrington said. "There is nothing he is weak at. He plays good defense, he passes – he's just a very good team player. He fits in very well with what Indiana wants him to do."

In the Butler game, he reverted to his high school days and moved from his usual guard spot into a posting position near the basket – because the man guarding him was 5-foot-8 Tim Bowen. "If Bowen had been on Greg (Graham), Greg would have done the same thing," Bailey said.

But it was Bailey, whom Knight has called one of the top Hoosier post players. Chris Reynolds, who drew the Bailey defensive assignment frequently in practice, tried to explain why he was so effective in a non-guard role. "He's strong, and he has a lot of athletic ability," Reynolds said. "People don't think he can jump or he's quick, but he'll fool you."

Graham also has guarded Bailey in the post. Graham gives away no height, as Bowen and Reynolds would, nor any edge in athletic or jumping ability, but he admitted he also has problems.

"You can't get around his farm butt," Graham joked.

When the Hoosiers went back in there for their 11th straight Hoosier Classic championship, Bailey took home the first MVP trophy he had won as a Hoosier.

Hoosier Classic, first round
Dec. 27, Market Square Arena, Indianapolis

BUTLER 48

No.	Min	3FG	AFG	FT	R	A	BS	St	TO	PF	Pts
12 Bowen, f	21		0- 2	0- 0	1	1	0	0	2	3	0
34 Beauford, f	24	2- 3	8-18	6- 7	10	1	0	1	3	2	24
44 Brens, c	31		0- 4	0- 0	4	2	0	4	4	4	0
14 Taylor, g	19	0- 1	1- 5	0- 0	4	2	0	1	1	5	2
22 Guice, g	23	1- 4	2-11	0- 0	3	3	0	1	3	1	5
30 Allen	10	0- 1	1- 6	0- 0	3	0	0	0	1	2	2
32 Miskel	14	0- 1	1- 6	0- 0	2	0	0	0	1	0	2
33 Reliford	26		3- 7	0- 0	2	1	1	2	2	0	6
20 McKenzie	21	1- 4	3- 6	0- 0	1	2	0	0	2	2	7
10 Bowens	10	0- 1	0- 2	0- 0	0	0	0	0	2	1	0
45 Phillips	1		0- 0	0- 0	0	0	0	0	0	0	0
Team					2						
Totals		4-15	19-63	6- 7	32	12	1	5	21	20	48

INDIANA 90

No.	Min	3FG	AFG	FT	R	A	BS	St	TO	PF	Pts
40 Cheaney, f	24	1- 2	8-14	0- 0	5	2	0	0	1	2	17
44 Henderson, f	26		5- 8	4- 5	4	4	2	1	3	4	14
24 Nover, c	26		7-10	3- 6	1	1	0	2	1	4	17
20 G.Graham, g	26	0- 1	4- 7	6- 7	3	2	0	1	3	0	14
22 Bailey, g	24	2- 3	5-10	5- 5	3	3	0	2	4	2	17
30 Leary	18	1- 4	2- 5	0- 0	1	0	0	1	2	0	5
34 Evans	16	0- 1	1- 4	0- 0	2	2	0	1	0	0	2
21 Reynolds	21		1- 3	0- 1	3	6	0	3	2	1	2
25 Knight	19		1- 1	0- 0	2	2	0	0	2	1	2
Team					4						
Totals		4-11	34-62	18-24	43	23	5	10	17	10	90

SCORE BY HALVES				3FG	AFG	FT
Butler (2-5)		13	35— 48	.267	.302	.857
Indiana (10-1)		37	53— 90	.364	.548	.750

Officials—Ted Hillary, Tom Rucker, Dan Chrisman.
Attendance—13,473.

Hoosier Classic, championship game
Dec. 28, Market Square Arena, Indianapolis

COLORADO 65

No.	Min	3FG	AFG	FT	R	A	BS	St	TO	PF	Pts
33 Hodges, f	32		5-14	2- 2	7	1	1	0	0	4	12
45 Allen, f	37	0- 1	6-10	1- 1	11	0	4	0	6	4	13
25 Robinson, c	30	0- 4	6-16	3- 4	3	4	0	1	3	4	15
12 Hefty, g	22	0- 2	1- 4	0- 0	4	2	0	2	4	2	2
24 Boyce, g	40	1- 3	7-19	1- 2	7	4	0	3	4	2	16
10 Pulliam	17	1- 3	1- 4	0- 0	4	0	0	0	0	0	3
21 Golgart	7		0- 0	0- 0	1	0	0	1	1	0	0
23 Williams	2		0- 0	0- 0	1	0	0	0	0	1	0
32 Stephens	4	0- 1	0- 3	0- 0	1	0	0	0	0	0	0
55 Schulte	9		2- 3	0- 1	3	0	1	0	1	0	4
Team					5						
Totals		2-14	28-73	7-10	43	15	6	7	19	17	65

INDIANA 85

No.	Min	3FG	AFG	FT	R	A	BS	St	TO	PF	Pts
40 Cheaney, f	31	0- 5	9-23	2- 2	5	2	0	1	2	2	20
44 Henderson, f	28		9-19	1- 3	12	3	3	2	2	3	19
24 Nover, c	30		6-11	2- 2	8	0	2	1	1	1	14
20 G.Graham, g	31	0- 1	3- 6	7- 8	7	6	0	3	5	2	13
22 Bailey, g	27	4- 6	6-12	1- 2	4	5	2	1	1	0	17
30 Leary	9	0- 2	0- 2	0- 0	1	1	0	0	0	0	0
34 Evans	20	0- 1	1- 0	0- 0	8	2	1	0	0	1	0
21 Reynolds	18		1- 1	0- 1	2	4	0	1	1	1	2
25 Knight	6		0- 2	0- 1	1	0	0	0	2	0	0
Team					2						
Totals		4-15	34-77	13-19	50	23	8	9	14	10	85

SCORE BY HALVES				3FG	AFG	FT
Colorado (5-2)		30	35— 65	.143	.384	.700
Indiana (11-1)		49	36— 85	.267	.442	.684

Technical fouls—Robinson.
Officials—Tom Rucker, Eric Harmon, Ted Hillary.
Attendance—13,289.

INDIANA 78

No.		Min	3FG	AFG	FT	R	A	BS	St	TO	PF	Pts
40	Cheaney, f	38	5- 6	12-19	0- 0	8	5	0	0	4	3	29
44	Henderson, f	37	0- 1	3- 9	4-10	13	3	1	0	2	4	10
24	Nover, c	37		8- 9	13-20	8	2	2	0	2	4	29
20	G.Graham, g	25	0- 1	2- 4	0- 0	2	0	0	0	2	2	4
22	Bailey, g	31	1- 4	1- 6	0- 1	4	3	0	1	1	1	3
21	Reynolds	23		1- 1	1- 5	2	1	0	2	1	3	3
34	Evans	5		0- 0	0- 0	1	0	0	0	2	0	0
30	Leary	2		0- 0	0- 0	1	0	0	0	0	0	0
25	Knight	2		0- 0	0- 0	0	0	0	0	0	0	0
	Team					1						
	Totals		6-12	27-48	18-36	40	14	3	3	14	17	78

KENTUCKY 81

No.		Min	3FG	AFG	FT	R	A	BS	St	TO	PF	Pts
24	Mashburn, f	40	6-12	11-24	1- 1	8	4	0	1	2	3	29
12	Rhodes, f	17	0- 3	1- 4	1- 2	0	1	0	0	0	4	3
4	Dent, c	12		0- 3	1- 2	4	0	0	0	1	3	1
5	Ford, g	37	7-12	10-15	2- 3	1	2	0	2	2	2	29
31	Brown, g	17	0- 4	0- 4	0- 2	0	0	0	1	1	2	0
23	Braddy	24	2- 5	2- 6	0- 0	5	2	0	0	1	3	6
10	Riddick	19		0- 1	1- 2	4	1	0	0	0	4	1
32	Prickett	15	0- 2	1- 7	1- 1	7	0	0	1	0	2	3
14	Brassow	10	1- 3	1- 3	0- 0	3	0	0	0	0	2	3
44	Martinez	9		2- 3	2- 4	1	0	0	0	1	5	6
	Team					2						
	Totals		16-41	28-71	9-17	35	10	0	5	8	30	81

SCORE BY HALVES			3FG	AFG	FT
Indiana (11-2)	36	42— 78	.500	.563	.500
Kentucky (9-0)	42	39— 81	.390	.394	.529

Officials—John Clougherty, Jim Burr, Jody Silvester.
Attendance—20,060.

Kentucky's Travis Ford was a gamelong headache for Greg Graham and Indiana.

As tight as the focus in Indiana basketball is on the Big Ten championship, there was no chance the one remaining pre-league game would be overlooked. It was against the best of the recent Kentucky teams, at Freedom Hall in Louisville, in a Sunday national TV game – No. 3 (Kentucky) vs. No. 4 (Indiana), the polls said.

No. 3 made the pollsters look good, winning 81-78, and as a result got an instant promotion to No. 2, with demotion only to No. 5 for loser Indiana.

This was a Kentucky team that was to go into Final Four Week looking like the best team in the land. It previewed that kind of tournament form in this game three months earlier, with a scorching stretch of 3-point firing that converted a 10-2 Indiana start into a 37-27 Kentucky lead – a 35-17 difference over that span. Included in it was a 7-for-8 stretch on 3s.

Indiana came back from that to go ahead 67-65 on a 3 by Cheaney, then 72-68 with 3:55 left. Travis Ford changed things fast for Kentucky with two 3s, and all-America Jamal Mashburn broke a 74-74 tie with another – his sixth, Kentucky's 16th. Indiana never quite caught up again.

Ford, averaging 7.9 points a game going in, had seven 3s and matched Mashburn's 29 points for Kentucky. Cheaney hit five 3s (in six shots) and tied Nover for Indiana scoring honors, with 29 each. Nover got his with 8-for-9 shooting from the field and 13-for-20 on free throws. He was the hottest Hoosier there. As a team, Indiana missed 18 of 36 chances.

Cheaney and Greg Graham, the Hoosiers' best free-throw shooters, did not shoot any of the 36.

"We just did not want to let the ball go to Calbert Cheaney," Kentucky coach Rick Pitino said. "From watching films, we felt that once Cheaney gets the ball in the lane, he is absolutely hell, he's so quick getting it off. If we got beat, we wanted to get beat by someone else."

Graham scored just four points in 25 minutes, Damon Bailey three in 31 minutes. Each had turns on Ford, although Graham had primary responsibility. "Without question, the key in the game was Ford," Knight said. "He just played a hell of a game." Pitino said, "What Bobby Hurley does for Duke, Travis Ford does for Kentucky. I would not trade Travis Ford for any point guard in America."

It was the low point of a senior year filled with highlights for Graham. This day, he felt he had been whipped pretty badly at that end of the floor by Ford.

His primary shortcomings, he self-analyzed – and had pointed out quite clearly by Hoosier coaches – "were basically not putting more pressure on him and not keeping the ball out of his hands. With the quickness I have, they know I should have been able to play a lot better than I did in pressuring the ball."

Two months later, he was named the Big Ten's Defensive Player of the Year.

Matt Nover had Wildcats on his back all day in a 29-point, 20-free throw performance.

Mother of all road trips

I t's a midwestern October rite. Big Ten basketball coaches in the main talk of unprecedented strength within their league, and Bob Knight chides them for short memories. Yes, the league is strong, Knight will say, but it always is. Has been for 50 years, will be for the next 50.

The talk was a little louder than usual prior to 1992-93 play. Only a few seniors were gone and perhaps the richest freshman class in league history (here we go again) was ripening in a conference that had sent two teams to the Final Four, three to the final eight, in 1991-92. "Our league, from top to bottom, is a nightmare," Minnesota coach Clem Haskins said. Michigan State coach Jud Heathcote said a national magazine writer told him his publication was ranking the Big Ten No. 1. Heathcote congratulated him for "a wonderful sense of the obvious."

All of that was in October. When it came time to start the league season, the polls amounted to ratification of the early raves. Conference play opened with Michigan No. 3 in the land, Indiana No. 5, Iowa No. 8 and Purdue No. 9, with Michigan State No. 14 and Minnesota, Ohio State and Illinois also receiving votes.

Indiana was the team with the immediate cause to hope the pollsters were wrong. In the first 14 days of league play, the Hoosiers were going to play No. 8 Iowa at home, then, on an eight-day "road trip," No. 3 Michigan, Illinois and No. 9 Purdue, in rat-a-tat-a-tat order.

Iowa came into Assembly Hall to open the Big Ten season 11-0, averaging 87 points a game, and leading the nation in rebounding. The first seven minutes of the game verified all those items. Iowa led 13-5 because it hadn't allowed Indiana even one offensive rebound and had scored 11 of its points on followups. Returning all-league center Acie Earl (6-10) and the team's leading rebounder, junior forward Chris Street (6-8), were providing the backboard dominance.

It came against the usual Indiana front line, but not the usual starting lineup. Upset by the defensive guard play that he saw as central to both the Kansas and Kentucky losses, Knight sat Greg Graham and Damon Bailey down and opened with Chris Reynolds and Todd Leary. His first substitution was Brian Evans for Reynolds, a one-guard lineup that sought to contest the Iowa inside edge. When Alan Henderson drew his second foul, Bailey got a call – the Iowa lead 17-11 at the time, 19-11 after another Street rebound basket.

Things changed in a hurry. Bailey jump-started the offense, hitting his first two shots, then two more – one a 3 – to push the Hoosiers in front, on the way to a 33-26 halftime lead that included another Bailey 3. "I thought he came in and played great," Calbert Cheaney said. "He's got to continue to do that for the whole Big Ten season."

"I think he likes our perimeter defense," Street said.

Graham's first call didn't come until just under four minutes remained in the half. The combination, Bailey and Graham, opened the second half. They scored the first five

Facing page: Todd Leary heads for a key basket against Iowa — 'a great moment in time' for witness Calbert Cheaney.

The game had its own role in history. The victory made Hall of Famer Knight, 52, the youngest college coach ever to win 600 games.

Indiana baskets, three of them 3-pointers, as the lead widened to 48-35. It was 63-55 with just under three minutes left when Knight took a rare time out to stress what he wanted: spread the court, work the 45-second shot clock down, and go for the basket.

The clock was nearing 10 when Leary, from high on the right side, saw an opening and went for the goal. Cheaney moved toward the basket from the left, available for the pass he expected from Leary when defenders Earl, the Big Ten's all-time leading shot blocker, and Kenyon Murray converged to challenge Leary.

Instead of passing, Leary took the ball through the Hawks, hit the layup and drew a foul that sent him reeling out of bounds, in Cheaney's direction.

What followed was a scene permanently burned into Knight's memory. Cheaney engulfed Leary in a hug, then hoisted him in the air to celebrate the play that had all but closed the door on the spunky Hawks. "One of my all-time great moments as a coach," Knight, months later, called that victory hoist. "One kid made the play and the other kid showed the enthusiasm and the exuberance for his having made the play. I really, really liked that."

Cheaney had a clear view of the play involved. Leary "was being hounded" by an Iowa defense desperately trying to pressure the ball, he said, "so the best bet is to just take it to the basket. He got it over three players. That was a great moment in time."

Iowa refused to surrender. The Hawkeyes were back within 73-67 with 20 seconds left when Murray missed with a 3. Somehow, the 6-3 Leary went up among the giants and came out with the basketball, though penned in by long arms as he teetered near the end line. His solution was a jump-pass, straight out of football – a long jump pass, toward the Indiana basket.

"I had two giant guys on top of me," Leary said. "I just heaved the ball to the other end. "And Jerry Rice ran under it."

Cheaney grabbed the rainbow and laid it in for the finisher to a 75-67 Indiana victory. It was a delayed dishoff, Cheaney laughed later. On the Leary 3-point play, "I *thought* he was going to throw it to me."

Even with that basket, Iowa had shut down the Hoosier front line with just 23 combined points: Cheaney 14, Alan Henderson five and Matt Nover four. "We held their great players," Street said, "but the other guys stepped up and played great games."

Leary had 12 points, his second-highest scoring total as a Hoosier – topped by a 14-point game his freshman year and challenged otherwise up to then by just an 11-point game that year, both of those against Iowa.

The sub guards hadn't done badly, either, Bailey with a team-leading 21 points (8-for-12 shooting, 5-for-7 on 3s) and Graham, who never left the game the second half, with 17 (6-for-9, including 3-for-6 on 3s).

The game had its own role in history. The victory made Hall of Famer Knight, 52, the youngest college coach ever to win 600 games.

"He started so young," Iowa coach Tom Davis said. "I remember being an assistant at Maryland when we had him down to speak to our basketball camp. He was the Army coach then (named to that job at 24).

"To win 600 games at his really young age is something I certainly

Jan. 6, Assembly Hall
IOWA 67

No.	Min	3FG	AFG	FT	R	A	BS	St	TO	PF	Pts
23 Winters, f	22	0- 1	5-10	6- 8	8	0	0	3	4	5	16
40 Street, f	23		2- 4	2- 2	7	0	0	0	3	5	6
55 Earl, c	35		3-15	5- 8	10	0	2	1	2	3	11
3 Murray, g	23	2- 3	2- 5	0- 0	4	0	1	0	0	2	6
20 Barnes, g	37	2- 4	8-12	0- 0	4	0	0	0	2	0	18
34 Lookingbill	23	0- 1	2- 5	2- 3	4	0	0	0	2	2	6
10 Smith	23		2- 5	0- 1	0	5	0	0	3	1	4
42 Webb	13		0- 1	0- 0	0	0	0	0	2	1	0
13 Glasper	1		0- 0	0- 0	0	0	0	0	0	0	0
Team					8						
Totals		**4- 9**	**24-57**	**15-22**	**45**	**5**	**3**	**4**	**18**	**19**	**67**

INDIANA 75

No.	Min	3FG	AFG	FT	R	A	BS	St	TO	PF	Pts
40 Cheaney, f	29	1- 4	6-13	1- 3	4	2	0	0	1	4	14
44 Henderson, f	29		2-11	1- 1	5	0	2	0	0	2	5
24 Nover, c	38		2- 4	0- 3	10	1	1	0	2	5	4
21 Reynolds, g	10		0- 1	0- 0	0	0	0	0	0	0	0
30 Leary, g	21	1- 4	2- 6	7- 7	3	4	0	1	1	1	12
34 Evans	18	0- 2	1- 5	0- 0	2	2	0	0	1	1	2
22 Bailey	29	5- 7	8-12	0- 0	2	3	0	0	6	2	21
20 G.Graham	24	3- 6	6- 9	2- 2	3	2	0	1	0	3	17
25 Knight	2		0- 0	0- 0	0	0	0	1	0	0	0
Team					1						
Totals		**10-23**	**27-61**	**11-16**	**30**	**14**	**3**	**3**	**11**	**18**	**75**

SCORE BY HALVES				3FG	AFG	FT
Iowa (11-1, 0-1)	26	41—	67	.444	.421	.682
Indiana (12-2, 1-0)	33	42—	75	.435	.443	.688

Officials—Gene Monje, Eric Harmon, Dan Crisman.
Attendance—17,020.

congratulate him on. He's a terrific coach."

The previous youngest to win No. 600, by about a year, was one of Knight's coaching idols, Henry Iba. The man who had been first to coach two NCAA champions, and back-to-back champions (Oklahoma A&M in 1945 and '46) also was a three-time U.S. Olympic coach – three-time *head* coach, which did not include the role Knight thrust upon him in 1984 as an emeritus but working assistant on that gold medal squad.

Ironically, just eight days after Knight reached 600, Henry Iba – 88, basketball's "Iron Duke" – died.

Tributes poured in from across the nation and around the world for Iba, but the one that led in national news accounts came out of Bloomington, where Knight said: "Of all the shadows cast across the history of the game of basketball, his was the biggest."

Between the Iowa opener and the foreboding three-game road trip, another bit of history came into Assembly Hall – Penn State, for its first visit as a member of the Big Ten.

Timing was unkind to Nittany Lions coach Bruce Parkhill, who had four straight 20-victory teams. The nucleus of that era had graduated, and Parkhill's Lions took a 105-57 lacing at Assembly Hall.

One more time, the Bailey-Graham combination came from off the bench and led the club in scoring: Bailey with 28 points in 23 minutes (9-for-11 overall, 3-for-3 on 3s, plus five rebounds and six assists) and Graham with 19 points in 18 minutes (8-for-11, including 3-for-6 on 3s).

To have that set coming off the bench "is an effective spark," Parkhill said. "They can really fill it up.

"Indiana is a hell of a team. As much as I hate getting beat like this, as a coach I really enjoy watching what they do, and the way they play together and execute, and defend.

"They're really good."

It was a freak of the computer age, a random happening, that strung Michigan, Illinois and Purdue as successive road opponents for the Hoosiers. In the 18 years since the Big Ten had gone to an 18-game round-robin schedule, Assembly Hall had been the toughest place for Big Ten teams to go (Indiana's league percentage there during that period .821), but the next three toughest were the teams on the Indiana trip – Purdue (.802), Michigan (.747) and Illinois (.698).

It was a make-or-break assignment that made this Indiana team the Big Ten champion.

There weren't a whole lot of games in the 1992-93 collegiate season as good as Indiana's 76-75 scrape past Michigan. It was a matchup of two marvelous teams playing hard and well, and it carried right to the last breathless second – when Michigan all-American Chris Webber, at his best with the ball in his muscular hands in slam-bang range of the basket, put a point-blank shot in the air and Indiana's Alan Henderson smacked it away.

Matt Nover shadows Iowa star Acie Earl to 3-for-15 shooting night.

Jan. 9, Assembly Hall
PENN STATE 57

No.		Min	3FG	AFG	FT	R	A	BS	St	TO	PF	Pts
24	Hayes, f	20	1- 2	5-14	0- 0	5	0	0	0	0	1	11
30	Carr, f	20		3- 5	0- 1	3	0	0	0	0	1	6
13	Amaechi, c	18	0- 1	2- 8	3- 3	6	0	1	0	1	3	7
00	Jennings, g	28	1- 2	3- 7	0- 0	3	0	1	0	2	1	7
22	Bartram, g	31	0- 2	1- 4	2- 2	1	2	0	1	2	3	4
45	Joseph	18		2- 3	0- 0	6	2	0	0	0	0	4
33	Dietz	15		1- 3	0- 0	1	0	0	0	2	2	2
4	Carter	9		1- 2	0- 0	0	0	0	0	1	0	2
20	Wydman	16	1- 3	1- 4	0- 0	1	2	0	0	6	1	3
15	Carlton	20	0- 2	5-14	1- 2	6	1	0	0	4	3	11
12	Williams	5		0- 3	0- 0	1	0	0.	0	1	1	0
	Team					3						
	Totals		3-12	24-67	6- 9	36	7	2	1	19	16	57

INDIANA 105

No.		Min	3FG	AFG	FT	R	A	BS	St	TO	PF	Pts
40	Cheaney, f	30	0- 5	7-13	0- 0	7	4	0	0	1	2	14
44	Henderson, f	22		6-11	2- 2	9	0	2	2	1	2	14
24	Nover, c	15		3- 4	1- 2	4	0	0	1	1	3	7
21	Reynolds, g	21		2- 2	2- 2	2	3	0	3	0	0	6
30	Leary, g	23	1- 3	4- 8	2- 2	0	3	0	3	1	1	11
20	G.Graham	18	3- 6	8-11	0- 0	2	0	0	3	0	2	19
22	Bailey	23	3- 3	9-11	7- 9	5	6	0	1	0	0	28
34	Evans	25	0- 1	1- 3	0- 0	7	5	0	1	1	1	2
25	Knight	23		2- 5	0- 2	2	3	0	0	2	2	4
	Team					1						
	Totals		7-18	42-68	14-19	39	24	2	14	7	13	105

SCORE BY HALVES			3FG	AFG	FT
Penn State (5-6, 0-2)	20	37— 57	.250	.358	.667
Indiana (13-2, 2-0)	53	52—105	.389	.618	.737

Officials—Tom O'Neill, Randy Drury, Mike Spanier.
Attendance—17,265.

"Credit Indiana and Henderson for that," Michigan coach Steve Fisher said. "Championship teams make plays like that.

"Henderson was as good as you could be tonight. He came up big at both ends of the floor."

Henderson had arrived in the Big Ten coincident with Webber and the rest of Michigan's "Fab Five." The greatest recruiting class in the history of the game, the consensus had declared Webber, Jalen Rose, Juwan Howard, Jimmy King and Ray Jackson after their drive to the NCAA championship game as an all-freshman starting lineup.

Henderson's rookie year wasn't bad. He started 26 of 33 games and averaged 11.6 points and a team-high 7.2 rebounds. The numbers ranked him with any freshman big man of the Knight era – Kent Benson (9.3 points, 8.2 rebounds), Ray Tolbert (10.1 and 6.9), Eric Anderson (11.9 and 6.1), Landon Turner (5.5 and 3.4) and Uwe Blab (7.5 and 3.7).

He had an engaging habit of playing well in key moments – 20 points against UCLA in his first college game, 20 against Minnesota in his first Big Ten game, 19 against Eastern Illinois in his first NCAA tournament game, and a season-high 24 in the biggest road victory of that year for the Hoosiers, at Ohio State.

He went to Michigan with his shooting hand chilly. Strong play around the basket had given him some easy baskets, but even with those he was 11-for-31 over the three-game stretch leading up to Michigan.

Outwardly, he didn't appear flustered. When a reporter asked him after the Penn State game what the problem was with his jump shot, Henderson responded playfully: "My jump shot's been off?"

But it had, and of course he knew it better than anyone. "I've been trying to figure out what happened to it," he said. "It's left me for a little while. I feel pretty confident it will be back soon."

Its return came with impeccable timing. Henderson kept Indiana alive early at Michigan with long-range baseline jump shots from both sides of the basket. He finished the night 10-for-15, including the shot from just inside the 3-point arc that changed a 75-74 Michigan lead to the 76-75 score that his block of Webber's shot preserved.

So very much more went into the game, carried nationally by ESPN. Michigan zapped the Hoosiers 13-4 over an early stretch that opened a 20-14 Wolverine lead. Then, Fisher said, the Indiana defense "sagged way off and teased us into taking the first shot that presented itself." Indiana moved out 43-33 early in the second half, but a lightning run by Michigan caught up at 45. The rest of the way was toe-to-toe, better-not-blink basketball. Indiana scored on seven straight possessions but came out of it down 68-67 because Michigan scored on seven of eight, and included two 3s in the burst.

The last tie was at 72. Webber broke it by hitting one of two free throws. Cheaney worked free with an acrobatic backward leap for a straight-out shot that put Indiana up 74-73. Rose, using his unusual guard size (6-8) well, drove right and put a left-handed jump shot up and over the 6-4 Graham for the 75-74 score that Henderson's 18-foot shot, at 1:35, changed.

Michigan senior James Voskuil tried to get the lead back with a driving shot that Matt Nover blocked. Henderson dived to the floor to

> 'Henderson was as good as you could be tonight. He came up big at both ends of the floor.'
>
> *Steve Fisher*

Jan. 12, Crisler Arena, Ann Arbor
INDIANA 76

No.	Min	3FG	AFG	FT	R	A	BS	St	TO	PF	Pts
40 Cheaney, f	39	1- 5	9-19	1- 2	3	3	0	0	4	2	20
44 Henderson, f	36	0- 2	10-15	2- 2	8	1	5	1	1	3	22
24 Nover, c	33		3- 7	2- 6	4	0	2	0	3	2	8
20 G.Graham, g	36	2- 2	5- 7	0- 0	5	5	0	1	2	0	12
22 Bailey, g	32	2- 4	2- 5	0- 0	3	10	0	0	0	1	6
21 Reynolds	6		0- 0	0- 0	2	2	0	0	0	1	0
30 Leary	6		1- 1	0- 0	2	0	0	0	0	1	2
34 Evans	11	2- 4	2- 4	0- 0	2	1	0	0	0	0	6
25 Knight	1		0- 0	0- 0	0	0	0	0	0	0	0
Team					4						
Totals		7-17	32-58	5-10	33	22	7	2	10	10	76

MICHIGAN 75

No.	Min	3FG	AFG	FT	R	A	BS	St	TO	PF	Pts
4 Webber, f	33	1- 4	8-17	1- 3	6	0	3	0	2	4	18
32 Voskuil, f	24	2- 5	3- 7	0- 0	4	3	0	0	0	2	8
25 Howard, c	35		8-12	1- 1	5	4	0	0	1	1	17
5 Rose, g	37	1- 2	9-18	0- 0	4	4	0	2	1	3	19
24 King, g	38	3- 7	4- 8	0- 0	2	5	0	1	1	2	11
14 Talley	3		0- 0	0- 0	0	0	0	0	0	0	0
3 Pelinka	13	0- 1	0- 3	0- 0	3	1	0	0	0	1	0
42 Riley	12		0- 2	2- 2	3	1	0	0	1	1	2
11 Fife	5	0- 1	0- 1	0- 0	1	1	0	0	0	1	0
Team					3						
Totals		7-20	32-68	4- 6	31	19	3	3	6	15	75

	SCORE BY HALVES			3FG	AFG	FT
Indiana (14-2, 3-0)		37	39— 76	.412	.552	.500
Michigan (12-2, 2-1)		31	44— 75	.350	.471	.667

Officials—Ed Hightower, Jim Burr, Phil Bova.
Attendance—13,562.

force a jump-ball call that the possession arrow returned to Indiana, with 32.6 seconds left.

Knight inserted Todd Leary, whose last free-throw miss in Big Ten play came three years ago (Jan. 28, 1990, at Minnesota). Indiana ran 18 seconds off the clock before Michigan gave up on stealing the ball and fouled – Leary.

He went to the line with 14.1 seconds left. He never got to find out what he could do. From the sidelines, Knight saw Greg Graham as the only Indiana deep defender, got Cheaney's attention and told him to join Graham deep. Cheaney left his rebounding position too late, according to Phil Bova, the official who handed the ball to Leary. The violation killed the free-throw opportunity and gave Michigan one more chance to shoot for the win. "When that happened, I *knew* this was our game," Michigan center Juwan Howard said. "All the praying we did . . . God just happened to help us right there."

Michigan put the ball in Rose's hands, to bring it up and either shoot or create a shot for someone else. Graham picked him up, so closely that the two lean athletes bumped chest-to-chest once as they advanced in tandem up the court. "We knew that's who they would go to," Graham said. "He's going to get the ball, and he's going to make a move to the basket or penetrate and dish it off to somebody."

Rose started to drive for the basket, but Cheaney – in textbook Bob Knight help-and-recover execution – stepped away from his man to make Rose pull up. Cheaney was guarding Voskuil, whose 3-point shooting had bedeviled Indiana in the past, and Voskuil was the man to whom Rose dished off his pass. From the deep left-corner, with Cheaney breaking back and extending a high, distracting hand, Voskuil fired.

"I thought it was good," Voskuil said. "The damned thing should have gone in."

It was short. The ball caromed back toward Voskuil, but Howard slapped it back at the basket – straight into Webber's hands. Normally, he would dunk, an unstoppable play with his size, quickness and strength. Unsure if he had that much time, Webber hurried the close-range shot back up – and Henderson made his play.

"I saw Voskuil shoot," Henderson said. "I saw it was going to be short, but I couldn't get to where I thought the ball was going to bounce. I tried to hold my position... I don't know how it happened, but it came into Webber's hands and I saw him go up. I just tried to take a slap at it, and fortunately I got a piece of it."

Graham credited Cheaney for "great help-and-recover, to stop the drive and get out on the shooter and make him rush the shot. That was really good. And Alan made a heck of a block."

It was a satisfying, defining moment and game for Henderson, product of an upscale life, a prep school (Brebeuf), son of a cardiologist and possessor of a 1,300 score on the

At Michigan, Alan Henderson said, and proved: 'I'm not as tall as some people, I don't weigh as much, but I'll bang with anybody.'

Close-knit Indiana (from left, Greg Graham, Damon Bailey, Calbert Cheaney, Alan Henderson and Matt Nover) was ready to take on the world on key road trip.

Scholastic Aptitude Test (SAT). His 2,419 points in four years at Brebeuf put him No. 6 on the state's all-time list. Teammate Bailey heads it (3,134) and three-time Purdue all-American Rick Mount is above Henderson (2,595), but the names below him fill the state's legend list – Oscar Robertson (1,825), George McGinnis (2,070), Steve Alford (2,116), Shawn Kemp (2,134) and Eric Montross (1,874), as a sampling, not to mention Jimmy Rayl (1,632), Don Schlundt (1,569) and Larry Bird (1,125).

After his rookie year, Knight had said, "Henderson probably more than any freshman that I've ever had pleased me with the way he played. He had all those tickets – Indiana All-Star, all-state, all the things than can amount to a kid being a real pain, which I thought for sure we were going to have. But it wasn't like that at all. He doesn't like to lose, he kind of pouts when he comes out – I kinda like that.

"He has a real quick mind to pick up things. You don't have to spend a lot of time getting Henderson to make the right move defensively or offensively."

Michigan's Howard knew what Henderson was bucking. "Everyone looks at Alan and says, 'He's not a tough kid.' He's got the heart. That's what a player needs.

"Alan's a great player."

Henderson heard that "not a tough kid" charge one more time and said, "I just go out there and play. I know I'm not as tall as some people. I don't weigh as much as some people. But as far as being physical, I'll bang with anybody."

Henderson said competition with Webber, Howard and the "Fab Five" didn't light any special fires for him. "I played against and with most of them in all-star games and in camps. We tried to approach this game like every other game – no matter who we're playing against, come out and play hard."

This night, along with his 22 points, he had eight rebounds (high for the game) and five blocked shots (Michigan as a team had three, all by Webber).

The Indiana box score included several other notable entries: 20 points for Cheaney; 12 points, five rebounds and five assists for Graham; just six points but 10 assists and no turnovers for Bailey.

Michigan lost on a night when it committed its season low of six turnovers.

"We probably played about as well as we're capable of playing," Knight said, .552 shooting and a surprising 33-31 rebounding edge supporting the idea. "We tried to do as good a job as we could of blocking out. If you don't, these (Michigan) kids are so quick they can beat you on the offensive board alone."

There was one last item of history to this one.

It was Knight's 500th victory at Indiana, where they have come for him at a rate of nearly 24 a year and a ratio of just a bit better than 3 to 1. He was the first to achieve that milestone at a Big Ten school. Second-best is 371, by the late Hall of Famer Ward "Piggy" Lambert in 28 dominant years at Purdue (1917 through 1945).

"That's where it started," Greg Graham said, "our three-game road trip. When we beat Michigan, I knew we were really developing as a team."

Probably, going into the three-game road stretch, Bob Knight would have been happy to come out of it 2-1. Even 1-2 probably wouldn't have seemed fatal. Iowa coach Tom Davis, who had his own title ambitions, had said on the eve of conference play, "This is my seventh year in the league. The most losses that a champion has ever had (in that period) was three. It seems like you can't lose many games if you're going to win the thing. But if you asked me to predict, I would guess that this year, the winner would lose a handful."

A fan looking at the Indiana road assignment would have rated the games in toughness Michigan No. 1, Purdue No. 2, unranked Illinois a rather distant No. 3. Knight wouldn't have. Because Michigan is so strong, because

Brian Evans latched onto his opportunity to make a big difference at Illinois.

Purdue is such a big rival, he knew at the least his team would be ready to play those nights. The in-between trip to Illinois scared Knight. It had gigantic potential for the kind of looking back on a big win, looking ahead to a rivalry game that Knight worries about and pointedly warns his teams against ("Look at the scores – you see teams doing that every day – *you* can't *ever* do that because you're *always* going to get the other team's best shot").

Lou Henson did have the Illini ready, in a year when Illinois was better than billed, sharing third place in the conference. The Illini went into the Indiana game the only other team unbeaten in league play.

Deon Thomas, the hub of everything for the Illini, also represents a point of contention for Knight, who tried hard to recruit the 6-foot-8 star out of Simeon High School in Chicago. Ultimately, that battle came down to Iowa vs. Illinois and became bloody. Illinois won; Iowa assistant coach Bruce Pearl turned in telephone tapes of conversations with Thomas that led to NCAA charges against Illinois; Illinois beat most of those charges but drew a penalty and paid additionally through loss of recruits (*e.g.*, Chicagoan Juwan Howard) while the NCAA investigation and potential penalty were hanging in the air; the distracted Thomas sat out his freshman year, mostly by Illinois choice, because of uncertainty about his status; Thomas sued Pearl – it was a general mess that lifted Iowa well past Indiana as the most hated basketball rival in Champaign.

Meanwhile, when Thomas finally got to play, he wasn't quite so dominant as all that furor had inspired Illinois fans to expect. A public picture emerged of a player not really hustling, a discipline problem for Henson. But the Thomas whom Knight kept seeing in tape studies posed major defensive problems in the post area, the starting point for any defense. When Knight said that, in postgame remarks at Illinois a year ago, a press corps sensitive to Knight-Henson sparring – at times electric – read the praise for Thomas as a jab intended to make Henson's job even tougher. The simple truth was that Thomas is a quick, effective, strong post threat, and he proved it one more time on Indiana's visit.

By halftime, he almost personally had put the whole Indiana front line in foul trouble – Matt Nover with three and Calbert Cheaney and Alan Henderson two each. It was the Hoosiers' first real exposure to the problems of a short bench.

Chris Reynolds and Indiana controlled things against inspired Illinois.

Jan. 16, Assembly Hall, Champaign
INDIANA 83

No.	Min	3FG	AFG	FT	R	A	BS	St	TO	PF	Pts
40 Cheaney, f	33	0- 2	8-14	14-16	2	1	0	1	4	3	30
44 Henderson, f	26		2- 8	2- 5	6	1	1	0	0	4	6
24 Nover, c	23		0- 2	0- 0	4	1	0	1	4	4	0
20 G.Graham, g	20	2- 3	3- 5	7- 8	4	4	0	1	1	1	15
22 Bailey, g	33	0- 1	1- 5	3- 3	3	5	0	1	1	2	5
21 Reynolds	7		0- 0	0- 0	0	1	0	0	0	1	0
30 Leary	28	2- 3	5-10	0- 0	3	2	0	1	1	1	12
25 Knight	1		0- 0	0- 0	0	0	0	0	0	0	0
34 Evans	29	3- 3	6- 8	0- 0	8	3	0	0	2	0	15
Team					1						
Totals		7-12	25-52	26-32	31	18	1	5	13	16	83

ILLINOIS 79

No.	Min	3FG	AFG	FT	R	A	BS	St	TO	PF	Pts
34 Kaufmann, f	28	2- 4	5-14	2- 3	7	2	0	0	5	4	14
30 Bennett, f	22		2- 7	0- 0	5	0	0	2	1	4	4
25 Thomas, c	36		8-12	7-10	9	1	2	2	2	1	23
24 Keene, g	25	3- 6	5-11	1- 3	4	1	0	2	1	3	14
11 Clemons, g	25		2- 6	2- 2	6	3	0	0	3	2	6
3 Harris	1	1- 1	1- 1	0- 0	0	0	0	0	0	0	3
4 Taylor	15		1- 1	0- 0	3	3	0	1	2	5	2
32 Michael	15	1- 1	1- 1	0- 0	1	1	0	0	0	1	3
33 Davidson	6		0- 0	0- 0	0	1	0	1	0	1	0
43 Cross	1		0- 0	0- 0	0	0	0	0	0	0	0
44 Wheeler	23	2- 5	4- 9	0- 0	0	2	0	0	3	3	10
52 Roth	1		0- 0	0- 0	0	0	0	0	0	0	0
20 Griswold	1		0- 0	0- 0	0	0	0	0	0	0	0
35 Rice	1		0- 0	0- 0	0	0	0	0	0	0	0
Team					1						
Totals		9-17	29-62	12-18	36	14	2	8	17	24	79

SCORE BY HALVES				3FG	AFG	FT
Indiana (15-2, 4-0)		31	52— 83	.583	.481	.813
Illinois (9-5, 2-1)		33	46— 79	.529	.468	.667

Officials—Sam Lickliter, Verl Sell, Mike Sanzere.
Attendance—16,299.

The bench answered. Brian Evans, at 6-8, came on to have his first big college game: 15 points, 6-for-8 from the field, 3-for-3 on 3s, plus eight rebounds. Along with him came Iowa-killer Todd Leary, whose 12 points included 2-for-3 on 3s. They had saved the Hoosiers from falling into a major hole in the foul-complicated minutes closing out the half, when Illinois and Thomas led 29-24 and seemed likely to build it up only to have the scoring of Evans and Leary keep the deficit to 33-31 at halftime.

Evans opened the second half by hitting a 3 that lifted Indiana in front. "When Brian came out and hit that one," Cheaney said, "I said, 'Oh, my goodness.' That was an excellent shot.

"He and Todd just played a great game off the bench."

Knight agreed. "We're not used to getting 27 points off the bench. Each has played well and helped us a lot over the course of the year, and tonight was the pinnacle for their contributions."

The 83-79 victory had one additional welcome wrinkle for the Hoosiers: the return of free throws as a major plus. Where Indiana had gone 4-for-13 on free throws in the Kansas loss and 18-for-36 in the Kentucky loss, against Illinois the Hoosiers were 26-for-32 on free throws to 12-for-18 for Illinois. And the difference in the success rate for Indiana, between that game and the two losses, was that Cheaney was 14-for-16 and Graham 7-for-8 – the two who had done almost none of the free-throw shooting in the two losses combining to hit 18 straight under game-ending pressure.

Knight had been careful to distract attention from the free-throw problem. Defense, he kept insisting, was the key reason the Kansas and Kentucky games got away. But, even in the big early conference wins, Indiana had hit just 11 of 18 free throws against Iowa and 5 of 10 against Michigan. In the last practice before the team headed for Champaign, Graham said Knight had brought the subject up, with one quiet, positive remark: "Let's end up being the best free-throw shooting team in the Big Ten."

"I think we got off to a great start (in that direction)," Graham said. The Hoosiers wound up second.

Those free throws "really killed us down the stretch," Henson said. "You can't give up 20 of 23 free throws (Indiana's second-half figure, 19-for-20 in the last five minutes) and expect to win the ball game."

Cheaney's free throws helped him to a 30-point night. Graham's helped him to 15. Meanwhile, there was Thomas with 23 points, nine rebounds (high in the game), two blocks, two steals – "I love the kid," Knight said. "He just works his butt off, he's got great timing in the post . . . He's not a big postman, but, boy, is he tough in there. I don't think you play against anybody all year who's a better posting player or a smarter kid inside than he is."

He mentioned the mail from Illinois he had received a year ago carrying clippings of press criticism he had drawn "from some of you people for talking about how good Deon Thomas was. It was kind of interesting, because about a month later, I got a flyer from the Illinois (sports publicity office) promoting Deon Thomas for all-Big Ten, which I thought he really deserved.

"It just amazed me how much he must have improved in the month after we were here."

Bob Knight holds himself in and Calbert Cheaney proceeds with business after a non-foul call.

Associated Press	
JAN. 19	
1. Kansas (45)	1,595
2. Indiana (7)	1,510
3. North Carolina (8)	1,483
4. Kentucky	1,362
5. Michigan (2)	1,358
6. Duke	1,339
7. Virginia (3)	1,232
8. Arkansas	1,164
9. Cincinnati	1,084
10. Seton Hall	1,026
13. Purdue	737
14. Iowa	694
21. Michigan State	327
24. Ohio State	141

At Purdue it was, as Bob Knight predicted, Calbert Cheaney's game.

Coaches' 600-win club

1.	Adolph Rupp	875
2.	Dean Smith●	774
3.	Henry Iba	767
4.	Ed Diddle	759
5.	"Phog" Allen	746
6.	Ray Meyer	724
7.	John Wooden	664
8.	Ralph Miller	657
9.	Marv Harshman	642
10.	Norm Sloan	627
	Don Haskins●	627
12.	Jerry Tarkanian	625
13.	Lefty Driesell●	621
14.	Bob Knight●	619
15.	Norm Stewart●	612
16.	Lou Henson●	609

Next in line

Gene Bartow●	592

Among the others

Guy Lewis	592
Tony Hinkle	557
Frank McGuire	549
Lou Carnesecca	526
C.M. Newton	509
Denny Crum●	518
Eddie Sutton●	502
John Thompson●	484
John Chaney●	478
Tex Winter	454
Pete Carril●	454
Johnny Orr●	452
Branch McCracken	450
Don Donoher	437
Tom Davis●	426
Digger Phelps	419
Clair Bee	412
Al McGuire	405

●Active

T he road trip had gone unexpectedly well. Last stop: Purdue, the site of the 1991-92 game that wouldn't go away for the Hoosiers.

There, a 61-59 last-day beating had snatched a Big Ten championship out of the grasp of an Indiana team that, for one of the rare times, was outhustled – and knew it. One more time, the Hoosiers thought about the unbridled hilarity that Purdue had enjoyed that day, how senior Craig Riley, at the end of an 8-10 Big Ten season, had said: "This just makes my whole career worthwhile. You dream about this when you're 9 years old. To come in here and win a game and ruin their championship hopes – it just means everything. You can't top it."

Riley's place had been taken by Glenn Robinson, clearly the best basketball newcomer in the Big Ten, really the nation. This Purdue team had gone 9-0 in pre-conference play to burst into the polls' Top 10, and despite league-opening losses to Michigan and Minnesota, still stood No. 13 in the country when Indiana came in.

Robinson of Gary Roosevelt and Alan Henderson of Brebeuf had been the two spotlighted Indiana players their senior year, both of them high in every national listing. They didn't face each other until the state championship game. That night in the Hoosier Dome, Robinson, with considerably more help, had all the fun – 22 points and 10 rebounds (to 14 and 10 for Henderson) in a 51-32 Roosevelt runaway. A "Mr. Basketball" race that had seemed even going in became a Robinson sweep.

Inevitably, their first collegiate collision drew pre-game attention.

Knight told his team that wasn't going to be this game's story line. "This will be Calbert's game," Knight said. "They don't have anybody who can handle him.

"Nobody does."

It was some forecast. In Indiana's 74-65 victory, Robinson played well, scoring 22 points, though Henderson – considerably more focused on defense than on his own offensive game – grimly stuck with the superbly talented Boilermaker and confined him to 9-for-22 shooting.

Cheaney topped that, by lots. He scored 33 points, his career Big Ten high up to then, and matched Robinson's 10 rebounds. "He was very good," Purdue coach Gene Keady said. "He's a fine young man. Seniors who come through programs and improve like he has – hats are off to him. He did play a super game."

Still, Purdue and Robinson had come

Jan. 19, Mackey Arena, West Lafayette

INDIANA 74

No.		Min	3FG	AFG	FT	R	A	BS	St	TO	PF	Pts
40	Cheaney, f	39	2- 3	11-15	9-10	10	4	0	2	2	2	33
44	Henderson, f	29		2- 7	2- 4	2	1	0	5	2	4	6
24	Nover, c	26		5- 7	0- 2	8	1	0	0	6	2	10
20	G.Graham, g	27	0- 1	2- 6	4- 4	1	4	0	2	1	4	8
22	Bailey, g	29		2- 7	2- 3	1	1	0	1	3	4	6
30	Leary	15	0- 1	0- 3	0- 0	1	2	0	0	1	0	0
34	Evans	21	1- 1	3- 5	2- 2	6	1	0	0	1	4	9
21	Reynolds	11		1- 1	0- 0	0	1	0	0	1	2	2
25	Knight	3		0- 0	0- 0	0	1	0	0	0	0	0
	Team					2						
	Totals		3- 6	26-51	19-25	32	16	0	10	17	22	74

PURDUE 65

No.		Min	3FG	AFG	FT	R	A	BS	St	TO	PF	Pts
13	Robinson, f	39	0- 2	9-22	4- 7	10	0	1	1	2	4	22
22	Martin, f	34		4- 7	5- 6	4	0	0	0	1	3	13
34	Stanback, c	26		1- 3	0- 2	4	0	0	0	0	4	2
11	Waddell, g	32	0- 1	2-10	5- 5	5	5	0	3	5	2	9
12	Painter, g	31	1- 2	4- 7	1- 2	3	3	0	2	4	3	10
00	Williams	9		1- 3	0- 2	5	1	0	0	1	2	2
23	Roberts	10	0- 2	1- 5	0- 0	0	0	0	1	4	2	2
30	Darner	8		0- 0	0- 0	0	0	0	0	0	2	0
21	Dove	6		1- 1	1- 2	1	0	0	0	0	2	3
35	McNary	1		0- 0	0- 0	1	0	0	0	0	0	0
33	Jennings	4		0- 0	2- 2	0	0	0	0	1	0	2
	Team					3						
	Totals		1- 7	23-58	18-28	36	9	1	7	18	22	65

SCORE BY HALVES			3FG	AFG	FT
Indiana (16-2, 5-0)	36	38— 74	.500	.510	.760
Purdue (11-3, 2-3)	23	42— 65	.143	.397	.643

Officials—Tom Rucker, Jody Silvester, Ron Zetcher.
Attendance—14,123.

College Player of the Year Calbert
Cheaney (40) and the 1992-93 Indiana
basketball seniors left behind a major
contribution to the rich Hoosier
basketball legacy. Cheaney set IU and
Big Ten records with his 2,613 career
points, and his 785 points as a senior set
an IU record. The senior group Cheaney
headed celebrated its first clear-cut Big
Ten championship on Senior Night at
Assembly Hall (facing camera, from left,
Greg Graham, Chris Reynolds, Matt
Nover and Cheaney). The four left with a
four-year record of 105-27, including 87-
16 over the last three years, the most
victories ever for a Big Ten school in a
three-season period.

*Matt Nover, who had his career high with
29 points against Kentucky as a senior
(left), shot over .700 from both the field
and the free-throw line in the Hoosiers'
final 10 games, after a knee injury to
Alan Henderson. Nover closed his career
with IU's field-goal percentage records
for both a season (.628 this year) and
career (.571).*

Calbert Cheaney's senior season moved him into No. 1 on many Indiana and Big Ten scoring lists, but equally as important in his College Player of the Year season, for Coach Bob Knight, was Cheaney's leadership. Knight called Cheaney the best combination of a player and a leader he has had in his 22 seasons as Indiana coach.

Calbert Cheaney stood up to close defensive attention from Michigan's Juwan Howard (left) and every other opponent in becoming the first Big Ten player in 17 years, and second Hoosier in history, to be named college basketball's Player of the Year. Cheaney swept all 13 major awards, as well as the Chicago Tribune silver basketball as the Big Ten's Most Valuable Player. On March 4 at Assembly Hall, Cheaney scored his career Big Ten high, 35 points, and became the all-time IU and Big Ten recordholder, and he was presented the game ball (below). He and Greg Graham (closing in on Penn State's Michael Jennings, right) were the highest-scoring duo in IU basketball history, with a combined 1,362 points.

For Calbert Cheaney and Greg Graham, a season to smile about

Greg Graham was named the Big Ten's Defensive Player of the Year, but he didn't spend all of his season as the player doing the guarding (with Minnesota's Voshon Lenard, left). Graham and Calbert Cheaney (above) became the first set of Hoosiers to be unanimous all-Big Ten selections since Randy Wittman and Ted Kitchel in 1983.

The on-court and off-court exuberance of Chris Reynolds created a role for him as the Hoosiers' instant ignition charge. Reynolds, a pre-law student from Peoria, Ill., also was the biggest Hoosier fan of four-year roommate Calbert Cheaney (right).

The description of Calbert Cheaney was by Matt Nover (above): "I think he really cares about everybody on the team a lot. If you'll notice, he's a really huggy kind of person at times, which is great. We all love that and appreciate that." Huggy was not the first word that Louisville star Dwayne Morton would have had for Cheaney after their brief first-half face-off in the Midwest Regional at St. Louis. Morton later termed it "just two young men expressing their emotions" and called Cheaney a "great player." Cheaney had 32 points as Indiana won, 82-69, in the first NCAA tournament collision of the two tourney perennials.

Just exactly what the Big Ten championship means to an Indiana player shows in the emotions of Calbert Cheaney and Greg Graham as they grasp the trophy Commissioner Jim Delany presented to them after they clinched the first outright championship of their four years. Cheaney (right) passes his own congratulations out to fellow seniors Chris Reynolds and Matt Nover.

from 12 down with just over 11 minutes left to trail just 55-51 when Brian Evans, left open on the right side, sank a 3-point shot. "*That* was frustrating," Keady said, "because if you're not a village idiot, you know after the Illinois game he can shoot it . . . and you don't leave him."

The closest Purdue got after that was 62-57, and Evans answered that by hitting a two-shot foul. That started the Hoosiers on an Illinois rerun: they put the game away by hitting their last 10 free throws (four by Cheaney, two each by Greg Graham and Damon Bailey, after the Evans pair).

The three-game road trip that looked so formidable from the front ended with a joyful two-hour busride back to Bloomington.

There, the joy ended. As the players got off the bus just after midnight at Assembly Hall, they heard the news that had rocked the college basketball world while they were traveling:

Iowa forward Chris Street, one of the best players in a strong Big Ten year and one of the most popular because of his competitive fire, had been killed in an Iowa City traffic crash.

The triumphal Hoosiers, with so much to celebrate and banter about, put their gear away in stunned silence and went home.

Purdue star Glen Robinson faced a red wall of (from left) Matt Nover, Damon Bailey, Brian Evans and Calbert Cheaney.

CHAPTER 4

The governor, and No. 1

' 'Offense wins
fans. Defense
wins games.'
That made me
feel good.'

Chris Reynolds

Chris Reynolds, the only non-Hoosier on Big Ten champion Indiana's playing roster, arrived at IU familiar with winning basketball games – bright, sharp, willing to lead, and a lousy shooter. At Washington, Ind., halfway through the post-season tour Indiana's four seniors took in April, Reynolds had a 58-point game – Chris Reynolds, who scored 44 points in the whole 18-game Big Ten season. It was, he said, truly amazing, the one time in his life "when I'd just shoot the ball and feel like every shot was going to go in… kinda like Calbert feels every day of his life, I guess."

No one knows roles better than Chris Reynolds, non-shooter and not the least abashed about it though shooting is the most defining and visible aspect of the game he plays. "It's not frustrating for me at all," he said. "It's frustrating more for other people. I'm very comfortable, but they're not.

"Somebody wrote a letter to me one time that made me feel real good. The person kinda compared me to Calbert. At the end, she wrote, 'Offense wins fans. Defense wins games.' That made me feel good." How his roomie felt about it – and be certain that he saw it – is unrecorded.

The roommate is Cheaney, with whom Reynolds shared an apartment all four of their Indiana years. He and Cheaney had met when they made their official recruiting visit the same weekend – Cheaney up from Evansville, Reynolds in from Peoria. "We talked a little bit," Reynolds said, "but he never talked much then. I don't know if he was introverted, shy or what – you can't shut him up now, but he wouldn't talk back then."

When the freshman recruiting group began settling the rooming matter, Reynolds said, "Pat Graham and Chris Lawson were friends. Greg Graham and Todd Leary were from Indianapolis. They just kinda left us."

Just as happenstance was the fact this poor-shooting contributor to an era of big basketball success wore the No. 21 jersey that – at another school, where jerseys or numbers of heroes are retired – would be flying from the Assembly Hall rafters in honor of another non-shooter but big winner from Illinois, Quinn Buckner.

Reynolds has met Buckner and heard enough about him to admire his playing greatness. But as for No. 21: "I wanted No. 20," Reynolds said. "I had that for four years in high school. Greg (Graham) wanted 20 also, and they gave it to him because he committed before I did. So I just took 21."

The comparison still is valid. The Buckner impact on a basketball game, in the mid-1970s when Indiana won 90 percent of the time, never really was properly described by box score numbers. Reynolds was even less of a numbers man, but he had a defined role and frequently over his four Indiana seasons played it.

Primarily it was to pick up the pace of a game – on offense, on defense, on anything that needed it. Sometimes it was reflected in steals, or in assists, or even occasionally in points scored. He had 14 points, plus seven assists and five steals in a 40-minute performance in his first college start at Notre Dame as a freshman.

Facing page: Bob Knight thought sparkplug Chris Reynolds 'almost singlehandedly' turned IU's Ohio State game around.

More representative was Indiana's 96-69 victory over Ohio State at Assembly Hall, when the Hoosiers had more problems than the score shows.

Indiana led 40-32 at halftime, and Buckeye coach Randy Ayers felt good about that. "I thought we had slowed down the tempo of the game some. When you go in at the half and Indiana is shooting 38 percent, you've got to be pretty pleased, only down eight." He figured to be even more pleased when his freshman-stacked team four minutes deep into the second half still was down just 49-41, after falling back to 49-34 and regrouping.

Enter Reynolds. At 6-feet, he took the ball off the Buckeyes' offensive board to provide one Indiana possession, then took a charge on defense to provide another. Now, the Assembly Hall crowd was perked up and so was the home team. Damon Bailey thwarted a Buckeye fast break by getting back quickly and effectively, drawing a traveling call against Ohio State freshman Greg Simpson. Then it was Bailey who pulled off a rebound and sailed a breakout pass to Calbert Cheaney for a dunk.

In three minutes, Indiana had re-established command of the game at 55-41 and started on its way to a blowout.

On that day, the one Reynolds himself picks as the game that sent him away feeling best about fulfilling his role, the box score showed him with two points, two assists and nothing else even that glorious.

But his coach that day said:

"I thought Reynolds almost singlehandedly turned the thing around. He made a couple of really good defensive plays and he seemed to get everybody else trying to play to his level. Our rebounding improved, our pressure improved, everything we were doing improved."

Alan Henderson felt Reynolds "picked up the whole team. Everybody just kept

Brian Evans (left) and Damon Bailey dig in to tie up Lawrence Funderburke.

Jan. 24, Assembly Hall											
OHIO STATE 69											
No.	Min	3FG	AFG	FT	R	A	BS	St	TO	PF	Pts
34 Funderburke, f	23		2-6	4-6	4	2	2	1	4	2	8
40 Dudley, f	9		2-2	0-0	3	1	0	0	0	5	4
4 Etzler, g	8	0-1	0-1	0-0	2	0	0	0	0	0	0
15 Skelton, g	25	0-3	4-10	2-2	1	1	0	0	3	2	10
20 Davis, g	25	1-1	4-6	0-0	0	1	0	2	1	4	9
41 Watson	23		3-5	0-0	4	0	0	1	2	3	6
3 Simpson	32	1-4	6-15	2-3	3	2	0	2	6	3	15
23 Anderson	25	0-3	1-7	4-4	2	3	0	0	1	1	6
31 Brandewie	9		1-2	1-4	2	0	0	0	0	1	3
33 Macon	13		3-3	0-0	4	0	1	1	1	3	6
44 Wilbourne	5		1-1	0-0	2	0	0	0	1	1	2
42 Ratliff	3		0-0	0-0	0	0	0	0	0	0	0
Team					3						
Totals		2-12	27-58	13-19	30	10	3	7	19	25	69
INDIANA 96											
No.	Min	3FG	AFG	FT	R	A	BS	St	TO	PF	Pts
40 Cheaney, f	31	1-4	10-22	6-6	11	2	1	1	4	2	27
44 Henderson, f	24		5-9	4-5	9	0	0	1	1	3	14
24 Nover, c	25		3-6	2-4	6	0	0	0	2	3	8
20 G.Graham, g	29	0-2	4-7	3-3	1	3	0	3	3	1	11
22 Bailey, g	25	1-3	2-7	4-4	3	2	0	2	0	1	9
21 Reynolds	20		1-2	0-0	1	2	0	0	0	3	2
34 Evans	24	1-1	4-4	5-7	6	1	0	1	1	2	14
30 Leary	16	1-1	2-3	4-4	2	1	0	1	1	1	9
25 Knight	6		1-3	0-0	0	1	0	0	0	0	2
Team					1						
Totals		4-11	32-63	28-33	40	12	1	9	12	16	96

SCORE BY HALVES			3FG	AFG	FT
Ohio State (9-5, 2-3)	32	37— 69	.167	.466	.684
Indiana (17-2, 6-0)	40	56— 96	.364	.508	.848

Technical fouls—Anderson.
Officials—Ed Hightower, Sam Lickliter, Jody Silvester.
Attendance—17,007.

trying to play as hard as Chris was."

Reynolds knows his job. "Coach always talks about hard play being contagious. Guys started moving a little faster, cutting a little harder, getting down and playing defense. For me to see other guys kinda feed off the energy I give out on the court makes me feel good – that I'm able to get guys like Calbert Cheaney and Greg Graham, all-Americans, to play harder and listen to what I say when I'm out there.

"I just try to pick everyone up so we can play as we're capable of playing. The first half, we didn't play like a Top 10 team. The second half, we knew because of their quick guard play, if we didn't pick it up, we might be in trouble. We went out and played as hard as we could. The score took care of itself."

Knight has been an open admirer of the Reynolds approach to basketball – all-out, always. That was the reason Knight, when he had his annual talk with IU students in October at the IU Auditorium, included Reynolds on the program, the first time he has had one of his basketball players share the speaking role.

"If we could get everybody to play the game like this kid does, we would be very difficult to beat," Knight told the students in introducing Reynolds. "Chris has a heart so big you have to fold it over about three times to get it inside his chest."

Reynolds told the students of his senior year at Central High in Peoria. "I had this teacher named Mrs. McCann, for trigonometry, one of the toughest, meanest teachers I ever had in my life. From the first day of class, she was on my butt. She would constantly call on me in class and have me go up to the board and do problems. Whenever I wasn't able to do a problem, she would make me come in after school and work it. And she wouldn't let me leave till I could not only do that problem but all the problems assigned that day.

"Our team was No. 1-ranked in Illinois, and my coach didn't appreciate me missing practice time. I told him this teacher was picking on me because I was a basketball player. He told me to deal with it the best way I could.

"So, whenever she told me to come after school, I'd smile at her and say, 'Fine. I'll see you at 3 o'clock.' In the back of my mind, I wanted to grab her and choke her to death.

"But I was so wrapped up in basketball I didn't realize how much I was learning in her class. No longer did I see her as a cruel and tough lady but someone who really cared about me.

"So then I came to IU. I got off to a pretty good start – the teachers were fine. And then Oct. 15 came, the first day of practice. I'm sitting there in my chair thinking, 'This isn't basketball practice. This is like class.'

"And about this time, I'm thinking, 'Mrs. McCann now rates a very distant second on my meanest and toughest teacher list.'

"The scary thing about Coach's 'class' is it doesn't just last a semester, it lasts four

Bedeviled by Ohio State's Doug Etzler, Todd Leary looks for a target.

years. Professor Knight requires us to think at all times. Practice is like a pop quiz. You always have to be on your toes. We learn in practice that few things can be accomplished without hard work . . . that preparation, perseverance and exactness are keys to success in any field.

"My freshman year, Coach brought a friend in to talk to us, Johnny Bench. He stressed to us that nothing magical happened to him. He was a success because he worked hard at it.

"As I shook his hand, I didn't see him as Johnny Bench, the great baseball player, but a person who would have been a success at anything he chose in life. Coach has brought in people like Tony LaRussa, Bill Parcells, Red Auerbach, D. Wayne Lukas – all great people and excellent role models. They didn't speak to us as if they were high and almighty. They showed us they were just ordinary people with extraordinary drive and determination.

"I want to go back to my community in Illinois and be a role model."

Probably, the good governor saw more from the Gophers than he anticipated in this game.

Minnesota followed Ohio State into Assembly Hall, and in St. Paul, Arne Carlson cleared an opening in state business, tuned in the TV set in the governor's mansion, and sat back to watch his beloved Gophers. The governor is a *big* Gopher fan, Minnesota coach Clem Haskins said. "We're good friends. We spend a lot of time together. We go out once or twice a month for dinner. We go fishing every year."

And, when the Gophers play at Williams Arena, "he's there every game. He's our No. 1 fan."

Probably, the good governor saw more from the Gophers than he anticipated in this game. Five minutes into it, the score was 16-4. Minnesota.

But, Greg Graham cut to a basket, Alan Henderson stole the ball and Graham hit a 3, Henderson claimed Indiana's first rebound of the night and Graham hit another 3. That quickly, it was a 16-14 game. The storm seemed over.

But it wasn't. Minnesota, usually a fast-break team that on this night played out each possession patiently and prudently, reclaimed that early margin at 30-18. It still was 48-39 with just 13 minutes left.

As the clock dipped under the 5-minute mark with the Gophers' lead 55-53, Minnesota ran off most of the 45-second shot clock and Voshon Lenard missed with a 3. Bailey went up with the big men and grabbed the rebound, then turned upcourt looking for a chance to pass for a quick score. He advanced at normal speed, then suddenly shifted to high and shot through the Gopher defense for a layup that became a 3-point play and the first Indiana lead of the night.

"Damon just put a burst of speed on and went to the hole," Henderson said. Haskins called it "just a heady play on his part. Damon Bailey really exploited us down the stretch."

With 29 seconds left, trailing 58-57 but possessing the ball, Haskins set up what he wanted at a time out. Arriel McDonald, a leader in the upset bid, got the basketball, with Greg Graham guarding him. Tightly. McDonald probed for an opening from the top of the key, then worked to his left as the clock moved inside 15 seconds.

"I knew when he kept coming at me and backing up they were trying to hold the ball," Graham said. "I wanted to stay close enough that I maintained pressure... I could hear the official counting ... "

Jan. 27, Assembly Hall
MINNESOTA 57

No.	Min	3FG	AFG	FT	R	A	BS	St	TO	PF	Pts
32 Walton, f	29		6- 9	2- 2	8	2	0	0	1	5	14
34 Carter, f	32		3- 6	0- 0	3	3	0	0	1	5	6
51 Kolander, c	25		1- 2	3- 4	3	0	1	0	2	4	5
10 McDonald, g	34	0- 2	6-10	2- 2	0	2	0	1	5	1	14
21 Lenard, g	22	0- 1	4- 9	0- 0	3	4	0	1	3	5	8
4 Tubbs	12		0- 0	0- 0	2	0	0	0	1	3	0
23 Orr	20	2- 3	2- 3	1- 2	1	1	0	2	1	1	7
25 Jackson	24		0- 1	3- 4	4	1	2	0	1	0	3
40 Washington	1		0- 0	0- 0	0	0	0	0	0	0	0
3 Wolf	1		0- 0	0- 0	0	0	0	0	0	0	0
Team					2						
Totals		2- 6	22-40	11-14	26	13	3	4	15	24	57

INDIANA 61

No.	Min	3FG	AFG	FT	R	A	BS	St	TO	PF	Pts
40 Cheaney, f	39	0- 1	2- 9	7- 8	5	2	0	0	3	1	11
44 Henderson, f	32		6-10	4- 5	3	0	1	4	0	3	16
24 Nover, c	28		1- 3	0- 0	2	0	1	0	0	1	2
20 G.Graham, g	37	2- 4	5- 7	0- 0	1	1	0	1	3	1	12
22 Bailey, g	31	1- 2	4-10	8-11	4	1	0	0	0	4	17
21 Reynolds	9		0- 0	0- 0	0	0	0	0	1	2	0
34 Evans	20	0- 2	1- 3	1- 3	2	0	1	2	1	2	3
30 Leary	3		0- 1	0- 0	0	0	0	0	0	0	0
25 Knight	1		0- 0	0- 0	0	0	0	0	0	0	0
Team					4						
Totals		3- 9	19-43	20-27	21	4	3	7	8	14	61

SCORE BY HALVES

			3FG	AFG	FT
Minnesota (11-5, 3-4)	35	22— 57	.333	.550	.786
Indiana (18-2, 7-0)	30	31— 61	.333	.442	.741

Officials—Art McDonald, Tom O'Neill, Sid Rodeheffer.
Attendance—15,696.

Whistle.

Five-second close-guarding call. Possession to Indiana.

Bailey hit one of two free throws at 0:08 for a 59-57 lead that still left Minnesota a chance. Lenard passed up a 3-point bid to take the ball to the basket, but on the way – against an Indiana defense that didn't fear a non-shooting foul because Minnesota wasn't yet shooting a one-and-one – he had the ball stripped away and Cheaney padded the score to 61-57 with two free throws at 0:01.

Damon Bailey goes to the hole against Minnesota's Jayson Walton.

Associated Press
JAN. 26

1.	Kansas (49)	1,603
2.	Indiana (7)	1,520
3.	North Carolina (9)	1,517
4.	Kentucky	1,436
5.	Michigan	1,391
6.	Cincinnati	1,254
7.	Duke	1,207
8.	Arizona	1,134
9.	Seton Hall	1,044
10.	UNLV	1,010
11.	Iowa	841
14.	Purdue	697

Greg Graham has Nate Tubbs' forearm and helper Townsend Orr to beat on a twisting drive.

Haskins was proud of his team's performance, which included checking Cheaney with just nine shots and 11 points. "They did a really good job on Cheaney," Knight said.

"That's as determined and tough-minded as I've seen Bailey play in the three years that he's been here. He really kinda carried us through when we had to have some things. A real offensive key for us in the second half was Bailey's determination.

"This was a great game for us. When we were behind, I thought it was a great game for us. We have to be able to play in that kind of situation. We've had a lot of games – too many games here at home, probably – that we've won too easily. I was really pleased with what we were able to do to come back. I think we played pretty well – maybe as hard and as well on defense as we've played all year. Minnesota is a very, very good basketball team, and they had things set up really well."

Haskins, the man who did that setting up, no doubt thought Lenard was fouled. Certainly, he objected to the five-second call, but he bit his lip. "We had a play in mind," he said. "My guards dribbled the ball a little too much, I guess."

Back home, the governor didn't handle it as coolly. He fired off a letter to Big Ten officiating supervisor Rich Falk, and released it for public viewing: "I was saddened to watch the Minnesota-Indiana game and see the referees take a victory from Minnesota. I have never written a letter like this, but, I must confess, I am still outraged. It was not a question of an occasional bad call here or there, which all basketball fans can expect. It had all the earmarks of a deliberate plan to simply take the game away from Minnesota. In all the years that I have been watching basketball, I can honestly say that I have never seen worse refereeing."

When Haskins saw the letter in print, "I was kinda embarrassed," he said. "I know people think 'Clem got him to do that.' No, I didn't. I was shocked to death. I read it in the paper the next morning and couldn't believe it.

"But he's a fan. He just got emotionally involved with the game and filed a letter.

"When I first started coaching, an old coach told me, 'Keep your mouth closed – and when you do talk, don't put anything in writing. You may say something and deny it, but if you put it in black and white, you've got problems.'

"Maybe I ought to pass it on to him."

The game had an April postscript. The College Basketball Rules Committee threw out the five-second close-guarding call, effective in the 1993-94 season.

Haskins is a member of the committee.

Alan Henderson, Calbert Cheaney engulf Damon Bailey after a go-ahead 3-point drive — 'just a heady play on his part,' Minnesota coach Clem Haskins said.

Almost three-quarters of the way through a 93-71 victory at Northwestern, Knight wasn't sure that Cheaney, after carrying the Hoosier load so long, wasn't beginning to run out of gas. He had followed the 11-point Minnesota game with just five points through a TV timeout with 11:46 left at Northwestern – Indiana in no particular trouble but still catchable, with a 55-43 lead.

"I almost put him on the bench," Knight said. "He was going to drift outside and be a jump shooter. He got the message."

The next TV break was less than four minutes later, and Cheaney used those four minutes to singe the Wildcats for 11 points. He tacked on six more quick ones for a 22-point game before sitting down with 2:41 to play, Indiana's lead doubled at 84-60.

"It looked like we had a shot," Northwestern coach Bill Foster said. "Then it was Cheaney, Cheaney, Cheaney."

Knight did feel some special factors were involved. "I think our team is tired," he said as the Hoosiers headed into a seven-day opening in their schedule. "In some of these games, Cheaney has been ridden so hard I thought about getting a saddle for him. I've seen him grabbed three or four times on the same sequence of plays with sometimes nothing being called.

"He's got to move, and people are taking a piece of him everywhere he goes. I think he has held up remarkably well, but I'm sure he will welcome a couple of days off."

Big Ten home-road

	League	Best at home		Best on road	
1993	60-39	.606	Indiana●	9-0 Indiana●	8-1
1992	60-30	.667	Indiana	9-0 Ohio St.●	7-2
1991	54-36	.600	Ohio St.●●	9-0 Indiana●●	8-1
1990	60-30	.667	Mich. St.●/Mich.	Mich. St.●	7-2
			Illinois/Pur.	8-1	
1989	63-27	.700	Illinois	9-0 Indiana●	7-2
1988	58-32	.644	Purdue●	9-0 Purdue●	7-2
1987	53-37	.589	Indiana●●	9-0 Pur.●●/Iowa	7-2

●Outright champion. ●●Co-champion.

The week of Indiana's Minnesota-Northwestern games had opened with No. 1-ranked Kansas taking a shocking whipping, 64-49 at home, by Long Beach State. While Indiana was playing Northwestern, North Carolina – No. 3 in one poll and No. 2 in the other, reversing spots with Indiana – was getting trounced by Wake Forest, 87-61.

On Super Sunday, the coaches in the CNN/*USA Today* poll swept Indiana into No. 1, and a day later, the sportswriter electorate of the Associated Press poll did the same thing.

Knight had joked about the inevitable after the Northwestern game. "It puts a target on your ass, that's all it does," he laughed.

Most would figure Knight as likely to disdain the "honor" as unwelcome baggage, but that wasn't at all the tone he took in sitting down with his team and discussing it, once the votes were in.

On Super Sunday, the coaches in the CNN/USA Today poll swept Indiana into No. 1.

"In 15 years, when you see another team is ranked No. 1," he said, "you'll be able to sit back and think, 'We were there once.'

"That's always the goal of our program. We'd prefer to have it when there are no more games to be played, of course. But whether we're there a game, a week, a month, or till there are no more games left, it's something for you to remember."

Jan. 30, Welsh-Ryan Arena, Evanston

INDIANA 93

No.		Min	3FG	AFG	FT	R	A	BS	St	TO	PF	Pts
40 Cheaney, f		32	0- 2	7-15	8- 9	5	0	1	2	2	2	22
44 Henderson, f		12		2- 6	0- 0	5	1	1	1	0	1	4
24 Nover, c		35		1- 2	8-12	4	1	3	0	4	2	10
20 G.Graham, g		30	1- 2	6-11	8- 8	5	2	0	2	1	0	21
22 Bailey, g		20	0- 2	1- 5	5- 6	0	2	0	1	2	2	7
21 Reynolds		27		1- 1	2- 2	2	5	0	1	3	2	4
25 Knight		7		2- 2	0- 0	1	1	0	0	1	0	4
30 Leary		13	2- 4	3- 5	2- 2	3	0	0	0	0	1	10
34 Evans		24	1- 3	4- 9	2- 2	6	1	1	0	2	2	11
Team						8						
Totals			**4-13**	**27-56**	**35-41**	**39**	**13**	**6**	**7**	**15**	**12**	**93**

NORTHWESTERN 71

No.		Min	3FG	AFG	FT	R	A	BS	St	TO	PF	Pts
4 Neloms, f		38	1- 2	9-25	1- 2	5	1	1	1	6	2	20
40 Howell, f		25		4- 6	3- 4	2	0	0	1	2	3	11
55 Rankin, c		35		3- 7	6- 6	10	4	2	2	1	2	12
23 Baldwin, g		37	0- 1	7-13	5- 5	2	4	0	4	2	4	19
24 Lee, g		16	0- 2	1- 4	1- 2	4	3	0	0	2	5	3
23 Purdy		9	0- 1	1- 2	0- 0	1	0	0	0	0	3	2
22 Simpson		4		0- 0	0- 0	0	0	0	0	0	1	0
30 Kirkpatrick		21	0- 3	1- 7	0- 0	3	3	0	1	0	5	2
33 Yonke		4	0- 1	0- 2	0- 0	1	0	0	0	1	1	0
34 Rayford		4		0- 1	0- 0	0	0	0	0	0	0	0
44 Williams		7		1- 1	0- 0	4	1	0	0	1	0	2
Team						5						
Totals			**1-10**	**27-68**	**16-19**	**37**	**16**	**3**	**9**	**15**	**26**	**71**

SCORE BY HALVES				3FG	AFG	FT
Indiana (19-2, 8-0)	41	52—	93	.308	.482	.854
Northwestern (5-10, 0-6)	29	42—	71	.100	.397	.842

Officials—Phil Bova, Randy Drury, Sid Rodeheffer.
Attendance—8,117.

Northwestern steals leader Pat Baldwin (center) and blocked shots leader Kevin Rankin can't stop Alan Henderson on a drive.

Paging Ivan Renko

The weekend his Indiana basketball team moved into No. 1 in the national polls, Bob Knight dropped a slow-fuse bomb that made No. 1 not even close to the hot conversational item in Bloomington, around Hoosier-loving Indiana, and even across the country. In the midst of his Sunday television show the day after the Northwestern game, Knight told interviewer Chuck Marlowe: "I spoke at a clinic in Europe last July. I was given some information over there on a kid from Yugoslavia. When I got back from the Northwestern game, on my desk was an indication that this kid has committed to coming to Indiana.

"He's a 6-8, 230-pound kid . . . anybody who follows the political situation of civil unrest in Yugoslavia can appreciate the fact that we'd just kinda like to leave it go at that. The kid's name is Ivan Renko. Let it suffice to say that we're very pleased."

By the next day, Ivan Renko had become an Indiana legend.

A wild, wild guess: The target of it all was the fast-growing group of charlatans who claim expertise in the evaluation of high school players – how they rate (you can get the power forwards ranked 1-through-70), who (supposedly) is recruiting them, where (supposedly) they're looking, their strengths, their weaknesses, their SAT scores. It's a lucrative larceny that adds enormously to the pressures and expectations that already are far too high for top recruits.

At a late-season press conference, Knight was laughing but wholly believable when he said, "There are a lot of people in the press that I truly like and respect, but as a group, you're not real high on my list. But you are higher than these recruiting people are. As long as those (bleeps) exist, you're a step at least in front of them."

So, on a Sunday in January, Knight threw the world Ivan Renko.

The gurus scrambled. One called Renko "a white Larry Johnson." Another said there was no such fellow one morning and went on radio that night verifying that Yugoslavian Ivan Renko would be going to Indiana. One said Ivan had been on the Indiana campus within the last two weeks. Another warned that Knight was risking an NCAA penalty by discussing a recruit's name publicly before he has signed a tender.

Indiana fans sensed the spoof early and joined in. One told an Indianapolis radio station he had seen the passenger list of a U.S. Air Indianapolis-to-New York flight and it included an Ivan Renko.

After Indiana's second game with Michigan, Knight commended Wolverine coach Steve Fisher's job of blending five touted recruits together. "You don't know what it is to have to coach a group of kids with some of the baloney that you people write about those kids," Knight chided his reporter/listeners.

"With all the really good teams that we've had here, I've never had to contend with all of that. I'll have it when I get Ivan Renko here. I don't know how I'm going to handle it, as good as the publicity will be on him.

"In fact, I'm honestly thinking about not letting Ivan come now."

One Indiana fan told an Indianapolis radio station he had seen the passenger list of a U.S. Air Indianapolis-to-New York flight and it included an Ivan Renko.

CHAPTER 5

A Nittany night, and daylight

Neither Ivan Renko nor their new No. 1 national ranking occupied Hoosier minds as they began their second lap around the league. Their first rematch was with Iowa, such a drastically changed team, physically and emotionally, in the exact month since they had played before.

The Hoosiers arrived in Iowa City in gloomy fog and stayed at the same motel where Chris Street and the Hawkeyes had eaten their game-eve dinner on Jan. 19, the night Street was killed. On the way to the game, the Hoosiers' bus passed through the intersection where driver Street, headed with his fiancee for a night class, had somehow failed to notice an approaching dump truck and had stopped for a sign, then driven straight into the truck's path.

At Carver-Hawkeye Arena, the Hoosiers stepped into a funereal atmosphere of loving grief. Street's family had picked this game, the Indiana game, for a ceremony retiring his No. 40 jersey. The game program, sold out a half-hour before the tipoff, had a full-length action picture of Street on the front cover, his close-up, smiling face on the back.

Mike and Patty Street, Chris's parents, and sisters Sarah and Betsy came onto the court for the pre-game ceremony. They stood together, facing the cheering fans with as brave a front as they could manage, their arms, behind them, intertwined in support.

And then it was time to play.

Fervently, almost desperately, that always loyal crowd wanted the Hawkeyes to honor Chris Street one last time with victory. The same crowd had willed Iowa to a performance above its capabilities just six days before, the first home game the team had played since the Street accident. That day, mighty Michigan had fallen, 89-80, the only Big Ten game the Wolverines were to lose other than their games with Indiana.

Months later, the passion of that Iowa crowd remained in Matt Nover's mind. So much, they wanted a win for Chris Street. "Yeah, I know," Nover said softly. "*I almost didn't want to beat them.*"

Nover was the one his teammates glanced at when the awful word came that night when they returned from Purdue. They knew that the summer before had made Matt Nover and Chris Street friends. They had heard Nover talk about what a good guy, as well as good player, Street was.

The two had played together on a Big Ten all-star team that toured Europe, Nover the team's leading scorer, Street its leading rebounder. "We got real close," Nover said. "We happened to be the first two to get to camp at

Patty and Mike Street accept an I blanket on the night Iowa retired the jersey of their son, Chris, killed in a Jan. 19 car-truck crash.

In first game, Matt Nover moves by Acie Earl and finds way blocked by friend Chris Street –'I just think he was a tremendous person.'

Iowa star Acie Earl gets sandwiched by Hoosiers Matt Nover (24) and Alan Henderson, as Greg Graham closes in.

Northwestern, and we started hanging out from there.

"In the practices at the camp, we really went at each other, rebounding and scoring inside. We each took it as a challenge, to outdo the other guy. There was mutual respect, I think.

"I really looked up to him as a player. I thought he had a great attitude – the things he said, the way he acted on and off the floor. I learned some things from him that I'll carry on into life outside of basketball. I just think he was a tremendous person. I said these things to my parents then, when I called home to talk to them. 'This guy just has a great outlook on life, how to treat people with respect.'

"That night when we got off the bus in front of Assembly Hall . . . (trainer) Tim Garl heard it over the phone and told me. I was just speechless, in total shock.

"I don't know if I slept at all that night. I just couldn't get it out of my mind. I was down for a long time. When someone's life is taken like that, you realize how precious things are."

The Hawkeyes were as zealous for victory as their crowd was. They jumped out 8-3, 19-9. "We came within a notch of getting knocked out right there," Knight said. Iowa led 24-14 when 3-point baskets by Damon Bailey and Calbert Cheaney highlighted a 10-0 spurt that tied the game. Iowa's last lead was 62-61 with just under five minutes left. Bailey went up with the 6-foot-10 Earl for a 60-foot pass Cheaney had lofted. Somehow, Bailey came out with it and took the ball to the basket for a two-shot foul that put the Hoosiers in front for good in a 73-66 victory.

It was the Hoosier seniors' fourth straight victory in a 10-year-old building where Iowa's percentage against everyone else was .823 – including 6-1 against previous Indiana teams. Cheaney was 12-for-15 in scoring 27 points, after going 13-for-17 (29 points) and 11-for-19 (30 points) the previous two years there. That's 36-for-51 (.706) shooting and a 28.7 average. "I don't think he needs my pat on the back," Iowa coach Tom Davis said, "but Calbert Cheaney is obviously terrific."

Cheaney and Nover had gone to the Hoosiers' lockerroom after the game when an Iowa manager entered and asked them to return to the court for a minute. The Street family had requested a chance to meet them – Cheaney, the Big Ten's best player (and Indiana's No. 40, by coincidence), and Nover, about whom the Streets in Indianola, Iowa, apparently had heard as much that summer as the Novers in Chesterton, Ind., had of Chris Street.

"That was really emotional," Nover said. "My eyes started watering when I went out there. His mom and dad are special people. They really have an inner strength, to handle it the way they have."

Knight learned that the Street family requested to have the ceremony at the Indiana game "because of the way that Chris felt and the enjoyment he got playing against Indiana. It pleased me immensely, maybe as much as anything that has been done as far as Indiana basketball is concerned over the years.

"The Iowa people have really rallied around the team and the family, but that's what I would expect from the people here. This is the 22nd time I've come out here, and there aren't any better fans. I'm sure they've been a real help to the family."

Tom Davis said yes, the pre-game ceremony had affected him, as had so many things in day-to-day life that reminded him and his team of their loss.

"I walk in the lockerroom and his locker is still there, his equipment is still there, his suit coat is still hanging in there, just the way he left it," Davis said. "Every time there's something like this, it just gets inside you. Sometimes you'd rather block it out, but I think it's better that we deal with it and go from there."

Somehow, gritty Iowa – obviously a considerably lesser team without a scorer, rebounder, defender and all-round contributor like Street – won 10 of the 14 games it played after the accident, and Tom Davis's team shared third place in the league.

Indiana stepped into a whole different kind of basketball environment at Penn State, just three nights after the Iowa game.

When Big Ten presidents made their surprise announcement in December 1989 that Penn State would be extended membership, Bob Knight had expressed his disapproval of the whole idea of expansion, when it included stretching the league's geographic borders. Penn State, Knight said, was such a tough place to get to in the winter time – basketball time – that it amounted to an overnight camping trip.

It was 1993 before the Lions could be integrated into the league basketball schedule. Knight's first trip in was a community festival, the campout theme dominant as the folks of University Park, Pa., prepared to "welcome" their logistical critic. Indiana's No. 1 ranking, plus the ease of the Hoosiers' 105-57 first-game victory at Assembly Hall, left little real hope of an upset in Happy Valley, but the arrival of Knight and his team nevertheless was an Event.

Penn State coach Bruce Parkhill, who went to dinner with Knight the evening before the game, had his team basketball-ready. Indiana led 34-32 at halftime. Up to then, John Amaechi hadn't been much of a Hoosier problem: two points, three defensive rebounds, nothing like the impact the 6-foot-10, 260-pound native of Manchester, England, had been making in a year that saw the Vanderbilt transfer lead the Big Ten in blocked shots and wind up No. 4 in rebounds and No. 14 in scoring, probably second only to Purdue's Glenn Robinson among the league's 1992-93 newcomers.

Amaechi opened the second half with an offensive rebound basket that tied the game. The rest of the way, Amaechi drew nine fouls, putting both Matt Nover and Alan Henderson out of the game and helping himself to a 19-point performance. On this night, the Henderson loss was especially costly for Indiana. Despite time lost to the fouls, he had his career Big Ten high of 17 rebounds, plus 16 points.

The double-overtime game became one for the ages because of the finish to regulation time. With 19 seconds left, Penn State led 68-66 and had the ball out of bounds on the sideline at the Indiana scoring end. After a Penn State timeout, Indiana's Chris Reynolds lined up with Greg Bartram, at about the Indiana free-throw line. "I'm kinda

Feb. 6, Carver-Hawkeye Arena, Iowa City

INDIANA 73

No.	Min	3FG	AFG	FT	R	A	BS	St	TO	PF	Pts
40 Cheaney, f	38	3-3	12-15	0-0	9	3	0	2	2	2	27
44 Henderson, f	33		4-11	1-2	8	1	2	2	2	2	9
24 Nover, c	20		2-5	1-2	5	0	1	0	2	3	5
20 G.Graham, g	38	1-4	3-8	8-10	4	4	0	3	0	2	15
22 Bailey, g	30	1-5	1-7	5-8	3	3	0	0	1	2	8
21 Reynolds	15		1-3	0-0	1	2	0	1	1	2	2
34 Evans	7	0-1	1-2	0-2	1	1	0	0	1	1	2
25 Knight	4		0-0	0-0	0	0	0	0	1	0	0
30 Leary	15	1-3	2-6	0-0	1	4	0	0	0	2	5
Team					4				2		
Totals		6-16	26-57	15-24	36	18	3	8	12	16	73

IOWA 66

No.	Min	3FG	AFG	FT	R	A	BS	St	TO	PF	Pts
23 Winters, f	24		1-3	2-4	4	5	0	2	3	3	4
34 Lookingbill, f	18	1-5	3-7	1-2	1	1	1	1	0	2	8
55 Earl, c	35		8-11	0-1	4	1	3	2	5	2	16
10 Smith, g	25	1-2	3-7	4-4	6	5	0	0	2	2	11
20 Barnes, g	34	0-4	5-16	0-0	5	2	0	0	1	2	10
42 Webb	9		2-3	0-0	2	0	1	0	1	3	4
52 Millard	19	0-1	1-5	4-4	4	0	3	0	0	1	6
13 Glasper	15	1-1	1-2	0-0	1	4	0	0	0	1	3
44 Bartles	6		0-0	0-0	1	1	0	0	0	0	0
3 Murray	15		2-2	0-0	2	0	0	1	0	5	4
Team					3						
Totals		3-13	26-56	11-15	33	19	8	6	12	21	66

SCORE BY HALVES			3FG	AFG	FT
Indiana (20-2, 9-0)	38	35— 73	.375	.456	.625
Iowa (14-5, 3-4)	37	29— 66	.231	.464	.733

Officials—Ted Hillary, Ron Zetcher, Rick Wulkow.
Attendance—15,500.

'The Iowa people have really rallied around the team and the family, but that's what I would expect from the people here.'
Bob Knight

face-guarding him," Reynolds said. "Bartram takes one jab step toward our basket, at the free-throw line, and I jump way over. He pushes me a little; he 'helps' me in that direction. There's no one down at the other end and he's got me by a couple of steps, so he takes off."

Reynolds sprinted after Bartram, and the ball headed their way. The game was carried nationally by ESPN, and one of the network's cameras caught a close-up view of Bartram going up to take the long pass, Reynolds' hand jerking at his shirt, and Bartram, trying to get free, pushing Reynolds away. The call, by official Sam Lickliter, at an angle on the play where he couldn't see Reynolds' grab but clearly could see Bartram's push, made the call he saw: foul on Bartram, Indiana's possession. It became the most controversial call of the Big Ten season.

Penn State's edge-of-the-court crowd reacts with doubt, disfavor and disbelief as Greg Graham, dumped on a 3-point shot, is awarded the biggest Hoosier free throws of the year.

"Instinct told me when he was going for the open basket to just grab him, like I would do on the playground," Reynolds said. "I knew where the referee was. I really wasn't that obvious about it. It looked obvious on TV, but from where the referee was standing, I knew he couldn't see what I was doing.

"But it *was* obvious that the guy pushed off on me. When the whistle blew, I knew the foul was on him. I just knew it was.

"On TV, they made me out to be almost a criminal."

Lickliter had more of a TV grievance. The play was run and rerun by ESPN, and the official was blistered coast-to-coast. Penn State fans screamed thievery – the call obviously wrong. Lickliter was taken off a game he was supposed to work at Purdue the next night, although Big Ten officiating supervisor Rich Falk said after many looks at the play on tape, "Lickliter doesn't see anybody grab a jersey because he's the official out in front. They can only call what they see."

There was a lot of basketball left after the foul.

Indiana used the possession to tie the game. Barely. Penn State's zone defense refused to let the Hoosiers get the ball to Cheaney, and as time ran out, Greg Graham went up with a 3-point try from the deep left corner. It missed, but the luckless Bartram smashed into Graham and knocked him down as the shot was in the air – and Graham, one of the nation's best shooters, went to the free throw line with three-tenths of a second left, with three shots to change Penn State's 68-66 lead.

"I knew he was jumping to pressure the shot, but I had no idea he would rush me like he did," Graham said. "I got the shot away, but there was no way I was going to hit it. My feet weren't set – it was just a prayer."

Parkhill used his last time out, the standard freeze-the-shooter attempt. Graham was far from frozen, ultra-confident that he was going to pull this pesky game out with three quick swishes. "I definitely felt pretty good," Graham said. "It brought back memories. In the high school regional, I was in the same situation: six seconds left and down one. I hit them and we won."

His first shot rimmed out.

Now, there was extreme pressure.

"I was so excited to get up there and shoot the first one I really wasn't concentrating, I guess," he said. "Then, it settled in and I realized I *had* to hit the next two. I turned and looked at the bench and everybody was looking at me like, 'Come *on*.'

"What really went through my mind was, 'If you miss these free throws, you've got to walk around campus all week telling people how you choked.' I was telling myself, 'I *have* to make these two.' "

He hit them, and still there was a lot of bullet-dodging ahead for the Hoosiers. In the first overtime, they dropped back 74-68 but 3s by Leary, Cheaney and Damon Bailey forced a second overtime. They trailed again, 83-79, with 1:30 to go, but Cheaney hit a 3, and the score was 84-84 when Brian Evans rebounded a missed Penn State free throw with 36 seconds left. Indiana ran the clock down, and with seven seconds to go, Evans – one-on-one with 6-4 Michael Jennings on the left side of the court – faked a drive to the basket, pulled up and hit the shot over Jennings that keyed an 88-84 escape for the Hoosiers.

Parkhill, whom the TV cameras caught several times gesturing angrily or glaring accusingly at Lickliter after the call, obviously was sickened by the giant upset that got away from a team that finished 2-16 in its first Big Ten season, last. He was classy in postgame interviews. "The only thing I wish I could do is just take the pain away from those kids – I don't know what to say to them," he said.

"They had their energy level up. I really believe the fact that they were playing the No. 1 team in the country was a great deal of it.

"Indiana's a great team. Everybody gets fired up for Indiana. And I'll tell you what: they did a great job to pull this game out. That's a sign of a first-class team, to be able to dig deep and pull it out of the fire like they did. They're really something.

"I really, really admire those players and their coach."

Their coach, the overnight camper, said, "They outplayed us, they outhustled us, they outsmarted us... If I were a fan, and I'm not, I'd have been rooting like hell for Penn State because I think it was a game they deserved to win. From our standpoint, we hung in there and tied the game up and we came back. We showed some things in being able to do that."

As shaky as the victory at Penn State was, it advanced Indiana into an elite group of teams that had gone 10-0 opening a Big Ten season.

In the league's 88th year, the Hoosiers were just the 16th team to do that, and the first in 17 years. It carried with it a positive omen: the previous 15 all had won the Big Ten championship.

This one, however, knew that the race was far from over. Michigan had shown it wasn't going to drop far back, and that Tom Davis forecast of a handful of losses for the champion was not going to happen.

On Valentine's Day, with four weeks to go, Michigan moved into

Brian Evans goes up and over Penn State's Michael Jennings for the game-winning basket.

Feb. 9, Rec Hall, University Park
INDIANA 88

No.	Min	3FG	AFG	FT	R	A	BS	St	TO	PF	Pts
40 Cheaney, f	50	2- 5	11-23	0- 0	8	3	0	0	4	2	24
44 Henderson, f	33		7-15	2- 2	17	1	2	0	2	5	16
24 Nover, c	27		3- 6	1- 2	3	0	1	0	1	5	7
22 Bailey, g	45	3- 9	4-12	2- 2	4	4	0	0	3	4	13
20 G.Graham, g	41	3- 6	5-12	5- 8	2	3	0	1	2	4	18
21 Reynolds	14		1- 1	0- 0	2	3	0	0	1	2	2
34 Evans	12		1- 2	0- 0	2	0	0	0	0	1	2
30 Leary	28	2- 4	2- 5	0- 0	1	6	0	1	0	0	6
Team					5						
Totals		10-24	34-76	10-14	44	20	3	2	13	23	88

PENN STATE 84

No.	Min	3FG	AFG	FT	R	A	BS	St	TO	PF	Pts
24 Hayes, f	46		8-16	0- 0	6	6	0	0	1	0	16
30 Carr, f	29		1- 4	0- 0	2	2	0	1	2	3	2
13 Amaechi, c	48	0- 3	4- 8	11-16	9	0	3	2	1	1	19
22 Bartram, g	38	1- 3	4- 9	0- 0	3	3	0	2	1	3	9
00 Jennings, g	41	2- 3	8-13	4- 7	10	7	0	1	2	0	22
15 Carlton	16	2- 2	5- 7	2- 2	2	0	0	0	2	3	14
20 Wydman	9	0- 1	0- 1	0- 0	1	2	0	0	0	1	0
45 Joseph	4		0- 1	0- 0	1	0	0	0	1	0	0
4 Carter	19		1- 5	0- 0	4	0	0	0	1	4	2
Team					1						
Totals		5-12	31-64	17-25	39	20	3	6	11	15	84

SCORE BY HALVES				3FG	AFG	FT
Indiana (21-2, 10-0)	34	34	9 11— 88	.417	.447	.714
Penn State (6-12, 1-8)	32	36	9 7— 84	.417	.484	.680

Officials—Gene Monje, Sam Lickliter, Dan Chrisman.
Attendance—7,540.

Assembly Hall for what amounted to a Big Ten championship game. It also was for No. 1 ranking. Indiana opened the week a firm No. 1, but No. 2 Kentucky and No. 3 Duke already had lost during the week as No. 4 Michigan stepped into The Hall with Indiana.

Michigan had played Duke, North Carolina and Kansas, plus Big Ten powers. The only team that had shot .500 against the Wolverines was Indiana, with .552 in that 76-75 victory at Ann Arbor. "They made open jump shots, and I'm going to underline open," Michigan coach Steve Fisher said. "Indiana knows better than anybody how to read and react to screens. If you don't communicate visually and verbally, eventually they'll get an open shot."

Michigan had one plus working for it, even with the scene shifted to Indiana's arena. Ray Jackson, the late bloomer among the "Fab Five," had missed that first Indiana game with an injury. An Ann Arbor *News* position-by-position assessment of the two teams flatly called the 6-foot-6 Jackson "the conference's best defensive player." His assignment obviously would be Cheaney.

Michigan's Juwan Howard leads with an elbow in scoring over Matt Nover.

The game began with Cheaney, just before stepping in for the opening tipoff, gesturing subtly but clearly for the packed Assembly Hall crowd to rev up. It revved.

But it was Michigan that controlled the tip and worked it down low to all-American Chris Webber for a basket. First-game hero Alan Henderson turned the ball over on Indiana's first possession, and first-game absentee Jackson scored for a 4-0 Michigan lead. The game was four minutes along before Cheaney got his first shot away. It missed, and his second was blocked by Jackson. Loose and easy Michigan was the team grimly and determinedly doing everything right.

James Voskuil, the senior whose 3-point miss closed out the first game, sank a 3. So did senior Rob Pelinka, an honor student who was these Wolverines' only link (as a freshman red-shirted but on the roster) with Fisher's 1989 NCAA-championship team. Then, Jimmy King hit a 3. Then Michigan switched inside and Howard scored seven straight Wolverine points. "I don't think they could have played any better," Cheaney said. "They couldn't miss."

Indiana was down 27-14 and reeling, with Michigan on a 114-point pace and looking icily capable of continuing it.

Matt Nover thought of that time, and other times when this Hoosier team was on the wrong side of a point run. They all had a common denominator. Never, in the entire season, including this testy moment in a highly meaningful game against Michigan, did Hoosier coach Bob Knight signal for a momentum-breaking time out.

At Ann Arbor after the first Indiana-Michigan game, Knight had kidded himself about his stubbornness where panic-time timeouts are concerned. "Nobody in the history of basketball has saved more timeouts than I have," he said. "I have almost a phobia about keeping them till the end of the game.

"I don't think we've ever been caught at the end of a game without a timeout. I'm sure we have once, but... "

It was a year when Indiana rode out the final seconds of a tournament victory over Xavier because the Musketeers were out of time outs . . . and when the national championship game had a bizarre ending because the trailing team, Michigan, was out of time outs in the final seconds but called one anyway, and drew a technical foul that assured defeat.

Nover thought of the time-out "phobia" in the broad sense of what that Knight confidence was based on: the poise that had built for this Indiana team, particularly its seniors. "That first year when we were 8-10 (in the Big Ten) was really a growing process for all of us," he said. "It takes something like that, unfortunately, to make you realize what you have to do – what kind of heart and mind you have to put into your game . . . how much determination it takes, to persevere and keep going when things are tough.

"That showed so much this year, when we'd get down and teams would make a run. It didn't faze us. We kicked it up a gear. We wouldn't have to take a time out to slow the momentum of the other team. We didn't do it, ever. I don't think any other team in the country would respond that way. That shows how tough and how competitive this team was."

Indiana was back within 43-35 with 3:33 left in the half, when Knight lifted Cheaney, who had played for a minute and scored four points after drawing his second foul – the almost-always point in the first half when a Hoosier comes out. By then, Greg Graham and Damon Bailey already were out.

Nover, Henderson and Brian Evans, the Cheaney-less front line, did all the scoring as Indiana reached halftime down just 46-44. Chris Reynolds and Pat Knight were the other two during the run. "I look over and I see Calbert, Greg and Damon on the bench," Reynolds said. "I told the guys, 'We've got to step it up and try to maintain this (eight-point Michigan) lead.' We really didn't plan on chopping the lead off. We didn't want

Matt Nover beats a Michigan posse of Jimmy King (24), Chris Webber (4) and Juwan Howard (25) for a key Hoosier putback.

MICHIGAN 92

No.	Min	3FG	AFG	FT	R	A	BS	St	TO	PF	Pts
4 Webber, f	33	3- 5	8-14	4-11	11	6	1	2	5	3	23
21 Jackson, f	21	0- 1	6-10	1- 3	2	2	1	0	0	5	13
25 Howard, c	32	0- 1	5- 8	5- 5	5	0	0	0	0	4	15
5 Rose, g	31	2- 4	4- 9	4- 4	2	3	0	1	3	5	14
24 King, g	35	4- 6	6- 9	0- 0	4	6	1	0	2	1	16
3 Pelinka	18	2- 3	2- 3	0- 0	2	1	0	0	0	4	6
32 Voskuil	10	1- 1	1- 1	0- 0	0	1	0	0	1	3	3
42 Riley	14		1- 2	0- 0	3	1	0	0	2	3	2
14 Talley	5	0- 1	0- 1	0- 0	0	1	0	0	1	0	0
11 Fife	1		0- 0	0- 0	0	0	0	0	0	1	0
Team					1						
Totals		12-22	33-57	14-23	30	21	3	3	14	29	92

INDIANA 93

No.	Min	3FG	AFG	FT	R	A	BS	St	TO	PF	Pts
40 Cheaney, f	36	1- 2	7-17	5- 7	9	4	0	0	2	2	20
44 Henderson, f	29	0- 1	4-11	4- 7	8	0	0	0	2	1	12
24 Nover, c	33		8-11	4- 5	8	0	0	0	2	2	20
20 G.Graham, g	29	2- 3	6- 9	2- 2	2	2	1	1	0	4	16
22 Bailey, g	21		0- 2	4- 6	3	2	0	0	1	2	4
21 Reynolds	18		0- 0	0- 1	2	3	0	1	1	2	0
34 Evans	28	3- 6	4-11	6-10	2	1	0	2	1	3	17
30 Leary	4		2- 3	0- 0	0	1	0	0	0	1	4
25 Knight	2		0- 0	0- 0	0	0	0	0	0	0	0
Team					4						
Totals		6-12	31-64	25-38	38	13	1	4	9	17	93

SCORE BY HALVES				3FG	AFG	FT
Michigan (19-4, 8-3)	46	46—	92	.545	.579	.609
Indiana (22-2, 11-0)	44	49—	93	.500	.484	.658

Officials—Jody Silvester, Steve Welmer, Tim Higgins.
Attendance—17,269.

them to get out to a 20-point lead."

Michigan hit eight of its first 10 shots in the second half and led 70-61 with 11:32 left. Over the next 10 minutes, Indiana outscored the super-talented Wolverines, 28-8 – "a huge run," Fisher called it. "We had not had that happen to us all season."

Nover scored the first eight of those Indiana points. Then Greg Graham scored seven in a row, dropping into the post against 6-4 Jimmy King in a matchup of marvelous athletes and twisting to the shot that tied the game 76-76.

Two 3s by Brian Evans boosted Indiana ahead 84-78 – and pushed Michigan to its second time out of the Indiana run. That left only one for clock-stopping in the wild final minute, which Michigan entered down 89-78 and Webber made sweaty for the Hoosiers with three 3s. King hit one, too, cutting the Indiana lead to 91-89 with the clock under 0:10. The Hoosiers ran off a few seconds, then got the ball in-bounds to Evans, who converted a foul at 0:02 into the last two clinching points – both of them needed because Webber launched his last 3 from just across the center line at the buzzer and hit it, for the 93-92 final score.

Indiana got 17 points from rookie Evans, a totally unnoticed signee in the recruiting season that brought in Michigan's "Fab Five." All five of those Wolverines scored in double figures, ranging from Jackson's 13 through Webber's game-high 23.

"Evans," Knight said, "has a nice personality to play this game. He's a little bit deceptive, kinda like he's camouflaged out there. I'm not sure he's ever shaved. You look at him (as an opponent) and you think, 'How's this SOB ever going to hurt us?'

"He played both ends well, he rebounded well, and he got some points for us when we needed them both in the first half and the second half."

Fisher noted that Evans, though 6-8, "is a guy you *have* to guard on the perimeter. A great part of the game, we had bigger guys on him. He used some moves to get himself open."

That was just a matter of following orders, Cheaney said. "Coach told him to try to take their big men to the basket. That's what he did."

I t was the second time in five seasons Indiana keyed a Big Ten championship with two one-point victories over Michigan. When it happened in 1989, the Wolverines went on to the NCAA championship. They took it as an omen again. Rose conceded the league championship to Indiana and said, "We've got to look at it like they're getting the silver and we're going for the gold."

These two Hoosier victories had two unlikely common threads. In both games, it was Indiana, not big and athletic Michigan, that had the rebound edge: 33-31 the first time, 38-30 this one. And, in both, Indiana's short bench outscored Michigan's displaced seniors: 8-2 the first time, thanks to Evans 21-11 the second.

Webber was to lead Michigan all the way to the championship game for a second straight year, share consensus all-America honors with Cheaney, but go into history for taking the fatal championship-game timeout. Long before that, Knight had made little secret of his admiration for both Webber and Michigan.

"Webber has the best and the quickest hands of any kid for his size that I've seen in a long time," Knight said. "Steve (Fisher) has done a great job with this team. You watch them play and they seem to be happy playing with each other – they seem to enjoy playing, they seem to have a good time."

A month after the championship game, Webber broke up the "Fab Five" by announcing he would turn pro.

Evans wasn't the only defensive problem for the Wolverines' big front line. "Nover," Fisher said, "came up big (20 points). That's what makes Indiana a great team. They've got a lot of weapons and options they can hit you with. It doesn't have to be Calbert Cheaney."

Knight called Nover "the key for us in terms of trying to get his quickness back into play offensively – getting him to the free-throw line, and then hoping he'd hit a couple."

For most of the year, Nover had been hoping that very thing.

Free-throw shooting hadn't been a hoping matter in Nover's past. He was a .707 career free-throw shooter entering his senior year. He had shot .714 – five out of every seven – his junior year.

Suddenly, in the year when his overall playing confidence was at a peak, he couldn't hit a free throw.

Brian Evans gets to the goal without the ball after a Chris Webber block.

"Things like that are a mystery," Nover said. "The whole country wonders why free-throw shooting went down this year."

He was *not* responsible for all of that. But, for much of his senior year, he contributed more than his share to the national decline.

"I don't know what happened. I missed some free throws, and I started thinking about it, what I was doing wrong.

"I tried everything . . . four or five different strokes. Nothing really helped."

He was 2-for-7 the day the Kansas game got away, 10-for-27 for the season (.370) when he missed five of his first six at Notre Dame. "Is it getting to be a mental thing with him?" Knight was asked after that game. "Do I look like a psychiatrist?" he responded. "It's mental with *me* when he goes to the line. I don't know what it is with him."

The problem wouldn't go away. He hit a few, 13-for-20 the day the rest of the team was 5-for-16 in the loss to Kentucky. Then he opened the Big Ten season 5-for-17 (.294) through the first seven games. And, of course it hurt.

"You can't help but hear the crowd start murmuring – 'Oh, no, no. Here he goes,' " Nover said. "You just block that stuff out.

"Finally, near the middle of the Big Ten season I got a different rhythm going. I didn't get in a crouch. I just stood up there and shot them in without thinking about it.

"Once I started making some, I gained confidence again. By the end of the Big Ten season, I thought I had made it back."

Starting with his 4-for-5 against Michigan, he was 32-for-43 the rest of the way – .744, down the Big Ten stretch and through the NCAA tournament.

"I was thinking about too many things," he concluded.

The Big Ten trip that Nover and Street had gone on paid Indiana big benefits. The Nover who came back from it, after being a team's No. 1 scorer for the first time since Chesterton High days, accomplished some things with that team that he hoped to do his senior year at Indiana. "I wanted to work on being assertive on offense and on the floor, playing with more confidence," he said. "That really helped me to do that and to carry them into this year."

The confidence was a long time building.

"I was not a star coming out of high school," he said. "A lot of people didn't think I'd be able to make it. I came here to prove to myself that I could compete against the best players in the country. I wanted to be a consistent contributor to one of the best teams in the country. I just worked my tail off my red-shirt year."

That was the year the Cheaney class signed up. All the openings that had seemed to be there for him filled fast when the highly touted freshmen reported.

"That worried me a little bit," he admitted. "I was unsure what the future held. There were a few low times. The beginning was the hardest. Not being a great player and not being highly regarded, I had to dig myself out of a hole. I had to take in a lot of things, but I had to stay positive. That was pretty tough, but I felt like it really helped me."

When Nover's senior year began, Knight expressed the hope that the Hoosiers could "get out of Nover the athletic ability that he has. He's quick, strong. In boxing terms, Nover would absorb a lot of punishment. But I want to see him knock somebody on his butt."

Knight seemed optimistic that all that would happen. In November he said, "Nover will be the key for us, particularly as a defensive postman."

Down the stretch, he was an offensive key, too. Nover hit 62 of the 87 shots he took from the field over the last 12 games, a .713 percentage. The kid who looked so hopeless as a shooter during his free-throw woes wound up with a stunning double that declared him the best – or at least the most accurate, the most efficient – shooter in Hoosier history:

■ His .628 shooting mark for the season (147-for-235) was an IU record, the first time any Hoosier regular ever shot .600 for a full year;

■ His four-year shooting average was .571, also a record. Cheaney wound up second with .559.

Nover finished his career just 22 points short of joining the 30 Hoosier players who scored 1,000 or more points.

Bellamy: An IU first in Hall of Fame

To Walt Bellamy went a signal honor May 10: the first player in Indiana University's storied basketball history to enter the National Basketball Hall of Fame solely on his playing skills. Bellamy's primary Hall of Fame criteria were his role with the 1960 U.S. Olympic team, widely considered the best amateur team ever, and his 20,941 points as a pro, still 16th-best in league history.

A key for the New Bern, N.C., native, however, was a trip he made to Bloomington in late-summer 1956. His high school coach, Simon Coates, doing postgraduate work at IU, invited young Walter to come up and see the place the summer before Bellamy's senior season.

While on campus, Bellamy played a little basketball with Hoosiers Wally Choice, Hallie Bryant and Gene Flowers. "The competitiveness of it was fascinating to me," Bellamy said. "The camaraderie, along with the fact that such an esteemed coach as Branch McCracken came out to acknowledge my presence – it was a culmination of all those things that led me back to Indiana. I had a rich and rewarding experience at Indiana."

Bellamy left in the spring of '61 with the IU rebounding records that he still holds (including the Big Ten mark of 33, in his last collegiate game, against Michigan) and as the school's No. 3 all-time scorer (1,440, which is 11th now).

He also left with that Olympic gold medal. Bellamy was one of the stars on the U.S. team that Pete Newell coached to a series of one-sided victories at Rome – a team of Oscar Robertson, Jerry West and Jerry Lucas, Hall of Famers, too.

"I have fond memories of each game," he said. That includes the 90-63 gold-medal game victory over Brazil, from which the big man called "Bells" was ejected "for allegedly flagrant use of the elbows," he recalls. "It was not. That was part of just coming off the board with the ball."

When he scored his 20,000th pro point in early November 1973, only five had done it before –Wilt Chamberlain, Robertson, West, Elgin Baylor and Hal Greer. Today, the number is just 18.

As the 1962 NBA rookie of the year, Bellamy scored 2,495 points and averaged 31.6, with 1,500 rebounds. He is second all-time among rookies in each of those categories, behind Wilt Chamberlain (2,707, 37.6, 1,941). Note the players who rank third: in points, Kareem Abdul-Jabbar, 2,361; in scoring average, Oscar Robertson, 30.5; in rebounds, Wes Unseld, 1,491. Michael Jordan led the NBA as a rookie with 2,313 points and a 28.2 average. Shaquille O'Neal was the wonder rookie of the '90s this year, with 1,893 points, a 23.4 average, and 1,122 rebounds.

Bellamy was a four-time all-star. He still stands No. 7 all-time in rebounds. Bellamy called his election "a culmination of any contributions that occurred over a basketball career."

It was also a heck of an honor. And an IU first.

New Hall of Famer Walt Bellamy's rookie season in the NBA – in 1961-62, his first year out of Indiana – outpointed every player in history except Wilt Chamberlain.

CHAPTER 6

A loss after a loss

Indiana came out of its Michigan victory No. 1 in the country, riding an 11-game winning streak, and Bob Knight – no prisoner of superstition – made a lineup change: Chris Reynolds at guard in place of Damon Bailey. "I didn't like the direction our defense had been going," Knight said. "We've not been as quick as we want to be – as good going up and down the floor as I'd like to see us."

Surely he saw what he wanted. The Hoosiers – with three early 3s and 13 points altogether by Cheaney in the first eight minutes – rocketed out to leads of 21-8, 27-10 and 37-14 on the way to 54-33 by halftime, against a team that had won eight league games in a row and was on its way to a third-place tie with Iowa in the final Big Ten standings.

The score was 64-41 four minutes into the second half when Reynolds did unto the Illinois offense just what he was out there to do – disrupt it. He swiped a pass, sped to the Hoosiers' scoring end and went up to cap the play with a smashing dunk..

Which he missed.

Every eye in the Assembly Hall stands swung to Knight, who – as Illinois picked up the rim-bruised basketball and hurried down to a basket of its own – quick-stepped up and back in front of his bench, obviously exasperated.

Only a few minutes later, Reynolds tried to take a charge from Illini Andy Kaufmann on a bullish drive to the basket. The foul call went against Reynolds, not Kaufmann, and lawyer-to-be Reynolds reacted with such pained disagreement that he got a technical foul on the play, too. Since technical fouls also are charged to the offender as a personal foul, one play became fouls No. 4 and 5, consigning Reynolds to the bench.

It was his good fortune that things didn't get really close on-court. Illinois didn't get the Indiana lead under 15 points until less than five minutes remained, and when it was at 14, Reynolds' friends on court responded with a 13-6 burst for a coasting 93-72 victory.

Knight did not wait to be asked his assessment of new starter Reynolds' evening. "He did some very good things . . . and a couple of really dumb things.

"You will not see Reynolds try to dunk the ball again. You can bet on that."

It has taken its special place in Indiana basketball history, that missed Reynolds dunk. For all the plays he made in four years of high-speed play, that's the Chris Reynolds Signature Play in a lot of Hoosier-loving fans' memories, Reynolds has learned.

On the post-season tour the seniors made around the state, Reynolds said, "Every place we went, I had to dunk, because people don't believe I can. At one place, this little

Alan Henderson, in his last game of full flight, goes way up and over Davin Harris of Illinois.

At last, on Senior Night, Chris Reynolds showed he really can dunk.

Feb. 17, Assembly Hall

ILLINOIS 72

No.	Min	3FG	AFG	FT	R	A	BS	St	TO	PF	Pts
30 Bennett, f	26		3-5	0-0	4	1	0	1	3	3	6
34 Kaufmann, f	21	0-1	2-7	8-11	2	1	0	0	5	3	12
25 Thomas, c	39		6-13	2-2	5	1	4	0	2	1	14
11 Clemons, g	32		3-6	2-4	3	2	0	2	4	2	8
24 Keene, g	27	1-5	5-11	0-0	1	1	0	1	3	4	11
44 Wheeler	18		4-5	6-6	3	1	0	0	2	5	14
33 Davidson	15		1-2	1-2	1	0	0	0	1	2	3
4 Taylor	10		1-1	2-2	1	1	2	0	2	3	4
3 Harris	5		0-0	0-0	1	0	0	0	0	0	0
32 Michael	7		0-0	0-0	0	1	0	0	0	0	0
Team					5						
Totals		1-6	25-50	21-27	26	9	6	4	22	23	72

INDIANA 93

No.	Min	3FG	AFG	FT	R	A	BS	St	TO	PF	Pts
40 Cheaney, f	34	4-5	10-20	5-7	9	0	0	3	1	3	29
44 Henderson, f	25		5-9	4-7	6	0	2	0	6	3	14
24 Nover, c	30		6-9	0-0	3	1	1	0	2	3	12
20 G.Graham, g	36	1-3	6-8	5-8	2	4	0	3	1	2	18
21 Reynolds, g	22		1-5	1-2	5	4	0	1	0	5	3
22 Bailey	28	1-2	5-7	3-5	2	5	0	1	3	1	14
30 Leary	13	1-1	1-1	0-0	1	2	0	0	0	3	3
34 Evans	6	0-2	0-2	0-0	2	1	0	0	1	0	0
25 Knight	6		0-0	0-0	0	2	0	0	1	0	0
Team					3						
Totals		7-13	34-61	18-29	33	19	3	8	15	20	93

SCORE BY HALVES			3FG	AFG	FT
Illinois (15-8, 8-3)	33	39— 72	.167	.500	.778
Indiana (23-2, 12-0)	54	39— 93	.538	.557	.621

Technical fouls—Illinois bench, Taylor, Cheaney, Reynolds.
Officials—Tom Rucker, Tom O'Neill, Sid Rodeheffer.
Attendance—16,336.

Associated Press
FEB. 23

1.	Indiana (63)	1,620
2.	Kentucky (1)	1,509
3.	North Carolina (1)	1,457
4.	Arizona	1,423
5.	Michigan	1,401
6.	Florida State	1,240
7.	Kansas	1,222
8.	Vanderbilt	1,125
9.	Duke	1,103
10.	Cincinnati	1,074
17.	Purdue	537
18.	Iowa	527

kid asked me, 'When did you learn how to dunk?'

"I told him you don't *learn* how to jump. Either you can jump or you can't."

Reynolds, 6-feet tall and explosive, can jump. And dunk.

"I had three or four dunks my senior year in high school," he said.

At Indiana, though, he never got around to trying one in a game until the opportunity was there that night against Illinois. "It's something I wanted to accomplish before I graduated from college: dunk in a game," he said. "It's no big deal, but it's something I wanted."

He was quite aware that in the Knight system, dunks are welcome, when they are the ultimate definition of a high-percentage shot – but no-no-*no* items when there is even the risk of a miss and there is a bit of showoff involved in the attempt, an intrusion of "I" into the "we" emphasis of the Knight game. Little guys are supposed to feed dunks to big guys, not take them themselves, and certainly not take them and miss. As great a player as Isiah Thomas bought himself some major Knight heat for blowing a dunk with the U.S. Pan American team in Puerto Rico in 1979. It didn't keep Isiah from dunking a few times as a Hoosier, but maybe it did keep him from ever missing another one.

"You've got to take chances in life," Reynolds said. "You might only get one chance."

As a matter of fact, he did.

"That *was* my first try here," he said. "I just took off from too far out."

The Knight promise ("You will not see Reynolds try to dunk again") held up, but the idea did cross the mischievous mind of a senior winding his career down amid championship glory. Once on the night the Hoosiers clinched at least a Big Ten title share against Northwestern, open court beckoned and "I *thought* about doing it," Reynolds said. "We were up by quite a few points."

He thought again and didn't. And he didn't, after that day against Illinois, ever attempt one in the privacy of practice, either.

"No, I didn't," he confirmed. "But one time I did take the ball up . . . and just laid a finger roll over the rim."

The career 0-for-1 dunker has no regrets.

"If I'd never tried, I'd never know if I could or not," he said. "At least I do have this on tape. I do have something.

"I know I tried."

The Illinois victory made Indiana 12-0 in the Big Ten. It meant the Hoosiers would be going for 13-0, and their 13th straight victory, against Purdue, in Boilermaker coach Gene Keady's 13th visit to Assembly Hall, the leader of his 13th Purdue team a great young talent in uniform No. 13, Glenn Robinson. There are 13 letters in that name, if you're counting.

There are 13, too, in Alan Henderson. On the Friday before all those 13s converged, luck turned awful for Henderson and Indiana.

It was a routine moment about halfway through a routine practice. The anticipated starters were in red and the back-ups – plus red-shirt Todd Lindeman – in white. Henderson took the ball to the basket, the shot missed and the whites started with the ball on a break. Near midcourt, Greg Graham stole the ball and saw Henderson – last man coming up the court because of his drive – wheel and become the first man down, ahead of everyone. Graham sailed him a pass, Henderson almost nonchalantly went up alone to catch it, one-handed, the lofted pass slightly behind him . . .

Somehow, in the jump and reach for the ball, Henderson lost his balance. He came down awkwardly, for an instant all the weight on his right knee. It buckled and he went down, his legs almost split.

Everyone on court knew it looked bad. And it was. Confirmation didn't come for a few days, but the early suspicion was the ultimate diagnosis: a tear of the anterior cruciate ligament, major knee damage that ultimately would require surgery.

Greg Graham slips behind Illini Deon Thomas and Tom Michael for a lob.

It was the knee of the best rebounder, the best shot blocker, the best big scoring threat on the team ranked best in the country. It was news that shot across the land within hours, and the immediate consensus reading was that without Henderson, Indiana's national championship chances would be dead.

"When I saw it, I wasn't thinking team at all," Chris Reynolds said. "I was just thinking Alan. I kinda went numb inside."

An irony of the situation was that it happened at the very point of the season when No. 1 Indiana seemed about to make a major step forward. Finally, 11 weeks after he had cracked that foot bone in Madison Square Garden, Pat Graham had clearance to play. His return almost had come in the Illinois game on Wednesday night, but the decision was to hold up, work through the rest of the week, and return against Purdue on Sunday.

Pat Graham was in the scrimmage, "about 20 feet away, in the play. I don't know why, but when he did it, I was looking right at his legs. I saw his knee buckle.

"As soon as it happened, I turned to go get a drink, because I thought I was going to get sick. When you see a kid go down, even if it's from another team – it just makes you sick because you know how long a road it is, how many bike rides and trips to the weight room he's going to have to make on his own without anybody around to help him and root him on.

"It really hurts when it's someone like Alan, and the team we have. With me coming back, I'd thought we had a better chance to play well."

Young players are resilient. They see startling things, athletic injuries, react to them but call on a reserve and get right back to work. Usually. That didn't happen this day.

"When I heard him yell, I thought it was just an ankle," Greg Graham said. "Then I saw him holding his knee. We were just so much in a state of shock we couldn't even practice that day. We were so worried about Alan and what was going through his mind. We're so close. We knew how much he wanted to be out there.

We were all shell-shocked."

Reynolds remembers that the practice went on "for about 30 more minutes. It was probably one of the worst practices we've ever had."

Henderson was taken from the floor to the training room just off the playing floor. He was thoroughly checked there, first by trainer Tim Garl, then by team doctor Brad Bomba. It was just the beginning of medical attention that ultimately brought in orthopedist Steve Ahlfeld (a guard in Knight's first Indiana recruiting class), a radiologist and other specialists, who verified within 24 hours the extent of the damage.

Knight has become far more practiced in the art of dealing with such team jolts than he'd like to be.

In 1975, his first real national championship contender at Indiana at almost the same point of the calendar lost its best player, Scott May, to a broken arm. That team was unbeaten at the time, No. 1 in the country, and it finished regular-season play that way. Its bid to win the championship, though, was cut short in the regional championship round, 92-90 by Kentucky.

In 1980, Indiana was No. 1 opening the season, and the Hoosiers were justifying the standing with spectacular early play. A certain all-American, Mike Woodson, went down in mid-December with a back injury that required surgery. A future all-American and

The Purdue game found Alan Henderson all dressed up with no place to go.

standout pro, Randy Wittman, cracked the same foot bone that Pat Graham did and went out for the year after surgery. That team still won the Big Ten. At full strength? The NCAA Final Four was in IU-loving Indianapolis that year, at Market Square Arena where Indiana to this day never has lost, the championship game on Indianapolis native Woodson's birthday. And this was the team that, a year later despite losing both Woodson and Butch Carter to the NBA, won the NCAA championship.

In 1982, any chances for a repeat ended with the one genuine tragedy of the list. A midsummer auto accident left Landon Turner, all-Final Four as a strong, quick 6-10 junior for the 1981 champions, paralyzed, his basketball career over.

In 1983, Indiana again was No. 1 early and it was on its way to a clearcut championship in the Big Ten when two-year first-team all-league forward Ted Kitchel had Woodson's luck: back injury, surgery, season ended. The team regrouped to win the Big Ten but its tournament bid ended against Kentucky in the regional.

And in 1992, the Hoosiers got to the Final Four, just a small boost away from possibly getting by eventual champion Duke, and did it without Pat Graham, whose first of three foot fractures came in November and led to a medical red-shirt season.

Now it was '93, and the Henderson injury lengthened the list.

Knight met with the team before its Saturday practice, Henderson there with his knee in a cast. Intentionally, Knight kept the atmosphere light. He joked that losing Henderson meant losing, oh, a lot of bad shots, and poor defense, and – how did we ever win with this guy?

And he turned serious to point out one more time just why those uniforms carry only one name on them. "Coach told us, 'The jersey doesn't say Henderson, it doesn't say Cheaney, it doesn't say Knight, it says Indiana,' " Pat Graham said.

Practice that day picked up considerably.

On Sunday, an emotional Hoosier crowd reacted loudly when Pat Graham ran out to warm up with the rest of the team. He didn't start. Neither did Evans, who had seemed the likely replacement for Henderson because at 6-8 he was the biggest man among the usual bench corps – and he had been playing well.

The choice, instead, was Reynolds, "because I didn't want Evans to think that he has to take Henderson's place, and do whatever we might have had Henderson do," Knight said. "We just brought him in off the bench."

Reynolds made it a three-guard lineup with Greg Graham and Damon Bailey, plus Calbert Cheaney and Matt Nover. That forced a tough choice: the 6-foot-3 Bailey guarded 6-9 Glenn Robinson.

At the first TV time out, Evans replaced Reynolds and inherited the Robinson defensive assignment from Bailey, who had done his job and got it back a few times during the day. Indiana trailed 11-8 when the change was made, and Robinson's sophomore roommate at Purdue, Cuonzo Martin, already had six points toward his eventual career-high 32.

Indiana trailed through 16-10 before – zap, zap – consecutive 3-point baskets by Evans, his first shots of the day, brought a tie. The Evans-for-Reynolds switch "hurt us," Purdue coach Gene Keady said. "We wanted to sag off Reynolds (with Robinson, who thus was freed to roam the

'The jersey doesn't say Henderson, it doesn't say Cheaney, it doesn't say Knight, it says Indiana.'
Bob Knight

The dunk counted, but the too-exuberant grasp of the rim cost Purdue's Glenn Robinson a technical foul.

basket area). We had to go out and cover Evans, and we didn't do it – with the same type of focus."

It was 18-18 when Indiana unloaded a barrage of 3s – Cheaney, Greg Graham, Bailey, then Graham again. In four minutes, the tie had changed to 32-20. Purdue was down 52-49 when Evans fed Nover for a layup, then hit a 3.

Purdue never got that close again on a day when many things happened but nothing so repetitively as Greg Graham driving, Greg Graham getting fouled, and Greg Graham sinking two free throws. He hit 10 free throws the first half, to go with those two 3s and give him 16 points. Six of his free throws came after he drew his second foul, and Knight left him in the game. "We were using our Greg Graham Shoots Fouls offense today," Knight quipped, "so we had to leave him in."

Graham didn't hit another field goal, but the last half, he shot 18 free throws and hit 16 – 26-for-28 for the day, IU and Big Ten records for free-throw conversions in a game, and the most in a game by any collegian, male or female, at any NCAA level this year.

It made for a rare box-score sight: two field goals, 32 total points. "I'll bet nobody ever scored 30 points in a college basketball game on two baskets," devout non-gambler Knight said.

The Hoosier game plan had included driving on the Boilermakers at every opportunity. "We got to the foul line, as we wanted to," Knight said. "We didn't anticipate one guy doing all of our free-throw shooting."

Robinson finished with the same shooting figures he had in the first game: 9-for-22, for 24 points this time with a game-high 14 rebounds. "Of the people we had guard Robinson, Bailey did the best job . . . a really good job in the first half," Knight said. Bailey said the defensive plan against the Big Ten scoring leader was not "a one-guy thing. I don't think we have anybody who's going to stop him. Everybody has to help. When we

Greg Graham takes a bump from Purdue's Linc Darner on Graham's record 26-for-28 free-throw day.

Feb. 21, Assembly Hall
PURDUE 78

No.	Min	3FG	AFG	FT	R	A	BS	St	TO	PF	Pts
13 Robinson, f	38	1- 3	9-22	5- 7	14	2	0	2	4	5	24
22 Martin, f	36		12-15	8- 8	4	1	0	1	2	4	32
34 Stanback, c	29		2- 3	0- 0	7	1	0	1	2	5	4
11 Waddell, g	21	0- 2	0- 4	0- 0	2	2	0	0	3	2	0
12 Painter, g	36	2- 5	5- 9	1- 2	1	7	0	1	1	4	13
21 Dove	4		1- 2	0- 0	1	0	0	1	1	2	2
30 Darner	19	1- 4	1- 4	0- 0	0	0	0	0	0	2	3
35 McNary	5		0- 1	0- 0	1	0	0	0	2	3	0
23 Porter	9		0- 1	0- 0	0	0	0	0	1	2	0
00 Williams	2		0- 0	0- 0	0	0	0	0	0	1	0
20 Foster	1		0- 0	0- 0	0	0	0	0	0	0	0
Team					4						
Totals		4-14	30-61	14-17	34	13	0	6	16	30	78

INDIANA 93

No.	Min	3FG	AFG	FT	R	A	BS	St	TO	PF	Pts
40 Cheaney, f	25	1- 2	6- 8	1- 2	2	3	1	1	1	5	14
22 Bailey, f	29	1- 3	3- 8	0- 0	5	6	0	2	3	4	7
24 Nover, c	39		5- 7	2- 2	9	0	0	1	4	2	12
20 G.Graham, g	40	2- 3	2- 7	26-28	3	2	0	2	2	2	32
21 Reynolds, g	8		0- 1	0- 0	1	1	0	1	0	0	0
34 Evans	35	3- 7	7-16	3- 6	7	4	1	2	1	3	20
30 Leary	14		0- 1	2- 2	1	1	0	0	0	4	2
33 P.Graham	9		2- 3	0- 0	1	0	0	0	1	1	4
25 Knight	1	1- 1	1- 1	0- 0	0	0	0	0	0	0	2
Team					0						
Totals		7-15	26-52	34-40	29	17	2	9	12	21	93

SCORE BY HALVES				3FG	AFG	FT
Purdue (15-6, 6-6)	36	42—	78	.286	.492	.824
Indiana (24-2, 13-0)	44	49—	93	.467	.500	.850

Technical fouls—Roberts, Robinson.
Officials—Jim Burr, Jerry Petro, Dan Chrisman.
Attendance—16,842.

(he or Graham) were fronting him, Matt or Brian was behind us."

Purdue, primarily Martin, confined Cheaney with 14 points, and just eight shots. He fouled out for the first time since the Duke game in the 1992 tournament and just the sixth time in his IU career – and the last.

The total situation left Knight marveling.

Henderson's injury meant the loss of "our best player to guard Robinson," he said. "And we had our best player (Cheaney) not play nearly to his capabilities. You say before the game that Cheaney is going to foul out and just play 25 minutes, you'd say, 'How the hell is Indiana going to win?' They just kept on playing. In fact, we really didn't lose anything with Cheaney out of there (the score was 70-60 when he drew his fifth foul, 93-78 at the finish).

"I told them that they ought to be really proud.

"We had a real good effort in preparation for the game. As much as all of us would like to have Henderson back tomorrow, that isn't going to happen. Injuries have been a part of athletics as long as games have been played. There are times when we just have to absorb an injury and play."

Keady, the first coach to go against Indiana without Henderson, said the injury cost the Hoosiers "a very competitive kid who rebounds well. Losing your leading rebounder always hurts you. He blocks a lot of shots and helps on D. He's a valuable key to their scheme of things.

"I don't think it changed a thing for them today. The other kids played harder. They've got the type of kids who are older and smart, and they understand that if they can pick it up a level, they can still win.

"We did try to pound it inside a little bit more than usual, and we wanted to be a better rebounding team. We thought we could exploit them there.

"We tried to get *them* in foul trouble, instead of vice versa."

The college basketball controversy of the moment was California's firing of coach Lou Campanelli, for harsh treatment of his players, superiors indicated. A similar allegation had brought the mid-year firing of former Knight player and aide Tom Miller at Army.

Late in this game, with Indiana up 80-65 and under orders to run the clock down and take only high-percentage shots, Evans fired a quick jumper, missed, and to his bad luck a TV time out came almost immediately. Knight met Evans a step or two in front of the bench. "If I'd been coaching at Army or the University of California, when I grabbed Evans, I'd have been fired on the spot," Knight said. "But Evans won't take that shot again when we're holding the ball, you can bet on that. That's what coaching is all about.

"And that I hope is what listening will be all about, as far as Brother Evans is concerned."

Even Knight liked just about everything else in Evans' career-best day: 20 points, seven rebounds, four assists, one block, two steals.

"I'm sure if I think a minute there'll be more than the *one* shot that ticked me off," Knight laughed, "but let's assume that was the only thing that irritated me.

"The kid played pretty good."

A high, high-percentage shot for Brian Evans, on his season-high 20-point day against Purdue.

Pat Graham made his first appearance when Cheaney picked up his second foul. The building rocked the second Graham came up off the bench and shed his warmup gear, and the noise picked up when he entered the game. Just 25 seconds later, the Hoosiers beat Purdue's press with a pass up the sidelines to Pat Graham, near the center line. Graham turned, hesitated for an instant, then drove between Matt Waddell and Ian Stanback to a layup.

The earlier noise levels suddenly seemed soft. Pat Graham's ears rang with his welcome back.

The brief hesitation after receiving the pass, Graham said, was strictly to size up the defensive situation, not for any injury-related reasons. "I said I wasn't going to come back and be tentative. I felt I did that the first two surgeries.

"I think I've learned my lesson. If it breaks again, we're going to do this all over again and I know it. If it's going to give, it's going to give, and it's not going to depend on how hard I play. So I might as well go out and play as hard as I can."

Knight had indicated in New York he might seek a special NCAA ruling for Graham, to permit him to have a second medical red-shirt year and save two seasons of eligibility. "We asked," he said. "It was turned down. Pat will not get back to 100 percent by the time the year is over, but it was good to get him back out there."

Graham said he knew he would get into the game. "I really didn't think it would be when I did – in crunch time, when Calbert got in foul trouble. I was very pleased about the way I came in and played, and the way it felt. I still have a little pain when I cut, but it felt really good in the game.

"I feel slow. I don't have that first-step quickness that you want to have, but I guess people who have been through three surgeries don't get their quickness back right away. I didn't start out with a heck of a lot.

"But I can't even put into words how happy I feel right now."

There's a price to being a glamour team in college basketball, a la Indiana, Duke, North Carolina, Kentucky, and in this era of the "Fabs," Michigan.

The paybacks are numerous, most notably national exposure that inevitably makes recruiting easier. The financial benefits are lessened by conference TV packages, but there still are some.

And the price is paid in scheduling. Because Indiana or Michigan meant big audiences, they were the two the networks that own Big Ten basketball national TV packages – CBS and ESPN – wanted on whenever they could get them.

The Big Ten schedule basically calls for Wednesday-Saturday scheduling, an 18-game schedule spread over 10 weeks leaving each team one Wednesday and one Saturday off during the year.

CBS has the big contract with the Big Ten, so it gets first shot at selecting the Saturday games it wants to advance to Sunday. Then, ESPN gets to look at the Wednesday schedule, to pick the games it wants to advance to its 8 p.m. (EST) Tuesday Big Ten slot.

Pat Graham's welcome-back was a press-beating drive between Matt Waddell and Ian Stanback for a basket in his first half-minute on the court.

Indiana coach Bob Knight reached a couple of milestones in his 22nd season in Bloomington and 28th as a collegiate coach. The 75-67 Hoosier victory over Iowa at Assembly Hall Jan. 6 made Knight, at 52, the youngest coach ever to win 600 major college games. Six nights later, with a key 76-75 victory at Michigan, Knight became the first to win 500 games at a Big Ten school. At season's end, his career totals were 516-163 at Indiana and 618-213 overall. Knight was inducted into the National Basketball Hall of Fame in 1991.

Rebounding in the Big Ten is an intense matter for big men such as Matt Nover (right) or Alan Henderson (opposite page), and small, such as Damon Bailey (above), crunched by Eric Pauley (51) and Richard Scott of Kansas.

Up close, it gets personal, and a bit bumpy, in college basketball – for (above) Calbert Cheaney, Purdue's Glenn Robinson and Alan Henderson, for (left) Alan Henderson and Colorado's Ted Allen, and for (right) Damon Bailey and Purdue's Porter Roberts.

Todd Leary (left) and Alan Henderson came to Indiana from metropolitan Indianapolis high schools after careers that finished for both in the state championship game – Leary with 1989 champion Lawrence North, Henderson with 1991 runnerup Brebeuf. Leary missed IU's 1990-91 season after knee surgery. Henderson, the Hoosiers' leading rebounder, had knee surgery May 6 to correct damage from a fall during practice Feb. 19.

Iowa's Val Barnes finds himself walled in by Hoosiers Greg Graham, Brian Evans and Pat Knight (above), while Calbert Cheaney of Indiana and Leon McGee of Western Michigan get arms entangled with Damon Bailey sandwiched (right). Nobody is around to stop Greg Graham (following pages).

There is no No. 1 assistant, associate head coach or recruiting coordinator on the Bob Knight staff, but involved in all facets of the Indiana game are aides Ron Felling (with Greg Graham above), Dan Dakich (with Damon Bailey, right) and Norm Ellenberger (sending Calbert Cheaney off with a slap, opposite page).

Indiana Basketball spans much more than the players on the floor or the coaches on the sidelines as these Hoosier backers show – included among them (far right, getting a greeting from Calbert Cheaney) Landon Turner, an all-Final Four selection for Indiana's 1981 NCAA champions.

The finish to Alan Henderson's sophomore season was a bummer, his face and the look of empathy from teammate Todd Leary say as the seconds wind down in Indiana's season-ending loss to Kansas at St. Louis. It might have been different if . . . Henderson hadn't had to spend his final games of the year with his right knee braced and protected, and his backup, freshman Brian Evans hadn't cracked the bone in his hand that Evans discusses with Chris Reynolds (above).

On the Indiana basketball team's Autograph Day April 15, Alan Henderson was a popular target (above), just as injured Pat Graham was a popular addition to the awards ceremony for Indiana's Pre-Season NIT champions at New York in November (from left, Calbert Cheaney, Brian Evans, Todd Leary, Matt Nover and Graham). Graham cracked a foot bone in the tournament semifinals after starring in an 81-78 overtime victory over Florida State that put the Hoosiers in the tournament finals.

Indiana coach Bob Knight found much to smile about (with team Dr. Brad Bomba, above) in a 31-4, Big Ten championship season – including an opportunity to sneak up from behind and bedevil one-time coaching rival Al McGuire during a CBS telecast from Assembly Hall.

Wednesday-Saturday games mean ample preparation time for both games. Wednesday-Sunday isn't bad. Saturday-Tuesday isn't bad. Those few times when teams operated with a Sunday-Tuesday squeeze – CBS backed a Saturday game to Sunday, and ESPN picked the same team to advance its Wednesday game to Tuesday – complicated things. It happened four times this year – to Michigan twice (at Iowa and at Michigan State the first time, at Ohio State and at home against Iowa the second), Ohio State once (at Indiana and at Michigan), and Indiana once – the weekend that began for the Hoosiers with the Purdue game and concluded at Ohio State.

Bob Knight knew his team faced a problem. Sunday-Tuesday was one thing. When the Sunday was spent with rival Purdue, it was another. When that Sunday with Purdue was preceded by the tension, strain and physical drain of the stunning events that began with the Alan Henderson injury, it was another. He knew he was taking to Ohio State a tired team, a team insufficiently prepared because the one day between games didn't permit heavy work against the Ohio State press, the Buckeyes' three-guard quickness, the things normally dealt with in preparation for a game. And, he knew his remaining players still were wrestling with the Henderson matter: concern for Henderson himself, uncertainty about what it meant to this team's strength, personal thoughts that each figured to have about what he himself – be it Calbert Cheaney, Greg Graham, Todd Leary, anybody – might be able to contribute above and beyond his previous norm to make up for the Henderson loss.

There also was the matter that showed up as Knight looked at the Buckeye tapes. Ohio State, under Randy Ayers, was a young team rapidly getting better, particularly freshman Derek Anderson, whose Big Ten takeoff had been hampered by an early-season injury.

Add one other item: Indiana is Buckeye guard Jamie Skelton's private pigeon. As a lightly used freshman, Skelton contributed two monumental 3-pointers to the Buckeyes' 97-95 double-overtime victory over Indiana at Columbus in 1991. A year ago, Skelton came from deep off the bench to score 11 points, including three 3-pointers, in helping to lead a 26-2 Ohio State charge at Bloomington, though Indiana countercharged to win. "Skelton gets my vote for all-time all-American, the way he plays against us," Knight said.

That was after Skelton's 22-point performance, including the night's biggest baskets, pulled Ohio State past the Hoosiers in overtime, 81-77, the only Big Ten beating for the 1993 league champions.

It was a night that left many memories, and some new Hoosier doubts.

"**R**eady to play" is the Knight standard for every game. Are we? Were we? He had ample reason to wonder when the Hoosiers jumped out 4-0, then turned the ball over four times – with unaccustomed problems against a press – as Ohio State put together an 11-0 two-minute run.

Then, Hoosier gears meshed for a 15-0 burst and a 27-15 lead that reached 41-27 on Brian Evans' 3 three minutes before halftime. It was 51-38 when rookie Anderson hit two 3s to tighten the game (51-46).

Up to then, Skelton had five points, none in 24 minutes since helping in that 11-0 early burst. For the last 17 minutes, the 6-2 junior was the dominant player on the floor.

Ohio State coach Randy Ayers is not sure he buys official Ed Hightower's decision to put time back on the clock.

The Buckeyes never quite caught up but trailed 67-66 when Chris Reynolds, the least likely Hoosier to do it, sank two clutch free throws with 50.1 seconds left to open the lead to 69-66. Skelton tried for a 3 but had to fake, twist inside the stripe and put up an off-balance shot from straight out. It rattled through, an ugly basket but a great and gutty shot. Now it was 69-68, and the Buckeyes fouled Bailey with 14.0 seconds left. He missed the first, hit the second. Ohio State rushed to the attack, found no opening, got the ball to Skelton – and from deep on the left, Buckeye bench-sitters close enough to touch him, he sailed a 3 high, and through.

The clock ran out, the courtside stands emptied, and Ohio State celebrated a 71-70 upset.

Wait, officials said; 1.4 seconds went back on the clock, and Indiana took the ball out of bounds at its end of the court.

Evans was the in-bounds passer. "We wanted to get Todd Leary the ball, because we knew everyone was waiting for Calbert to shoot it," Reynolds said.

"I was at half-court, with Todd and Calbert in front of me. The plan was for me to pick Leary's man, and after that, Calbert's man. Before the play even started, I had looked at the guys who were guarding Todd and Calbert. A freshman (Anderson) was guarding Calbert. I knew if I went up and picked him, he would not see me because he was so intent on guarding

Lawrence Funderburke wears a look of triumph after a jump-ball call gave the Buckeyes possession in the final seconds of overtime.

Calbert – 'Calbert's *not* going to score on me.'

"I knew he was going to run into me. I just *knew* he was."

Cheaney broke up the sidelines, Evans threw for him – and with the pass in the air, a whistle blew. Anderson, eyes locked on Cheaney and sprinting straight up-court to stay with him, had run right over screener Reynolds.

That was the good and the bad news for Indiana. Apparently beaten when the crowd was covering the floor minutes before, the Hoosiers had two chances to tie and win. Reynolds had hit two big free throws earlier in that tense final minute, but even with those he was a career .620 free-throw shooter as he went to the line.

Certainly, he had worked at being better. He shot them one way for a while, then another. "I tried every different way possible – every way except underhanded," he said. "I worked before and after practice, just shooting free throws. Coach Knight worked with me, on getting my shoulders back. I *tried* to do it the way he wanted me to."

And now he was shooting two with the game at stake.

"I was at half-court, getting ready to walk to the free-throw line, and I was thinking to myself: 'You dream about this kind of situation, but you think you're going to be nervous. I'm not even nervous.' And I wasn't."

He hit the first, and the game was tied. Now, he was shooting for victory.

"The worst feeling in the world would be to miss both of them. I think I was so excited about making the first one, I didn't concentrate as much on the second one. I had told myself, 'If I make the first one, I'm *going* to make the second one.' I concentrated so *hard* on making the first one.

"I thought for sure the second one was going to go in. It almost did. It rattled around."

It rattled just enough that the Buckeye inside rebounders mistimed their jumps. From behind, Evans slipped through for a perfectly timed tip that eased up, rolled teasingly across the rim at its flange, and rolled on out.

Overtime.

A minute into it, Indiana was down 77-71. A minute and a half later it was 77-77 and the Hoosiers had the ball back. Cheaney worked open on the baseline, but his shot bounced out.

Now it was Ohio State with the ball. Senior guard Alex Davis, who had opened the overtime with a 3-pointer, missed a shot, ran the ball down in the corner, hoisted it all the way to the top of the key to Skelton and . . .

From NBA range, well above the stripe, with 40 seconds left, Skelton broke the night's last tie with his last of four 3s. Indiana worked Evans open for an attempt to tie, but his miss became a jump ball call that gave possession to Ohio State. At 0:05, the Buckeye who had begun collegiate basketball with the Hoosier seniors, Lawrence Funderburke, sank the first of two free throws to clinch victory.

Without Henderson, Funderburke said, "they had a tremendous void. That really hurt them by not having a 6-9 frame. It's really tragic he couldn't play because he definitely would have been a factor.

"But, hey, regardless of who's playing, we still want to win the ballgame. And we did."

Ayers spent a few immediate postgame moments checking out TV tapes of the Reynolds screen. "It was a legitimate play," he said. "The screener allowed him two steps. Give them a lot of credit. They executed when they had to.

"You learn from those situations. Derek will learn from that. Certainly Coach Ayers is going to learn something about setting screens and going long."

Anderson, who had 20 points, closed the season well, but teammate Greg Simpson (12 in this game) beat out him and Illinois guard Richard Keene for Big Ten Freshman of the Year. Greg Graham had 21 points – and six of the Hoosiers' 18 turnovers, their Big Ten season high.

"Usually the team that makes the fewest mistakes wins," Knight said. "I think that's exactly what happened tonight. I don't think anything else had a thing to do with the outcome."

"Anything else" specifically included fatigue, ruled out by Knight as an excuse. "I don't think so, not the kinds of mistakes that we made."

IU's Big Ten starts
BOB KNIGHT YEARS

Year	Start	First loss	Finish	Record
1973	5-0	at Ohio St., 70-69	Champion••	11-3
1975	18-0		Champion	18-0
1976	18-0		Champion••	18-0
1987	5-0	at Iowa, 101-88	Co-champion•	15-3
1989	6-0	at Illinois, 75-65	Champion	15-3
1991	4-0	Ohio St., 93-85	Co-champion	15-3
1992	6-0	at Mich. St., 76-60	Second••	14-4
1993	13-0	at Ohio St., 81-77	Champion	17-1

•NCAA champion; ••Final Four

Feb. 23, St. John Arena, Columbus
INDIANA 77

No.	Min	3FG	AFG	FT	R	A	BS	St	TO	PF	Pts
40 Cheaney, f	43	0-2	5-12	2-2	9	0	0	1	3	0	12
22 Bailey, f	34	0-1	5-8	1-2	5	4	0	0	2	2	11
24 Nover, c	32		4-8	1-4	6	0	0	0	3	5	9
20 G.Graham, g	42	2-5	8-14	3-5	4	4	1	0	6	2	21
21 Reynolds, g	36		2-3	4-6	5	4	0	0	3	2	8
34 Evans	27	1-5	4-11	4-4	5	4	0	0	1	4	13
30 Leary	9	0-1	1-2	1-1	2	1	0	1	0	1	3
33 P.Graham	1		0-2	0-1	0	0	0	0	0	0	0
25 Knight	1		0-0	0-0	0	0	0	0	0	0	0
Team					2						
Totals		3-14	29-60	16-25	38	17	1	2	18	16	77

OHIO STATE 81

No.	Min	3FG	AFG	FT	R	A	BS	St	TO	PF	Pts
34 Funderburke, f	35		4-12	4-9	7	1	1	0	3	1	12
15 Skelton, f	34	4-8	8-17	2-3	3	3	0	2	0	4	22
41 Watson, c	16		2-2	0-0	2	0	1	0	2	4	4
3 Simpson, g	41	0-3	4-8	4-4	1	9	0	2	2	3	12
23 Anderson, g	33	2-2	7-8	4-4	3	3	0	3	2	5	20
40 Dudley	6		0-0	0-0	0	0	0	0	0	0	0
20 Davis	22	2-4	3-8	0-0	3	1	0	0	0	3	8
33 Macon	26		1-5	1-2	5	0	1	1	3	3	3
42 Ratliff	5		0-0	0-0	0	0	0	0	0	0	0
31 Brandewie	7		0-1	0-0	2	0	0	0	1	1	0
Team					3				1		
Totals		8-17	29-61	15-22	29	17	3	8	13	24	81

SCORE BY HALVES					3FG	AFG	FT
Indiana (24-3, 13-1)	43	28	6—	77	.214	.483	.640
Ohio State (13-10, 6-8)	36	35	10—	81	.471	.475	.682

Officials—Eric Harmon, Ed Hightower, Tom Rucker.
Attendance—13,276.

CHAPTER 7

Effort. Memorable. Record.

More than the possibility of an ultra-rare 18-0 Big Ten season disappeared with Indiana's loss at Ohio State. So did any sense of being home free with the Big Ten championship, the Indiana lead down to two games with four to go and runnerup Michigan unlikely to lose again.

The first of those four games left was a mean one: Minnesota, at Williams Arena, where another probable championship began to slip away for the same Hoosier group a year before.

It didn't happen this time. Indiana broke a halftime tie with seven of its shiniest minutes of the year and handled the Gophers, 86-75. A month later, when deep in NCAA tournament play Bob Knight was discussing key moments in the evolution of his No. 1-ranked team, he said:

"We had a very interesting week when we played at Ohio State and at Minnesota. You've got to look at that and say, 'Indiana has a better chance to win at Ohio State than at Minnesota.' We were a little bit tired when we went to Columbus, Ohio State played very well, we had a chance to win and didn't…

"We're in a real bind now. We go up to Minnesota and play and we just got a great effort, one of the really memorable efforts that I've ever had a team give."

The subject changed to other things, but it came back when writer Steve Warden of the Fort Wayne *News-Sentinel* asked what made that Minnesota game so special.

"Damn, Steve, that was great *effort*," Knight said.

"Did you ever see a guy go from first to home on a single? You never saw Enos Slaughter go from first to home in the '46 Series on a single?

"Damn.

"Effort.

"Memorable."

The E for effort was all Minnesota's when this one began. Williams Arena was packed (16,638), Governor Arne Carlson was in place, and the mood of vengeance that Carlson's letter to the Big Ten had helped to build sent a charge of extra voltage from the loud fans to the Gophers.

Knight gave Brian Evans his first college start, partly out of concern for the big and muscular Gopher front

Damon Bailey and Minnesota's Ryan Wolf, old high school rivals from Bedford-Martinsville days, tangle on a Bailey drive.

Big Ten Defensive Player of the Year Greg Graham closes in on an interception as Arriel McDonald breaks.

Feb. 27, Williams Arena, Minneapolis

INDIANA 86

No.	Min	3FG	AFG	FT	R	A	BS	St	TO	PF	Pts
40 Cheaney, f	32	2- 3	5- 9	3- 4	5	2	0	4	3	3	15
34 Evans, f	16	0- 1	1- 3	0- 0	4	1	0	0	0	3	2
24 Nover, c	39		5- 6	7- 8	9	0	1	0	1	2	17
20 G.Graham, g	37	2- 3	6- 9	5- 6	2	4	0	0	2	2	19
33 P.Graham, g	27	1- 2	4- 7	0- 0	1	3	0	0	2	3	9
22 Bailey	28	2- 3	4- 8	7- 8	4	6	0	0	2	3	17
25 Knight	9		0- 1	1- 2	1	1	0	0	0	1	1
30 Leary	8	1- 2	2- 4	1- 1	0	0	0	0	0	0	6
21 Reynolds	4		0- 0	0- 0	0	2	0	0	1	1	0
Team					2						
Totals		8-14	27-47	24-29	28	19	1	4	11	18	86

MINNESOTA 75

No.	Min	3FG	AFG	FT	R	A	BS	St	TO	PF	Pts
4 Tubbs, f	32	1- 2	4-10	0- 0	6	3	0	1	1	2	9
34 Carter, f	25		6-10	3- 4	11	0	0	0	3	4	15
51 Kolander, c	17		0- 1	3- 8	6	1	1	1	0	4	3
21 Lenard, g	33	5- 9	7-15	3- 3	2	2	0	3	0	4	22
10 McDonald, g	36	2- 6	5-16	4- 4	1	4	0	2	1	3	16
32 Walton	15		2- 5	0- 0	3	1	0	1	2	3	4
53 Nzigamasabo	17		2- 3	0- 0	3	0	1	0	0	2	4
25 Jackson	16		0- 0	0- 0	1	1	0	0	1	1	0
3 Wolf	6		0- 0	0- 0	0	1	0	0	2	2	0
11 Crittenden	1		0- 0	0- 0	0	0	0	0	0	0	0
33 Baker	1		1- 1	0- 0	0	0	0	0	0	0	2
30 Roe	1		0- 0	0- 0	0	0	0	0	0	0	0
Team					1				1		
Totals		8-17	27-61	13-19	34	13	2	8	11	25	75

SCORE BY HALVES				3FG	AFG	FT
Indiana (25-3, 14-1)		39	47— 86	.571	.574	.828
Minnesota (15-9, 7-8)		39	36— 75	.471	.443	.684

Officials—Phil Bova, Randy Drury, Tom Clark.
Attendance—16,638.

'I figured it would be four or five games before I could really start playing the way I enjoy playing, playing well and hard.'

Pat Graham

line. He also started Pat Graham, his first start in more than two years. Graham's 3-point basket got Indiana scoring started, but Minnesota was storming the backboards so hard and so productively that – make or miss – the Gophers scored on every possession in going up 12-6.

The lead became 29-23 on guard Voshon Lenard's 3-point play that sent Cheaney to the bench with two fouls, 7:50 left in the half. It was a point in the game that invited a Gopher pullaway, but the Indiana bench troops – Chris Reynolds, Todd Leary, Pat Knight, plus a blend of usual starters Matt Nover, Damon Bailey and Greg Graham – pulled even with the Gophers at halftime, 39-39.

"The team that drew us back to a tie did an excellent job in just keeping us in it," Cheaney said. "We made a vow to ourselves just to go out and play our behinds off."

Pat Graham came off a screen, took a pass from Damon Bailey and sank the jump shot that snapped the halftime tie.

To the Hoosiers, to Knight, it was a signal and a reminder all at once – a signal that Graham, so newly returned to competition and so far from peak shape, was making progress, and a reminder of what two years without Graham had meant. Knight had preferred to use Graham, through most of his first two seasons, as an instant offensive boost from off the bench. The start at Minnesota was just the ninth of his collegiate career, though he scored in double figures 23 times and topped 20 twice.

Even from the bench he made others better, Knight felt. "It isn't just Pat's play, it's what he does to everybody. If he comes in to take my place, I know that I'm being replaced by somebody at least as good as I am. When I get another chance, I'd better play my ass off or he's just going to stay there."

This day, Cheaney followed Graham's tie-breaker with a baseline jump shot, then a 3 that pushed Gopher coach Clem Haskins to a time out, down 46-39. The time out did not arrest the Hoosiers. Pat Graham scored, then Cheaney knocked the ball away and Greg Graham scored – now an 11-0 start to the half and a 50-39 Indiana lead that became 60-43 and forced another Haskins timeout. A very good Minnesota team – a month away from taking out its umbrage over an NCAA tournament snub by rolling to the NIT championship – had been turned aside.

The Gophers did get back within six points a few times. "I probably went a little bit too long with the kids we had playing in the second half," Knight said. "I wanted to have them hang in there because it was essentially the same group, with the exception of Pat Graham, that made some bad plays in our game at Columbus."

Haskins said the addition of shooter Pat Graham to the Indiana lineup scuttled his plan to play more zone defense. "I was surprised they started him," Haskins said. "When you have guys who can shoot the basketball, you can't stay in the zone long."

"I'm really happy right now with how everything has been going," said Pat Graham, who scored nine points. "I figured it would be four or five games before I could really start playing the way I enjoy playing, playing well and hard.

"Coach gave me the chance, and I was just really happy with how the team played and how I played. It was a huge win."

It was a blend of satisfaction and joy he hadn't felt since the injury. "I'm not saying I haven't felt like a part of the team, but it's playing with the team, and knowing that you're an instrumental part of the team. You can't have that sitting on the bench in your street clothes."

Never, Graham said, during those periods of rehabilitation did he join in the growing doubt among outsiders than he would ever get back, at least in this season.

"I *knew* I would. Dr. (Steve) Ahlfeld told me, 'We're going to look at this thing being eight to 12 weeks.' It ended up being 11. I couldn't wait. I wanted to get back as soon as possible.

"I came back at a time when I got a little feeling of everything. We beat Purdue, then we lose, and then we beat Minnesota in a big game. In three games, I've felt everything everyone has felt all year."

At season's end, with all the season to scan, Nover pinpointed the victory at Minnesota as "a really pivotal game for us – without Alan, and the way that team plays against us." It gave the Hoosiers a chance to clinch an outright Big Ten championship by winning games at home against Northwestern and Michigan State. But there also was the matter of re-establishing team confidence without Henderson. "If we had lost," Reynolds said, "it could have started snowballing. When you start losing, it's easy to keep losing. We had to get back on the winning track.

"It's awfully hard to play at Minnesota, because they play so well at home. We knew we had to just go in and take them out, particularly at the start of the second half. They don't play anybody as hard as they play us. And they're really good."

Greg Graham considered it "a must win, if we wanted to win the Big Ten outright. We didn't have that attitude going into the Ohio State game. We had the attitude at

Bob Knight makes it plain what he wants from Pat Graham (33), Matt Nover, Todd Leary and Calbert Cheaney in a 'memorable' victory at Minnesota.

Minnesota that 'We're going to win here today. That's just the bottom line.'

"That was the topic of our halftime: the game is going to come down to the first five minutes of the second half. The way we jumped on them there – they were really becoming impatient and I think we scored on every possession."

It was expected, going into his senior season, that Calbert Cheaney would come out of it as Indiana's all-time scoring champion, barring an injury. In February, the count-down got serious. From the double-overtime victory at Penn State through the win over Illinois, Cheaney scored in the 20s five straight times, averaging 24.4 points per game and shooting .522 over the stretch to reach 2,392, only 46 short of Steve Alford's record. Two good games away.

Then he had a 14-point game against Purdue, 12 against Ohio State, 15 at Minnesota. Where he had averaged 18 shots a game during his string of 20-plus games, he averaged just over nine those three games.

The spotlight that came with the approaching record gave that slowdown visibility, too, and started some questions. Was Cheaney tired? Was he catching even more of a defensive concentration without the threat of Henderson around?

Alford, the only man alive who had been through what Cheaney was experiencing, felt the record had become "a huge distraction. It's not the record so much. I think more than anything it's where you're doing it – at a place that is second to none when it comes to tradition.

"There's a scary feeling. You're about to become the top of a scoring list of just some absolutely incredible players who have played there.

"That's what I felt the most. I was about to become No. 1 on a scoring list at a place where as a little kid I dreamed about playing. As confident as I was in my game, I never fathomed the idea of being the No. 1 scorer in the school's history. I dreamed about playing for Coach, and playing at Indiana.

"Calbert's just like any other kid growing up in Indiana. He's had those same aspirations, and now not only is he living them out, he's about ready to become the top scorer in the school's history."

The form that launched two thousand points, and then some, for Calbert Cheaney.

Alford had gone into his senior year needing 504 points to beat a record the late Don Schlundt, the center on Indiana's 1953 NCAA champions, had posted 32 years before, 2,192 points. The best scoring stretch of Alford's career – 31 against Purdue, a career-high 42 against Michigan State, 30 against Michigan – jumped him to 2,177. One game to go, it seemed.

It took two. He and that eventual national championship team both struggled at Northwestern before Indiana escaped, 77-75, despite 15 points from Alford – 4-for-13. The 15 tied him with Schlundt. The Hoosiers went to Madison, where Alford took care of the record-setting early, but the game was a nightmare for him and his team. He was 4-for-19; he missed more shots than he took in two-thirds of the games that got him to the record. In two games on the brink of the record, he hit 8 of 32 shots, 25 percent, for a lifetime 53 percent shooter.

An Indiana player, the evidence suggested, is not used to having individual feats take on such attention. "That's exactly right," Alford said. "I got a ton of coverage before, but it was always how I was helping the team and how the team was doing. And now you get close, and all of a sudden the team stops getting mentioned and it's you, you, you.

"I don't remember *feeling* anything. It's kinda like Calbert. He hasn't been quite as assertive as he normally is, to where he just takes over periods of the game. I felt I was like that.

"I remember Coach telling me after the Northwestern game, 'Look, if you just showed up tonight to play as hard as you usually do, this game's over in the first 10 minutes.'

"At Wisconsin I got great shots, and they didn't go in. I can remember looking at Coach and going, 'I don't *know* why they aren't going.' And I was a player who never, *ever* played the game and looked over to see what Coach was doing. At Wisconsin, I was looking over at him all the time."

When the record-setting was behind him, Alford remembered, "I immediately started shooting the ball better." He averaged 23.0, above his best season's average, in the Hoosiers' six-game drive to the national championship.

As Cheaney reached the Northwestern game at Assembly Hall needing six points to set the mark, Alford was otherwise occupied. In his first full season of coaching at Manchester College, he was named his conference's Coach of the Year. The Spartans, after winning just four games last year, improved to 20-8 and won the Indiana Collegiate Athletic Conference tournament. The school's first bid ever to the NCAA Division III tournament followed. Alford's team was playing its tournament game at Wisconsin-Whitewater the night of the Indiana-Northwestern game.

"I wrote Coach a letter and told him I don't *wish* I could be there, but I wish I could," he said. "I was definitely going to go if we were out of it."

Alford had sent Cheaney a letter, too.

"When I broke Don Schlundt's record, he sent me a letter and one of the things he said was that I was more than a basketball player, that he was glad a class individual was breaking his record.

"That's how I feel with Calbert. It's been a great pleasure to watch him develop as a player over the last four years. But, more than that, it's great to have somebody breaking your record who is just a first-class individual and somebody who has been a part of the Indiana basketball family.

"I think he exemplifies what it means to be an Indiana basketball player."

The points came fast and every way for Calbert Cheaney on his record-setting night against Northwestern.

Associated Press	
MARCH 2	
1. North Carolina (49)	1,600
2. Indiana (8)	1,517
3. Arizona (5)	1,491
4. Michigan (3)	1,435
5. Kentucky	1,390
6. Duke	1,263
7. Vanderbilt	1,246
8. Kansas	1,131
9. Utah	1,065
10. Seton Hall	978
15. Iowa	735
24. Purdue	128

t happened so quickly. For something so very long in the building, it happened in a flash.

"Did he come out on *fire*?" Northwestern coach Bill Foster said later. "I had barely sat down from the national anthem and he had his record."

Foster didn't overstate by much. Cheaney controlled the opening tip, took a pass in return and scored from the baseline 10 seconds into the game. Indiana got the ball back, and on a quick break downcourt Cheaney swished a 3. Already, 40 seconds into the game, he had tied Alford's 2,438.

On the third Hoosier foray, Greg Graham missed, but Cheaney was there for a soft tip-in that – after just 66 seconds of play – made him IU's scoring recordholder.

It was one special moment in a special night. Very special.

When Alford was such a statewide darling as the all-American on the 1987 Indiana team, some saw in the popularity a stigma. It's because he's white, skeptics said. That's Indiana.

Now his record was falling to a young black man. The love affair, border to border, was the same. To the crowd inside, to the hundreds of thousands around TVs and radios throughout Indiana, this was Calbert's night.

That, truly, is Indiana.

The response when Cheaney was introduced in the starting lineup was loud and loving. The first basket sent up an explosion of sound, topped somehow by the followup 3. When the tip-in came so fast, the tribute from the shot that tied the record was still dying down and a new, higher crest of sound overrode it.

There was, of course, a game to be won. A victory meant at least a Big Ten co-championship was assured. Every Knight season at Indiana has had a first-place finish in the Big Ten as the only stated goal.

Northwestern is the one school that never has won at 22-year-old Assembly Hall, but the Wildcats hadn't won anywhere in the Big Ten for seven years and 59 games before they won at Purdue just four days before. *They* hadn't come to be stooges to a Calbert Cheaney show.

The opening fusillade put the Hoosiers up 7-2. Northwestern has an able scorer of its own in sophomore forward Cedric Neloms, an Alabaman who – fast start and all – scored his eighth point before Cheaney got his, then got his ninth, 10th and 11th with a 3 that moved Northwestern in front, 25-24.

The shot that made Calbert Cheaney the Big Ten's highest scorer ever – a 3-pointer on a 35-point night.

Just ahead of Neloms' 3, Cheaney had faked a 3, stepped inside the stripe and hit a jump shot that broke a 22-22 tie and moved him to 2,441 – one point shy of the 2,442 that had given Michigan all-American Glen Rice the Big Ten career record in 1989.

Throughout The Hall, signs saluted Cheaney. At the south end of the court, the one Indiana was using the first half, a fan near the pep band had come prepared with a Cheaney-o-meter. It had started at "Cheaney Needs 10" and now it read "Cheaney Needs 1."

With Indiana up 26-25 (after a Matt Nover go-ahead basket) and 6:12 to go in the half, Damon Bailey faked a penetrating move, zipped a pass to Cheaney deep on the left side of the court, behind the 3-point stripe, and . . .

History.

After a hero's salute from the crowd, Calbert Cheaney gets a smile and a hug from Craig Hartman.

The hush with the ball in the air almost let the swish be heard. No one could have heard the ball hit the floor. The Hall erupted.

The Alford Effect was as predicted. Both Cheaney and the Hoosiers played from there as if their shoes had shed cement. Indiana led 45-35 at halftime, and Cheaney opened the second half with a 3 that started a 12-0 dash to 57-35.

Now, the championship-clinching was over, the record was in the books, and the night was a festival. Cheaney tipped in a shot, hit some jump shots, slammed home a couple of dunks, drove to a layup, did just about anything he wanted as his scoring total mounted to 35 – his Assembly Hall high, his best total ever in a Big Ten game.

With 4:13 left, Knight did what he never does – stood up and signaled for a time out. During it, by hastily arranged agreement, veteran Big Ten official Ed Hightower, a frequent Final Four official who was back there again in April at New Orleans, represented the Big Ten in presenting Cheaney with the ball he had used to set the league record.

Before the night was over, Mother – Mrs. Gwen Crawley, who watched from the center stands opposite the players' bench – had that basketball, to put alongside what would be a proliferation of trophies generated by Cheaney's College Player of the Year season.

Calbert had taken the ball from Hightower with his back to his mother's side of the stands. But, as the ovation washed down on him, he turned and waved – to all, to Mom. "Yes, we made eye contact," she said. "It was just a great moment."

I t was the first time Knight ever interrupted a game to recognize an individual feat. He did it, he said, because Cheaney's achievement "is an absolutely outstanding honor for a great kid.

"I don't think there's ever been a kid more deserving of setting a record like Calbert set tonight than he has been, because he has been able to score every way possible. Mike Woodson (who missed seven weeks and 15 games his senior year, 1979-80, and finished 131 points short of Schlundt's record) would have set the record, had he not gotten hurt. Mike was another kid who could score every way possible, but I think Calbert is probably a better athlete than Mike was.

"Calbert has scored on tip-ins, on lob passes, on 3-point shots, on drives, on posting – probably nobody that we've had has been as versatile a scorer as Calbert Cheaney. Yet, I think Calbert really recognizes the fact that, while his name will be the only one with the accomplishment as having broken the record, that there are a lot of other names that belong there.

"These kids have done a hell of a job working with Calbert. Calbert has received the bulk of the publicity, and he has handled it really well.

"This was a very deserving honor for him. The next should be Player of the Year in the Big Ten … then Player of the Year in the country."

Everything came, from every source that picked one or the other.

"He has worked hard," Knight said. "He has rebounded, he has played defense, and he has scored. I think he played pretty well in all phases of the game tonight.

"It's a hell of a burden for a kid to be a scorer, to know that everybody is counting on him. We're telling him that: 'Calbert, you've got to move,

March 4, Assembly Hall
NORTHWESTERN 69

No.		Min	3FG	AFG	FT	R	A	BS	St	TO	PF	Pts
4 Neloms, f		26	2- 3	8-13	5- 5	5	2	0	0	4	4	23
44 Williams, f		17		2- 5	0- 0	2	0	2	1	1	2	4
55 Rankin, c		29		5-13	0- 0	3	2	0	0	4	3	10
23 Baldwin, g		33	0- 1	3- 6	2- 2	4	6	0	0	1	3	8
30 Kirkpatrick, g		31		4- 5	2- 2	3	4	0	2	0	4	10
3 Purdy		11	1- 2	1- 2	0- 0	1	3	0	0	1	1	3
40 Howell		9		2- 6	0- 0	1	0	0	0	0	1	4
24 Lee		19	0- 2	0- 5	0- 1	6	1	0	1	2	1	0
34 Rayford		14		2- 3	0- 2	1	0	0	0	0	2	4
22 Simpson		4		0- 0	0- 0	0	0	0	1	1	1	0
33 Yonke		5	1- 1	1- 2	0- 0	1	0	0	0	1	0	3
10 Ling		1		0- 0	0- 0	0	0	0	0	0	0	0
12 Kreamer		1		0- 0	0- 0	0	0	0	0	0	0	0
Team						1						
Totals			4- 9	28-60	9-12	28	18	2	5	15	22	69

INDIANA 98

No.		Min	3FG	AFG	FT	R	A	BS	St	TO	PF	Pts
40 Cheaney, f		34	3- 4	14-19	4- 6	6	1	2	1	3	3	35
33 P.Graham, f		23	0- 2	5- 9	1- 2	3	1	0	2	1	2	11
24 Nover, c		29		3- 4	2- 3	5	3	0	0	0	1	8
20 G.Graham, g		30	4- 6	5-10	5- 6	4	6	0	1	0	0	19
22 Bailey, g		29	1- 3	3- 6	2- 4	7	7	0	0	4	2	9
30 Leary		9	1- 3	2- 5	2- 2	0	0	0	0	0	1	7
21 Reynolds		20		2- 2	2- 5	1	4	0	2	0	1	6
34 Evans		18	0- 1	0- 2	1- 2	6	0	0	0	1	2	1
25 Knight		8		1- 1	0- 0	1	2	0	1	2	1	2
Team						4						
Totals			9-19	35-58	19-30	37	24	2	7	11	13	98

SCORE BY HALVES

				3FG	AFG	FT
Northwestern (7-17, 2-13)	35	34—	69	.444	.467	.750
Indiana (26-3, 15-1)	45	53—	98	.474	.603	.633

Officials—Ed Hightower, Tom O'Neill, Ted Valentine.
Attendance—16,704.

you've got to work, you've got to get open. We've got to have you scoring. We don't have you out there to set screens.'

"Boy, has he responded really well to the pressures of being the leading scorer.

"Steve's scoring was amazing because he was almost exclusively a jump shooter. That's why I make a little distinction between Steve and Calbert because of Calbert's total ability to score in any way possible.

"He had a hell of a slump this year. He was 5-for-26 at one time with 3s (going into the Iowa game). We were almost at a point where we weren't going to let him shoot it any more. Norm (Ellenberger) worked with him. From that point on, he has shot them pretty well – right around 50 percent, I would bet (from that second Iowa game through the end of the year, .538).

"So you've got to guard him. Then he's quick enough to get past you. He can play in the post. He does everything just better than anybody else does right now."

Knight also graded Cheaney top-rate in the area of leadership he thrust on him in his senior season.

"That was another great quality Alford had. He was a leader and a scorer. It would be a hell of a lot easier to be one or the other, but when you're both, it's a very, very tough thing to handle."

If anyone enjoyed the evening as much as Gwen Crawley, it was Chris Reynolds, Cheaney's biggest needler, and fan.

"It's been a privilege for all of us, playing with a great player like Calbert," Reynolds said after the hubbub.

"I've had people ask me, 'Who's the best guy you ever played against in the Big Ten?'

IU President Tom Ehrlich stands and cheers a decisive moment at Minnesota, with help from Dr. Dan Grossman, retired vice president Ed Williams, and (right) vice president Terry Clapacs.

CNN USA Today
MARCH 8

1. North Carolina (32)	848
2. Indiana (1)	805
3. Michigan	759
4. Kentucky	748
5. Arizona (1)	700
6. Vanderbilt	674
7. Kansas	650
8. Duke	599
9. Cincinnati	559
10. Seton Hall	546
17. Iowa	264
18. Purdue	176

To Calbert Cheaney, Steve Alford was 'a great scorer... Sorry, Steve.'

I start thinking about Ohio State and Michigan, who they have.

"We take Calbert for granted sometimes. *He's* the best basketball player I've ever played against.

"We his teammates forget that, because we watch him every day in practice. It's just unbelievable watching him score.

"He knows he's our scorer. We don't have to tell him that. During the guts of the game, he has to be the horse to carry us."

Reynolds laughed as he thought back to those freshman days when the whole Cheaney class was breaking in.

"We had lots of guys who were *Parade* All-Americans, McDonald's All-Americans," he said. "I never really heard of Calbert. I think *my* name was ahead of Calbert on the all-American lists in high school.

"During the fall, we play pickup games. Calbert just seemed to hit all of his shots. He was 6-6, 6-7 back then, and he was drilling 3-pointers. I had expected him to be an inside player.

"When the Big Ten started, we had lots of trouble. People tend to forget that, but we lost a lot of games in the Big Ten. But Calbert seemed to score 20 to 25 points a game. He was really the only scorer we had at the time. He stepped forward, and we all kinda rallied around him. We tried to pick and get him open, do all we could, because he was our guy.

"People think he just comes out and shoots 3-pointers and gets open, but he puts a lot of work in. He comes in and watches tapes. No one puts in as much time as Calbert Cheaney on our team. He deserves all the publicity he gets."

Cheaney said, sure, he knew from the crowd reaction when he passed each of the key milestones. "You've got to recognize that," he said of the elevated noise level. "It's a great feeling.

"When I came here as a freshman, I just wanted to contribute, play hard, play my heart out. I never had any type of aspirations to all this. It's surprising to me."

He said he had watched the Alford team on TV. "I really didn't watch them most of that '87 season until they got to the tournament. Alford was a great scorer. He worked very hard."

A wide grin, not really of guilt, crossed his face.

"Sorry, Steve."

Nolte, Friedkin bring Hollywood to Hall

Actor Nick Nolte, director Bill Friedkin and screen writer Ron Shelton have impressive screen credits – *Prince of Tides* and *Down and Out in Beverly Hills* on Nolte's long list, *The Exorcist* and *The French Connection* on Oscar winner Friedkin's, *Bull Durham* and *White Men Can't Jump* on Shelton's.

They're linked for the first time in *Blue Chips*, a Paramount Pictures film that went into production in May. When it comes out next fall, it will have a pronounced Hoosier look, including a feature role for Matt Nover and parts as well for Nover's fellow seniors on the 1992-93 Hoosiers: Calbert Cheaney, Greg Graham and Chris Reynolds. And film star Nolte, in all probability, is going to come out coaching a great deal like Bob Knight.

Nolte and Friedkin spent more than a week in Bloomington in March, sitting in on coaches' meetings and Knight's sessions with Hoosier players for games with Northwestern and Michigan State.

Going to IU was Friedkin's idea. He had met Knight a few years ago through mutual friend Red Auerbach of the Boston Celtics. At the time, Friedkin was attempting to put together a TV movie on the life of former Hoosier star Landon Turner, a project Friedkin says still could come to fruition.

In *Blue Chips*, Nolte is Western University coach Pete Bell, an aging coach who, Nolte said, "has won two national championships, been to the Final Four three times, won about eight conference championships, but the last couple of years he's been in tough shape . . . three losing seasons in a row . . . recruiting problems. That's how we open the picture – a very frustrated coach, with the most pressures we can possibly put a coach in."

Friedkin said "Winning at any cost has corrupted almost everything in his life. I don't believe Bobby Knight has that problem."

But, Knight was the pattern he and Nolte picked because, Friedkin said, "Right now the best basketball coach in the world is Bobby Knight. He really knows what he is doing."

Nolte moved in to see all that he could see in Knight mannerisms and coaching techniques. "It's just been a sheer pleasure," Nolte said in a press conference. "I'm learning every day. He's let us in on the whole process.

"He's been pretty specific about what you can do and what you can't do, like, 'Nick, come on in here for our meeting – just *you*, Nick,' or 'Nick, why don't you go sit over there for a while now.' "

"He hopes that we can get the damned film right. If we don't, I don't suppose we'll be back in Indiana.

"It's really fascinating. You're watching – I hope I'm not being too flamboyant with this – a man at the peak of this. He knows what he's doing in every place. He won't tell *you* every time. I'm trying to figure it out.

"We're not going to do Bobby Knight *per se*. Pete Newell, Red Auerbach, Bob Cousy – there's a bunch of them." But, Friedkin noted, Knight was the only coach Nolte spent extended time with. "Don't be surprised if Nick undertakes a great number of his characteristics."

Nick Nolte's research for his coaching role in Blue Chips *brought him to Bloomington and to Bob Knight.*

It's really fascinating. You're watching – I hope I'm not being too flamboyant with this – a man at the peak

CHAPTER 8

'Finest guard in America'

In the six league games that were left after Alan Henderson's injury, Greg Graham averaged 25.0 points a game.

Greg Graham, Michigan State coach Jud Heathcote said, 'made our guys look like they had their feet nailed to the floor.'

Minnesota coach Clem Haskins had the sound of a man who had come across a secret and had to tell somebody. He was preparing his team to meet Indiana for the second time this year, the eighth time he had gone against the Hoosier seniors. He had gone over Indiana game tapes, looking, looking. He saw, of course, Calbert Cheaney do some wondrous things and he pondered ways to keep them at a beatable minimum. And he looked some more and there was that secret that he hadn't heard anyone mention.

"Greg Graham," he said, starting and finishing the sentence right there while those tapes ran through his mind again.

"I think Greg Graham at this stage is the finest guard in America – as far as being productive on offense and defense.

"Am I wrong?"

There *was* an element of a Stealth bomber to Gregory Lawrence Graham, who – though few seemed to notice it – left Indiana as the author of more points (1,590) than all but seven players in the storied Hoosier history.

As a senior, he scored 577 points. Only nine players in Indiana's rich history scored more than that in a year, and all Indiana remembers them: Don Schlundt, Archie Dees, Jimmy Rayl, George McGinnis, Scott May, Mike Woodson, Steve Alford, Jay Edwards and Calbert Cheaney. Great scorers, each, known as scorers. Greg Graham stands 10th, ahead on that list – on both IU lists, career and one season – of other great and remembered scorers: new Hall of Famer Walt Bellamy, Tom Bolyard, Tom and Dick Van Arsdale, Steve Downing, Isiah Thomas, Ted Kitchel, Randy Wittman.

But Greg Graham was Lou Gehrig when Indiana had its Babe Ruth. He almost slipped through undetected by conferrers of honors until he did some things down the stretch of a championship season that were impossible to overlook.

Calbert Cheaney was the nation's Player of the Year. Purdue's Glenn Robinson was the Big Ten scoring champion. Greg Graham was better than both, better than anyone in the league, as a scorer during the six games that were left to make or break Indiana's season after Alan Henderson went down and out with a knee injury.

Greg Graham was having an outstanding senior year, averaging 14.2 points a game, when Henderson was out there as an inside target in the balanced inside-outside attack that was producing double-figure scoring from all five starting positions and winning games not every time out, but awfully close to it.

In the six league games that were left after Henderson's injury, Graham averaged 25.0 points a game. Cliches of the day talk non-descriptively of stepping up, of taking a game to another level. For description, consider those two Greg Graham averages: 14.2 before, 25.0 after.

Consider, too, that his career high in a collegiate game, prior to the Henderson injury, was 25. He had done it once, against Ohio State at Assembly Hall his junior year,

Matt Nover, once a 7-foot high jumper, gets just high enough for a rebound.

the one game that season when Henderson, flu-stricken, did not play and a step-up, a fill-in, another level was needed.

Graham finished the season as the first player ever to lead the Big Ten in both shooting and 3-point shooting. He wasn't far from a shooting triple, finishing third in free-throw shooting.

And Big Ten coaches voted him the league's *Defensive* Player of the Year, as well as first-team all-league. Suddenly, he seemed likely to go in the first round of the NBA draft. Indiana's Stealth bomber finally had made a blip on some meaningful screens.

Graham and fellow seniors Cheaney, Matt Nover and Chris Reynolds went into their final Assembly Hall game in a near-perfect way: already crowned as at least co-champion of the Big Ten, able on this last night before the home crowd to clinch an outright championship.

The opponent was Michigan State, which was 3-3 against Indiana during the seniors' years, the last league opponent with a chance to finish with an edge over the Hoosiers in that era.

Michigan State had a luckless year. The Spartans arrived in Bloomington 6-10 in the league and dead for NCAA tournament consideration. Their last four games had been losses – by three points, two points, three points, and in overtime, the overtime at Michigan when the Spartans had two point-blank shots blocked by Wolverine all-American Chris Webber in the final seconds of regulation time. The Spartans had lost three other league games by four or fewer points, and one more in overtime (to Iowa, in its first game back after the death of Chris Street).

There was nothing to agonize over for the Spartans in this one, which ended 99-68. Greg Graham, who had games of 22 and 23 points against Michigan State the year before, made very sure very early that Senior Night was going to be merry in Assembly Hall.

Both Michigan State and Indiana scored on four straight trips, opening the game. Indiana came out of that stretch up 11-8, because Graham sank 3s on three straight trips – three in 55 seconds that started him toward a career-best 23-point first half.

"After hitting your first shot, and then your second . . . you just go into a zone," Graham said. "It feels really good."

Maybe that wasn't the best first half a team ever played at Assembly Hall, but it's a contender. Indiana, in going up 56-30, shot .659 and didn't commit a turnover.

Graham went on from his 23-point half to match his 32-point Purdue game. Cheaney scored 17 points, Nover 15 and Reynolds six – a cumulative 70 points for the seniors, enough to win.

Heathcote called Graham's performance "outstanding. He made our guys look like they had their feet nailed to the floor. He is *extremely* quick.

"They played so well the first 10 minutes it was unreal."

In just over 10 minutes, the Hoosiers opened a 31-18 lead, and Graham already had 16 points. Indiana shot .684 over that period, .610 for the game. "Hey, they kicked our ass," Michigan State center Mike Peplowski said. "Let's not mince words."

The victory capped the sixth unbeaten home season for the Hoosiers in their 22 years at Assembly Hall. It extended the nation's longest home-court winning streak to 31 and improved the seniors' four-year record there to 51-6. The record IU streak there is 35, which spanned the only other set of consecutive unbeaten home seasons, 1974-75 and 1975-76.

It was the 19th Big Ten championship and 11th outright for Indiana, both league records. It was Knight's 11th, tying him with the late Ward "Piggy" Lambert (Purdue, 1917-45). Knight has had eight outright champions and three co-champions; Lambert's teams won six outright and shared five.

For the first time, the championship trophy was there to be presented when it was clinched. Big Ten Commissioner Jim Delany, who played on a Final Four team for Dean Smith at North Carolina, brought the trophy with him from Chicago and gave it to the four senior captains at the start of the postgame ceremony.

In the final minutes of the game, the seniors were pulled, one by one, to give them one last exiting ovation. They had been sitting for a while when one last substitute stood up to shed his warmup gear and go in. Nothing all night brought the crowd reaction that did, because the sub was Alan Henderson.

It was purely a cameo role, Knight seeking to reward a major contributor to the Big Ten championship by letting him go on court for at least the closing seconds of the clinching game.

It almost didn't happen. Henderson sat at the scorer's table as the seconds ticked down. With six seconds left, Pat Knight did the unthinkable – on any other night. Knight stopped the clock with what really was an intentional foul, and Henderson, his injured knee braced and protected, ran on court to one more booming ovation.

He lined up as a rebounder for the Spartan free throw, but Knight – the coach, father of the quick thinker – hurriedly altered that. Knight waved Henderson out of the action, all the way down to the Indiana end, far from any potential contact.

"I was trying to set him up for a 3-point shot," Knight fibbed.

Greg Graham left to a hug from Calbert Cheaney and a hand clasp from Alan Henderson.

March 10, Assembly Hall
MICHIGAN STATE 68

No.	Min	3FG	AFG	FT	R	A	BS	St	TO	PF	Pts
31 Stephens, f	29	0- 2	1- 5	0- 0	3	5	0	0	0	2	2
34 Miller, f	22		2- 5	0- 0	6	0	0	1	1	1	4
54 Peplowski, c	30		7-12	1- 2	13	1	1	0	4	3	15
13 Snow, g	18		3- 6	2- 2	0	2	0	1	2	5	8
24 Respert, g	32	0- 2	7-13	0- 0	3	0	0	0	4	2	14
3 Weshinskey	25	1- 2	5-11	2- 2	6	0	0	3	1	3	13
23 Beathea	7		1- 3	0- 0	0	0	0	0	0	0	2
40 Brooks	23		3- 6	2- 2	5	0	1	0	1	3	8
25 Zulauf	7		1- 3	0- 0	1	0	0	0	0	0	2
22 Nicodemus	4		0- 0	0- 1	1	2	0	1	0	1	0
4 Hart	3		0- 0	0- 0	0	0	0	0	0	0	0
Team					1						
Totals		1- 6	30-64	7- 9	35	16	2	3	15	18	68

INDIANA 99

No.	Min	3FG	AFG	FT	R	A	BS	St	TO	PF	Pts
40 Cheaney, f	34	1- 1	7-13	2- 2	4	4	1	0	2	0	17
34 Evans, f	14	0- 2	1- 3	0- 0	2	1	0	1	0	3	2
24 Nover, c	32		5- 6	5- 6	5	2	0	0	1	2	15
20 G.Graham, g	37	4- 6	11-16	6- 7	3	3	2	2	1	1	32
21 Reynolds, g	16		2- 2	2- 2	1	4	0	1	1	2	6
33 P.Graham	22	3- 5	4- 7	0- 0	2	3	0	0	0	2	11
22 Bailey	26	1- 3	2- 6	2- 2	4	3	1	0	1	1	7
30 Leary	12	1- 2	4- 5	0- 0	1	2	0	1	0	2	9
25 Knight	6		0- 1	0- 0	0	1	0	0	0	1	0
44 Henderson	1		0- 0	0- 0	0	0	0	0	0	0	0
Team					2						
Totals		10-19	36-59	17-19	24	23	4	5	6	14	99

SCORE BY HALVES			3FG	AFG	FT
Michigan State (14-12, 6-11)	30	38— 68	.167	.469	.778
Indiana (27-3, 16-1)	56	43— 99	.526	.610	.895

Officials—Jody Silvester, Gene Monje, Sam Lickliter.
Attendance—16,863.

Knight the Coach was also Knight the father to sophomore Pat, who rarely played more than a few minutes but made his dad proud with several of them.

In the Hoosiers' victory at Purdue, the early Indiana lead was starting to slide during a long field-goal drought late in the first half. The Hoosiers got the ball out to Knight on a break, but Purdue defenders got back. Knight took the ball toward the basket, then threw it almost directly behind him to Cheaney for a 3-point basket that stopped the Hoosier skid.

He also was involved in the Hoosier comeback during the last part of the first half at Minnesota, and in a similar stretch against Michigan. But for one play, the foul he made against Michigan State pleased his dad about as much as anything he did all year – because it was done to help teammate Henderson get in the game.

"We win the Michigan State game without Henderson," Knight the Coach said. "Yet, without Henderson playing in the first 12 games, we don't have a chance to win the championship. Here's a kid who has to sit and watch the other guys lock up the championship, without being involved in the game himself.

"So, I wanted to get Henderson in the game. And it's one of those rare times when a whistle isn't being blown. Pat is quick enough and smart enough to make that play. Henderson gets in the game, and people are able to recognize Henderson for his contributions to that team. I really liked that."

Calbert Cheaney's shirt, his smile, the scoreboard, and his fellow seniors tell a championship story on IU's Senior Night.

In a mid-season interview, Pat said he considered his decision to go to IU a good one. "Sure, it's been hard sometimes," he said. "I'm aware that I could've probably gone to a small Division I school and maybe played 30 minutes a game and scored in double figures.

"But I'd trade all of that for being with good friends and having a shot at being on an NCAA championship team."

Pat spent a year at New Hampton Prep School in New Hampshire after graduating at Bloomington North. That's when he made his final decision to take on the "Bobby's kid" jeers and play for his dad.

"My (New Hampton) coach, Mark Tilton, coached his son and talked to me about it," Pat said. "He let me know that, while it can be difficult, it can build the father-son relationship into something even closer and more special. Coach Al McGuire, who coached his son, Allie, basically said the same thing.

"This summer we're planning to go to Alaska together. I'm really looking forward to that."

Even so brief a role by Henderson cheered the Hoosiers, including the seniors who took their turns at the center-court microphone after the game in the 19th Senior Night program of the Knight years.

"I want to thank Alan for coming out and working real hard," Reynolds said. "The last couple of weeks, I've seen in Alan a lot of character and integrity. I'm thrilled to death he's walking. We picked him up off the ground.

"He's really been an inspiration. Alan has never had his head down. He's been working hard in the weight room. He's real optimistic and positive. He wants to get back out there as soon as he can. He's doing everything right now in order to do that."

Graham and Nover were the seniors' comedians.

Nover said, "I know it seems like I've been here since the Branch McCracken years. And I'd like to thank him for recruiting me." The late Coach McCracken, a Hall of Famer and two-time NCAA championship coach for whom the Assembly Hall court is named, coached his last IU team in 1965.

Graham had his own secret that he shared with the 16,000: "Some of you loyal IU fans may have thought on some occasions that you met Calbert Cheaney in the mall. I'm sorry to disappoint you. I've been called Calbert so many times, I learned to go along with it. For the sake of not disappointing you, I went ahead and signed Calbert's name a few times."

Knight gave the seniors his own tribute:

"I want to thank you… You have been four outstanding basketball players. You've been four tremendous people to have here at Indiana. You're four people who are going to graduate… who have represented basketball here at this university the way we expect it to be represented.

"You're four guys I'm very proud of. You're four guys I hope I'm going to be coaching for several weeks."

Dave Bliss, the New Mexico coach who was a Bob Knight assistant during the foundation years of the Knight program at Indiana, remembers Knight's ability to see ahead, plan ahead, and be right.

'I know it seems like I've been here since the Branch McCracken years. And I'd like to thank him for recruiting me.'

Matt Nover

The first year the Big Ten went to an 18-game double-round robin schedule, 1974-75, Indiana opened its league season at Michigan State. The Spartans' black players walked out of a team meeting and boycotted the game, which went on and Indiana – unbeaten at the time and about to become No. 1-ranked for the first time in the Knight era – was untested in a 107-55 victory. From there, the Hoosiers went to Michigan for the back half of a Saturday-Monday trip.

"Before the game at Michigan," Bliss recalls, "Bob told me, 'If we win this one, we'll go undefeated.'" There were 16 games to go after that, seven trips into unfriendly arenas. Indiana beat Michigan and went undefeated, an 18-0 trip around the league matched only by virtually the same club the next year, when it went all the way through season and NCAA tournament play without meeting a conqueror.

Only three times since then had a Big Ten champion gone even 16-2. Nobody thought in 18-0 or 17-1 terms. But, as early as five games into the schedule, the Michigan-Illinois-Purdue road trip behind it, the unthinkable had crossed Knight's mind: this team, in this year when so many felt the league was so strong, could go 18-0.

An overtime slip at Ohio State ended that possibility, but the Hoosiers went to Wisconsin for their final regular-season game with, for special motivation, only that reach for history – the chance to have the best league record in 17 years, to do what not even four NCAA championship teams had done in the intervening years.

Damon Bailey breaks upcourt in schedule-ending win at Wisconsin.

Knight had hoped the Hoosiers wouldn't be going into that final game under any sort of gun. The pressures of a long year had been ample preparation for the NCAA tournament. A chance to ease off, play for the sake of playing, a fling at 17-1, sounded pretty good as a tournament tuneup.

The NCAA Tournament Committee was winding up its session in Overland Park, Kan., when Indiana and Wisconsin took the floor at Madison – and when No. 1-ranked North Carolina began its Atlantic Coast Conference tournament championship game against Georgia Tech. A No. 1 seed for Indiana probably meant a first-round assignment to the Hoosier Dome, as had happened in 1987 when Indiana began its national championship drive there. Certainly, there were logistical advantages to getting a close-to-home start, and Knight wondered right up to game time if the Hoosiers really were playing for something, that No. 1 seeding, even though they surely had built a strong enough claim for it, win or lose on the final day.

Knight knew something about games played after championships had been clinched. His senior year at Ohio State, he recalled in Madison, the Buckeyes "came up here 12-0. We had won the Big Ten. Wisconsin beat us by 19 points, and put the ball in their trophy case. And that was a pretty good team." Not bad. Basketball Hall of Famers Jerry Lucas and John Havlicek were starters, Hall of Famer Fred Taylor was the coach, and Hall of Famer Knight was a front-line sub.

"I'll never forget," Knight's reminiscing went on. "The referee's name was George Ellis; he was an NFL official, too. He was from Akron, Ohio, and he had worked games I had played in high school. He came over to me with a minute and 24 seconds to go in the game and said, 'I think Taylor thinks the game is lost. He told me *you're* the captain.'

One defender down, Calbert Cheaney focuses in on a dunk.

New Wisconsin coach Stu Jackson, a Rick Pitino aide with Providence's 1987 Final Four team and Pitino's aide, then successor, with the New York Knicks, has hit a popular chord with Badger fans. Ancient Wisconsin Fieldhouse was sold out a few times, very early for the Indiana finale. And Jackson discovered that predecessor Steve Yoder had left him a few nuggets. Point guard Tracy Webster, quick and strong, led the Big Ten under Jackson in both assists and steals, and 6-6 sophomore Michael Finley became the No. 2 scorer in the league – just behind Purdue's Glenn Robinson, just ahead of Indiana's Calbert Cheaney, a very classy neighborhood.

Wisconsin, the 1941 NCAA champion, hasn't made it back to the tournament since 1947. Jackson seemed on the verge of delivering a breakthrough tourney invitation when the Badgers beat both Michigan State and Illinois to stand 14-9 overall and 7-7 in the league. Then games against Northwestern and Penn State, the league's bottom teams, got away, so Wisconsin played Indiana with no NCAA stars in its eyes and an NIT bid virtually sure – Jackson's link with the Knicks an obvious asset.

Wisconsin's Louis Ely (33) and Michael Finley make sure nothing comes easily for Calbert Cheaney.

Indiana came out loose, but ready. Guards Greg Graham and Damon Bailey beat the Badgers to their specialty and hit the game's first 3s in a 12-2 Hoosier breakout on the way to 36-21.

Graham was having his second huge first half of the week. His two free throws with 1:23 left in the half gave him 19 points and Indiana a 48-31 lead. It was 50-31 when Indiana ran the clock down for a final shot at the half. The Wisconsin student section began a countdown "5 . . . 4 . . . 3," about four seconds ahead of the clock – and it worked. From well out on the court, not really open, Graham jumped up just ahead of the countdown and sank a 3.

Truly, Graham knew right then, he had *everything* going for him in this blissful stretch of his life. He was confused by the crowd's chant because he couldn't see – and still he hit the shot.

"I got hit in the eye by Calbert as I was coming out (to use a screen)," Graham said. "I was wondering if I still had my contact lens in. I was thinking if I missed the shot, I had an excuse.

"I knew time was running down but all I heard was the crowd yelling. They did what they were supposed to do, and I reacted the way they wanted me to.

"Unfortunately for them, I hit the shot."

The 23-point first half against Michigan State had sent him into halftime feeling hot. The 22 this time was more sneaky. "I didn't realize it was that big," he said. "It didn't hit me till after the fact." They were the two biggest halves of the season by a Hoosier, Cheaney and all.

It would have taken some comeback for Wisconsin to overcome that Graham-supplied 22-point halftime margin, but the Badgers gave it a try. With seven minutes left, Finley's fourth basket of a 15-point second half and 23-point game cut the Indiana lead to 71-65. Damon Bailey's 3 helped Indiana edge out to 78-68, but another Finley basket put Wisconsin close again at 78-72 with 4:20 left.

Bailey tried one more 3. It missed, but the littlest man on the court, Chris Reynolds, blocked out on the side of the basket opposite the shooter, just as the textbooks say, and claimed the rebound, starting the Indiana offense over again. This time, the Hoosiers got the ball to Cheaney, who surprised the Badgers by going up for an apparent jump shot but passing instead to Matt Nover for what became a layup and 3-point play – "probably the biggest offensive play by far that we made in the second half," Knight said.

Right behind it, Graham just beat the 45-second clock with a slashing, jumping, twisting jump shot that became a 3-point play and an 84-72 lead. The final was 87-80, and Graham had 27 points.

"Greg has done a great job in the last five or six games," Knight said. "He has been very good offensively. He has taken the ball inside and scored outside. He has really helped in taking some of the offensive pressure away from Cheaney.

"Cheaney (22 points) made a couple of really good defensive plays. I think Bailey (13 points, and five assists) made more defensive plays and played better defensively in this game than perhaps in any game this year. And Nover (16 points and 10 rebounds) did a hell of a job."

W hile the Hoosiers were winging home on the day the tournament seedings and pairings were to be made, the ACC tournament ended: Georgia Tech 77, North Carolina 75.

No. 1 had fallen. No. 2 was Indiana.

The season ended as only four others in history had, with Indiana No. 1 in the land. The final Associated Press poll on Monday confirmed it, giving the Hoosiers permanent standing as No. 1 for the 1992-93 regular season.

That got an Assembly Hall banner for the 1974-75 Hoosiers, that and an unbeaten regular season, including 18-0 in the league. This one was 29-3 and 17-1.

And No. 1.

G reg Graham had heard the question so often he wished he had a better answer. How *did* he achieve such an instant improvement when Alan Henderson went out?

"It's not something I planned on doing," he said. "We knew everybody would have to step up their game a little bit, just for the lack of size we have without Alan. I really asserted myself and stepped up my level of play. When you do that, you hope the other players on the team will step up theirs.

"I'm really not a vocal player. I try to lead by example, and just hope some of the players follow. There comes a time when you have to assert yourself as a vocal leader, but with this team, you really don't have to say much. If they see you playing hard, they'll start playing hard."

Graham mentioned another factor: Henderson's usual replacement was a perimeter player (even the 6-8 Evans), rather than someone to play the role Henderson had inside. The result was "a different look with us. It's like we're playing with one inside player and four around.

"With the loss of Alan, there were some things that we were missing. But when you spread it out among all the players, we can make up for it. Like, Nover has been doing a great job of rebounding, and Calbert has, too. That makes up for Alan's part. As far as scoring, everybody has picked up some.

"Our inside play is really just Nover. Matt can be a great offensive player, but his job is mainly to rebound, screen and get everything off the backboard. He's not a go-to guy in the post. Alan is a scorer in the post, where Matt is a hard-nosed, physical player in

---

March 14, Wisconsin Fieldhouse, Madison

INDIANA 87

No.		Min	3FG	AFG	FT	R	A	BS	St	TO	PF	Pts
40	Cheaney, f	40	1- 3	9-15	3- 3	4	4	0	2	3	1	22
22	Bailey, f	30	2- 3	5- 9	1- 1	5	5	1	1	1	2	13
24	Nover, c	36		6- 7	4- 5	10	1	1	0	0	2	16
20	G.Graham, g	37	4- 6	10-16	3- 5	3	2	0	0	0	1	27
21	Reynolds, g	33		0- 3	3- 5	6	5	1	2	3	1	3
33	P.Graham	5	0- 1	0- 2	0- 0	0	0	0	0	2	2	0
34	Evans	8	0- 2	1- 3	0- 0	3	0	0	0	2	2	2
30	Leary	10		1- 3	0- 0	0	2	1	0	0	0	2
25	Knight	1		0- 0	2- 2	1	0	0	0	0	0	2
	Team					3						
	Totals		**7-15**	**32-58**	**16-21**	**35**	**19**	**4**	**5**	**9**	**11**	**87**

WISCONSIN 80

No.		Min	3FG	AFG	FT	R	A	BS	St	TO	PF	Pts
24	Finley, f	38	1- 6	9-21	4- 4	4	3	0	0	2	2	23
33	Ely, f	22		4- 6	1- 1	5	0	2	1	1	4	9
41	Harrell, c	16		0- 4	2- 2	1	0	0	0	0	1	2
11	Webster, g	38	3- 4	6-11	0- 0	3	9	0	1	1	3	15
15	Kilbride, g	31	6- 9	7-11	3- 3	4	2	0	0	2	2	23
4	Kelley	14		0- 1	0- 0	5	2	0	0	1	3	0
3	Johnson	9	0- 2	0- 2	0- 0	1	0	0	0	1	1	0
43	Petersen	20		3- 6	0- 2	1	0	1	1	0	3	6
10	Carl	2		0- 0	0- 0	0	0	0	0	0	0	0
22	McDuffie	1		0- 0	0- 0	0	0	0	0	1	0	0
52	Johnson	9	1- 1	1- 1	0- 0	0	0	2	0	0	1	2
	Team					6						
	Totals		**10-21**	**30-63**	**10-12**	**30**	**16**	**5**	**3**	**9**	**20**	**80**

SCORE BY HALVES				3FG	AFG	FT
Indiana (28-3, 17-1)	53	34—	87	.467	.552	.762
Wisconsin (14-13, 7-11)	31	49—	80	.476	.476	.833

Officials—Tom Rucker, Phil Bova, Eric Harmon.
Attendance—11,500.

Associated Press
FINAL, 1992-93 (MEDIA)

1.	Indiana (39)	1,580
2.	Kentucky (9)	1,518
3.	Michigan (9)	1,504
4.	North Carolina (7)	1,488
5.	Arizona	1,328
6.	Seton Hall (1)	1,325
7.	Cincinnati	1,193
8.	Vanderbilt	1,143
9.	Kansas	1,073
10.	Duke	1,052
11.	Florida State	895
12.	Arkansas	758
13.	Iowa	757
14.	Massachusetts	748
15.	Louisville	724
16.	Wake Forest	640
17.	New Orleans	464
18.	Georgia Tech	447
19.	Utah	425
20.	Western Kentucky	312
21.	New Mexico	306
22.	Purdue	218
23.	Oklahoma State	175
24.	New Mexico State	120
25.	UNLV	107

the post. We get it to him when we can, but basically the shots are going to come from the perimeter, and we have Matt and everybody else rebounding."

That does mean more 3s, Graham said. "But we try not to overlook what really got us there, and that's being patient and running our offense. We're always going to look inside before we take a 3, unless it's just something that's absolutely open. We're not going to say, 'We're going to jack up so many 3s.' Some teams live by the 3s. We utilize it within our offense."

Graham hit just seven 3s in his whole sophomore year, shooting .241 – well below The Knight Line for putting them up: .400. Graham stepped it up to 32-for-75 (.427) last year but kept working on it till he became not only his team's but his league's best. "I have *great* confidence in it now," he said. "It has really helped me out a lot. And hitting the shot outside really opens a lot inside for Matt and Calbert.

"My first two years, everybody played me for the drive. Now they have to respect the outside shot. I can shot-fake and drive, or if they back off, I can shoot the 3. It's just an added dimension to my game."

And, to Indiana's. The Hoosiers averaged 22 points a game on 3-point shots in the closing six-game stretch, compared to 15.8 before the Henderson injury. Graham was the main reason for the jump, hitting 18 of 29 tries over the stretch, .621.

Far more than his own hot streak, Graham was happy with the championship that was a result of the stretch run.

"It's great for us, because we had a lot of disappointing moments," he said. "I think back to last year when we had the chance to win it outright and just totally gave it away.

"This one is really important, because it's our first outright championship, without sharing it with anybody. It's really special. I think it's one we're going to remember for a long time."

Hall of Famer Al McGuire shares a CBS microphone with all-Big Ten Hoosiers Calbert Cheaney and Greg Graham.

A rocky introduction to Hall for rookies

Just as the departing Indiana seniors previewed their Hoosier careers with an Assembly Hall appearance for an AAU team in 1989, the new wave coming into IU played The Hall for the first time April 20. Californians Richard Mandeville, Monte Marcaccini and Rob Foster were there, plus Ohioan Robbie Eggers and Hoosier Steve Hart, who spent the year in prep school in New Hampshire.

Also present but unable to suit up because of NCAA limitations on all-star appearances was the sixth IU recruit, Sherron Wilkerson of state champion Jeffersonville.

It was far from a perfect night for the young Hoosiers. They lost to a team built around freshmen headed to other Big Ten schools, 118-102, completing a two-game sweep for the opponents. Illinois recruit Jerry Hester of Peoria was named his team's MVP for an 18-point performance, and Michigan State-bound guard Ray Weathers of Jackson, Mich., led both teams with 28 points.

Two nights earlier, the Indiana-hubbed team lost in overtime at Fort Wayne, 117-111.

It was a particularly rugged experience for Mandeville, a 7-foot center who hoped to have a more enjoyable time in his first Assembly Hall game. Just two weeks before, he had returned to the court for the first time since his high school career ended with a broken leg in February.

He had just two free throws and three rebounds after 25 minutes in the Assembly Hall game. "I just feel awkward," he said. "I'm used to just getting the ball and going.

"I was frustrated with myself. I just have to think positive and go on from here, and remind myself what I have to do. It just shows me I have to work my butt off all summer."

Steve Hart

Eggers, a 6-10 all-Ohio player from Cuyahoga Falls, had 14 points and eight rebounds – and a strep throat problem, but he was happy to play. "Definitely it's a thrill, just to get on the floor and play a game," he said. "That was exciting. I definitely have to work on the weights."

Hart was the Hoosiers' standout, with 27 points (2-for-4 on 3-pointers), three assists and three steals. His year of prep school has added some strength and maturity, he said. "I've only been playing basketball since the ninth grade. I really didn't have much basketball knowledge. The year in New Hampshire helped me a lot."

Wilkerson saw the difference. "I played against him a couple of times in high school. He's stronger, he's more mature, he has a scorer's mentality and a passer's mentality. In high school, he was good, but nowhere near how he is now."

Marcaccini was a crowd favorite with 14 points and a Pete Rose playing style. He arrived with a proper sense of reverence. "It's an honor to play on this floor – just stepping out onto this floor gives you chills," he said.

He realized Indiana people aren't used to seeing their favorites lose in The Hall. "I think there was some humbling going on out there tonight, which is probably a positive thing," he said. "You might be a superstar in high school, but here, at this level, you'd better be prepared to fight for anything you can get."

Foster had seven points, seven rebounds and four assists.

Wilkerson said he had an empty feeling on the sidelines. "I was telling myself, 'Don't you wish you were out there? How stupid can you be? The chance of a lifetime.' I've got four more years. I'm looking forward to it. I can't wait."

Robbie Eggers

CHAPTER 9

One step short

NCAA Tournament Committee members dealt out no surprises in pairings and seedings for the 1993 tournament. The top four teams in the final polls were the No. 1 seeds – Indiana, Kentucky, Michigan and North Carolina, the first time the Big Ten ever had two No. 1s and only the fourth time any conference did.

Indiana got its Indianapolis routing and headed to the Hoosier Dome on Thursday for a practice on the court where the Hoosiers and Wright State, tournament champion of the Mid-Continent Conference, were to meet at 10 p.m. Friday. Even the practice made some history. It was just a brief session for some shooting and light running, but that was enough to put more than 25,000 people in the stands. Dome manager Mike Fox, a Richmond native who was an Indiana basketball manager under Knight, calculated the turnout and gave it perspective: the walk-in, practice crowd was bigger than ever had seen a first- or second-round NCAA tournament *game* at any site other than the Indianapolis Dome.

Knight did nothing special to acknowledge the turnout for about the first half-hour on court. After the Hoosiers had shot at both ends of the court and run a few drills, loudly cheered for almost every move, Knight called them to center court and talked. The results tipped off what he said, essentially:

These people out here tonight are what you are playing for now. This is what Indiana basketball is all about. I want you to give them a little show.

Granted, it doesn't sound Knightlike, but that's what the Hoosiers left him and did: a series of flashy, athletic dunks, two of the best by Cheaney, always capable of such things but rarely showy.

Then Knight called the Hoosiers back together in center court and said: This is what we're going to do.

From a fringe spot in the huddle, Alan Henderson cocked an eye that said, "Am I hearing him right?" Some of the Hoosiers laughed. "We *all* thought he was kidding and kinda laughed it off," Matt Nover said. "He was serious about it.

"It turned out to be a real neat thing to do."

To accomplish "it," players fell to the floor, and Knight became a choreographer of strewn bodies. A couple here at the start, perpendicular; now three here, and . . .

Even from courtside, it quickly became clear what he was doing. And the fans in the most distant seats, high, high up, knew best of all. The stretched out bodies, outlined against the playing floor, were spelling out THANKS!

The exclamation point was Knight.

The Hoosiers left to the biggest tournament-practice roar in history.

Pat Graham and Alan Henderson hem in Xavier's Brian Grant in NCAA's second-round game at the Hoosier Dome.

To 25,000 on practice night at the Hoosier Dome, the Hoosiers said Thanks, with an exclamation point.

Greg Graham works around Wright State star Bill Edwards, while Damon Bailey, (in background) Wright State coach Ralph Underhill watch.

Wright State was in the tournament for the first time, representing the league that had sent another first-time entrant, Cleveland State, to the 1986 tournament. Indiana became that team's first-round victim. The Hoosiers' 1992 drive to the Final Four also began against a first-time Mid-Continent representative, Eastern Illinois.

The Hoosier seniors were battle-ready. Before going out to the court, Calbert Cheaney spoke up. "We got up at 6 o'clock in the morning in the summertime to lift weights. There were times we didn't like it – as a matter of fact, *every* morning we didn't like it. But we've worked very hard to get to this point, and we're going to see if we can go any farther. This is a big thing for us, our last go-round. We're going to try to make the most of it."

Wright State trailed only 15-13 when, 12 minutes before halftime, Cheaney drew his second foul and sat down. "That was a big point for us," Knight said. Nover made it big with four straight Hoosier field goals, sandwiched by scoring from Pat Graham, as Cheaney-less Indiana leaped ahead 36-17.

It was 45-29 at halftime. Wright State scored the first six points of the second half. Cheaney scored the next 13. "He was well rested," Knight quipped. Cheaney, by then already the recipient of the first of the 13 national Player of the Year awards he was to sweep, finished with 29 points in 21 minutes. Wright State guard Andy Holderman, a product of Manchester High School and ardent Indiana fan, called Cheaney "a great player. He deserves to be Player of the Year." Mike Nahar, a 7-foot center from the Netherlands, said, "We've played against Kentucky and Jamal Mashburn and some other real good players, but Cheaney is the best."

NCAA tournament, first round
March 19, Hoosier Dome, Indianapolis
WRIGHT STATE 54

No.	Min	3FG	AFG	FT	R	A	BS	St	TO	PF	Pts
32 Herriman, f	30	0-2	3-7	0-0	2	0	0	2	2	3	6
42 Edwards, f	33	1-4	6-23	5-6	8	1	0	1	3	4	18
52 Nahar, c	30		4-8	1-1	6	0	0	0	2	3	9
22 Woods, g	34	1-3	6-15	1-1	0	5	0	1	3	0	14
30 Holderman, g	24	0-4	0-4	0-0	2	0	0	2	0	2	0
23 Blair	1		0-0	0-0	0	0	0	0	0	0	0
24 O'Neal	5		0-2	0-0	2	0	0	0	1	2	0
25 McGuire	16	0-1	1-2	0-0	0	4	0	0	0	3	2
34 Willis	3	1-1	1-1	0-0	0	0	0	0	1	0	3
35 Ramey	5	0-1	0-4	0-0	0	0	0	0	0	0	0
40 Unverferth	11		0-0	0-0	3	1	0	1	1	1	0
43 Skeoch	5		1-2	0-0	3	0	0	0	1	0	2
44 Smith	3		0-1	0-0	0	1	0	0	0	0	0
Team					4						
Totals		3-16	22-69	7-8	30	12	0	7	14	18	54

INDIANA 97

No.	Min	3FG	AFG	FT	R	A	BS	St	TO	PF	Pts
40 Cheaney, f	21	1-3	12-17	4-6	8	0	0	1	1	2	29
22 Bailey, f	25	0-2	2-6	0-0	4	9	0	3	2	3	4
24 Nover, c	31		7-10	3-5	5	0	1	1	3	2	17
20 G.Graham, g	30	1-4	2-8	4-4	5	1	0	0	1	2	9
21 Reynolds, g	16		0-2	0-0	6	4	0	0	1	0	0
25 Knight	5		2-2	0-0	0	1	0	0	0	0	4
30 Leary	11	2-2	3-3	0-0	2	2	0	0	2	0	8
33 P.Graham	26	2-2	3-5	4-4	4	2	0	2	2	1	12
34 Evans	27	2-4	4-6	0-1	9	3	1	1	0	1	10
44 Henderson	8		2-6	0-0	3	0	0	0	1	0	4
Team					4						
Totals		8-17	37-65	15-20	50	22	2	8	13	11	97

SCORE BY HALVES			3FG	AFG	FT
Wright State (20-10)	29	25— 54	.188	.319	.875
Indiana (29-3)	45	52— 97	.471	.569	.750

Officials—J.C. Leimbach, Stanley Pate, Michael Smith.
Attendance—38,387.

Pat Graham, with 12 points, had his biggest point total since the first of his foot fractures, since he had scored 13 points March 16, 1991, at Louisville in a second-round victory over Florida State – two years, three nights and three operations ago.

Bailey scored just four points but had nine assists in "a pretty stingy place for assists," Knight said. "He did a good job of getting the ball for us where it had to go." Wright State coach Ralph Underhill cited the Bailey problem. "We knew we had to stop Bailey's penetration. He got in a seam a couple of times."

Wright State had its league's Player of the Year in 6-foot-8 Bill Edwards, who averaged 25.5 points a game and was predicted to be an NBA draft pick. Edwards scored 18 points.

Xavier, which had dominated Midwestern Collegiate Conference play until Jim Crews' Evansville team upset the Musketeers in the MCC tournament championship game, smacked New Orleans aside, 73-55, to qualify for a second-round matchup with Indiana.

Xavier's basketball history is long, but its modern identification is with its peppery, funny, splendid eighth-year coach, Pete Gillen, who joked that Custer had a better chance at the Little Big Horn than his team did against No. 1 Indiana in Indianapolis. No, no, he said, that didn't mean he was conceding in advance. "Custer just had a bad day. Another day, Custer might have had a chance. We have a chance."

The Muskies had a whole lot more than that. In 6-9 Aaron Williams and 6-8 Brian Grant, they had a big and skilled set of inside players who previewed the problems Indiana, without a functioning Henderson-Nover tandem, would have against Kansas.

Indiana led just 35-31 at halftime, and a Williams dunk with 5:41 left cut the Indiana lead to 59-58. Two free throws by Greg Graham and a Graham steal cashed in by Calbert Cheaney pushed the Muskies back, 63-58, and forced Gillen to call time out – his last.

The ball is a long stretch away for Calbert Cheaney.

Only once after that did Xavier get the basketball with the Indiana lead under four points – in catching range. At 66-64 with just over a minute left, Graham posted low and went up with a turn-around shot that bounced out, claimed by Williams.

Xavier set up its half-court offense. Michael Hawkins, who hit four 3-point baskets, tried to dribble behind a Grant screen and accidentally bounced the ball off Grant's foot. The ball glanced free. Chris Reynolds, inserted seconds before, was the opportunist on the spot.

"It really wasn't anything I did," Reynolds said. "I saw the ball loose and went and picked it up." Gillen called it "a big, big play, the big play of the game, no question."

Reynolds' instinct was to dash off on a break, but the discipline of four Knight years put on the brakes. "We just wanted to control the ball as long as we could and get a good

XAVIER 70

No.	Min	3FG	AFG	FT	R	A	BS	St	TO	PF	Pts
25 Hawkins, f	33	4- 8	6-12	0- 0	1	2	0	0	2	4	16
44 Williams, f	36		6-13	5- 8	10	2	1	2	1	4	17
33 Grant, c	36		5-13	1- 2	16	2	3	2	1	1	11
12 Gentry, g	29		1- 5	0- 0	5	2	0	0	0	5	2
22 Gladden, g	36	3- 9	6-16	3- 4	1	3	0	1	4	2	18
34 Walker	19		2- 4	0- 0	3	0	0	0	1	4	4
54 Sykes	7		0- 0	0- 0	0	0	0	0	0	1	0
21 Mack	2		0- 0	0- 0	0	0	0	0	0	1	0
50 Edwards	1		0- 0	0- 0	1	0	0	0	0	1	0
5 Poynter	1		1- 1	0- 0	0	0	0	0	0	0	2
Team					2						
Totals		7-17	27-64	9-14	39	11	4	5	9	23	70

INDIANA 73

No.	Min	3FG	AFG	FT	R	A	BS	St	TO	PF	Pts
40 Cheaney, f	39	0- 1	8-17	7- 9	8	1	2	0	2	1	23
34 Evans, f	15	0- 1	0- 2	0- 0	4	1	0	0	0	1	0
24 Nover, c	30		3- 5	0- 0	8	0	1	0	0	4	6
20 G.Graham, g	33	2- 3	7- 9	3- 3	2	3	2	2	4	3	19
22 Bailey, g	28	0- 2	2- 8	7-10	1	3	0	1	1	1	11
21 Reynolds	19		1- 3	0- 3	2	4	0	2	0	0	2
33 P.Graham	19	1- 1	4- 5	1- 1	2	2	0	0	0	2	10
44 Henderson	7		0- 2	0- 0	2	0	0	0	0	1	0
30 Leary	10	0- 2	1- 3	0- 0	0	0	0	0	0	0	2
Team					3						
Totals		3-10	26-54	18-26	32	14	5	5	7	13	73

SCORE BY HALVES			3FG	AFG	FT
Xavier (24-6)	31	39— 70	.412	.422	.643
Indiana (30-3)	35	38— 73	.300	.481	.692

Officials—Larry Lembo, Tom Lopes, Charlie Range.
Attendance—37,411.

shot," Reynolds said. Bailey was fouled with 51.6 seconds left, hit both free throws, and two more by Cheaney at 29.0 eased the situation more, 70-65.

It was 71-65 when Hawkins sank a 3 for Xavier. The ball went through with about 12 seconds left, but Xavier, with none left, couldn't make the obvious timeout call. The ball after passing through the net bounced to the floor, uncaught. It rolled near the free-throw line. Bailey, not poky but not rushing, trotted out to pick it up, then jogged to the out-of-bounds area. Not until he was there, in position to pass the ball in-bounds, did the five-second obligation to make a pass begin for him. Three or four seconds had spun off the clock by the time the official's count began, and Bailey coolly let the time run down some more before forcing a pass in that was knocked back out of bounds – now three seconds left, the clock stopped.

His second in-bounds pass was to Cheaney, who was fouled with 1.7 seconds left, and he hit the two free throws that clinched an ultimate 73-70 victory.

Bailey's leisurely pace in getting the basketball, burning off about nine seconds when the allotted norm is five, raised TV charges of home-court favoritism – officials, surrounded by 30,000 wearers of red in Indiana's second basketball home, accused of bending the rules.

"I guess some of the commentators felt that Damon should have sprinted out of bounds and thrown the ball to Xavier," Knight said. "What Bailey did was a very, very smart thing. If we don't go after the ball, the official can stop play. But when we pick up the ball we are absolutely entitled to take it out of bounds at a normal pace.

"Bailey did a great job of that. We were able to use up eight or nine seconds."

Bailey did know the rules. "I *wasn't* in any hurry," Bailey said. "We knew they had no way to stop the clock.

"It just so happened that the ball went out to the free-throw line. That was fortunate for us."

Also cited as evidence of Indiana-slanted officiating was a 23-13 differential in fouls. Gillen declined an invitation to comment.

"I'm tremendously proud of our team," Gillen said. "We played the No. 1 team in the United States, with the No. 1 player in the Unitd States, Calbert Cheaney, in their home state, in front of probably 30,000 of their fans. We played them to the wall and had a chance to win.

"They respond. Calbert Cheaney's an unbelievable player. Damon Bailey is much maligned; they expect him to be Sir Lancelot, but he makes a lot of big plays. Graham is a super player. They have a great coach. I think they're going to win it all."

The Dome was first used for the state high school basketball tournament in 1990, largely because Bedford North Lawrence had a player of enormous popularity and there was a chance he would have the Stars playing there – maybe even against reigning champion Lawrence North and its star, Eric Montross. Damon Bailey and BNL did make it to the Dome, filled the place, and won the tournament, with Bailey bringing his team from six points down in the last 2-1/2 minutes by scoring its last 11 points.

Bailey enjoyed his return, too. "It's a nice place to play," he said, "especially when there are 35,000 or 40,000 people there all rooting for you."

Sir Lancelot Bailey is not, nor has Indiana been all Camelot to the most popular, most storied player ever to come out of the Indiana high school program.

Bailey was a national name before he played his first high school game as a freshman at Bedford North Lawrence High. The previous summer, *Sports Illustrated* named him the national freshman of the year and ran an excerpt from *Season on the Brink* which included Bob Knight's trip to Shawswick Gym to see Bailey play as an eighth grader.

In four seasons under an intense spotlight at BNL, Bailey set a state scoring record with 3,134 points, and his team went 99-11, including the 1990 state championship. The winning has continued in his three Indiana years – 87-16, a three-year Big Ten record in wins for the Hoosiers, giving the Bailey senior group a shot at the four-year mark, too (108, by the Quinn Buckner-led Indiana class of '76). He is the 10th Hoosier to score his 1,000th career point before entering his senior year, and his 1,152-point total ranks seventh among those.

"Bailey I think has improved a great deal as an all-round basketball player," Knight said this year.

"He was a center in high school. It has been a tough adjustment for him to do everything that is required of him playing basically as a guard in our system. He has made some very good adjustments. He still has some way to go in terms of consistency of concentration and effort. That in the final analysis will determine what kind of player he eventually is."

No Hoosier, not even Player of the Year Calbert Cheaney, was the subject of more postgame questions than Bailey. Knight fielded one during the NCAA tournament, asking how he expected Bailey to play next year. Knight started to answer the question seriously ("If I could determine what the hell he's going to look like next year... "), then reached for a crystal drinking glass in front of him, peered into it as if it were a crystal ball and said:

"I see... I see Bailey... it's fading... it's coming back, coming back... yes... yes, I see Bailey... I see Bailey being *better*."

The questioner wasn't satisfied. "Do you see him being a better playmaker next year?"

Knight went back to the glass.

"There's something for me here... it says... 'What a bleepy question.'

"Wait!"

He picked up another glass:

"This glass likes the question. It sees Bailey being better . . . sees Bailey being a leader... sees Bailey getting... *lots* of 3-point shots... "

Bailey, who was selected during the spring to play for an NIT all-star team on a late-summer European swing, had a less-mystical view of the difficulty of the Hoosiers' tournament road, reacting with anything but apologies for the Hoosiers' 73-70 second-round scrape past Xavier.

"Don't think Indiana can't get beat because we're Indiana, or Duke can't get beat because they're Duke,"

Damon Bailey brings Xavier's Jamie Gladden from the skylights with a fake.

Bailey said. "A lot of teams *live* for the chance to beat an Indiana or a Duke – that's something we face all season long.

"You can watch all the film you want but you can't really know how scrappy and tough people are until you're out on the floor playing against them. Xavier had three 6-footers who were quick, tough guys. They play awful hard. Williams is very strong, big and a good jumper. We can't simulate that (Williams' shot-blocking ability) in practice very readily, with Alan hurt."

One more postscript. Gillen, like Minnesota coach Clem Haskins, is on the College Basketball Rules Committee. Another new rule voted in for next year stops the clock after every basket scored in the last minute. Call it the Damon Bailey Rule.

Indiana moved on to St. Louis, a sentimental journey for Knight and longtime Knight-watchers. The Hoosiers were returning in the 20th anniversary year of their first Final Four trip under Knight. In all, the Hoosiers were 5-1 there under Knight, including three when they won the little noted nor long remembered Conference Commissioners Assn. tournament in 1974.

Louisville's Clifford Rozier tries, but on this night Calbert Cheaney was unstoppable.

The regional originally was assigned to the Hoosier Dome, and creaky St. Louis Arena was down for first- and second-round games. Then they checked contracts at the Hoosier Dome and realized the state tournament was booked there on the NCAA's regional weekend. They requested and got a trade-down, so they could keep both the collegians and high schoolers. That, they marveled in St. Louis, describes basketball's grip on Indiana.

Louisville was the other winner coming out of the Hoosier Dome and heading for St. Louis, setting up an improbable first: the first NCAA tournament game ever between Indiana and Louisville.

Bob Knight and Denny Crum took over at their schools the same spring (1971), and each had his team in the NCAA field for the 17th time. Crum took six teams to the Final Four, Knight five. Each coached in his 50th tournament game at Indianapolis, Knight improving his record to 37-13 and Crum, to 35-16.

But with all that traffic, their paths never crossed.

They really had come close to colliding only once. In 1983, they were a game away from meeting in the final game of the Mideast Regional at Nashville, Tenn. Louisville won but Kentucky beat Indiana, and Louisville beat Kentucky in overtime to go on to Albuquerque and a high-flying semifinal loss to Houston.

Cheaney already had been declared the winner of most major national awards as the regional began. Any votes still out surely swung his way after a 32-point performance that led the Hoosiers through, 82-69.

Greg Graham scored 10 points in the first 6-1/2 minutes to get Indiana out front 18-16 in an unexpectedly offensive battle. "I thought we were going to score 160," Knight said. "But I thought Louisville was, too."

"We wanted to come out and really assert ourselves – step the tempo up," Graham said. "We know Louisville likes to run. We like to run also.

Matt Nover, Louisville's *Troy Smith go eye-to-eye before two of Nover's 15 points.*

We wanted to jump out on them and make a statement to them."

Crum got Graham's early message. "When the game started, he was in charge," Crum said. "His game early was really good. He's a heck of a player."

Indiana shot .739 for the half, but the Hoosiers led only 47-43 as they ran the clock down for a last shot. A charging foul against Chris Reynolds aborted the attempt, with 9.6 seconds left, but Brian Evans forced a Louisville turnover that gave the ball back to Indiana near midcourt with three seconds left.

It was just enough time for Bailey to take an in-bounds pass and fire a 3-point shot that sent Indiana to halftime up by seven.

"Bailey made a hell of a cut, and Evans hit him with a perfect pass," Knight said. "Obviously, that was big. It amounted to a five-point play. Evans made a hell of a play at midcourt to get the ball back."

Indiana was 17-for-23 that half, with Graham 6-for-7 in scoring 16 of his eventual 22 points. "That was an awesome display of shooting," Crum said. "It wasn't that we weren't *trying* to guard them. They had to hit a 3-pointer at the buzzer to be up seven. We were right in the game."

After missing just six shots the first half, the Hoosiers missed their first six opening the second. Louisville wasn't scoring, either. It was 62-59 with nine minutes left when, Crum said, "Calbert just took the game over."

Cheaney hit a 3, then from 67-62 hit three shots in 71 seconds for a sudden 73-62 Indiana lead that pushed Crum to a time out, only 5:25 left. "It seemed like every time down the floor he shot the ball," Crum said. "He didn't miss a shot when it counted."

Cheaney had sat out the last 5:39 of the first half because of an Indiana player rarity: a technical foul. Louisville star Dwayne Morton swept to the basket with a dunk in mind, and Cheaney met him there bent on a block. Cheaney got the block but was called for the foul, and suddenly the two stars stood with their faces an inch apart – in playground parlance "woofing."

Brace and all, Alan Henderson enjoys one taste of old times in going high and blocking Clifford Rozier's shot.

NCAA tournament, Midwest Regional semifinals
March 25, The Arena, St. Louis

LOUISVILLE 69

No.	Min	3FG	AFG	FT	R	A	BS	St	TO	PF	Pts
24 Smith, f	29		3- 4	2- 4	6	6	0	2	2	2	8
50 Morton, f	29	1- 4	4-14	3- 4	3	3	0	1	3	5	12
44 Rozier, c	34	0- 1	8-14	0- 0	10	2	0	0	2	2	16
10 LeGree, g	27	0- 2	1- 5	0- 0	3	4	0	1	2	3	2
23 Minor, g	36	5- 7	5- 8	0- 0	6	0	0	0	1	4	15
11 Brewer	26	2-10	4-16	3- 4	0	1	0	0	0	4	13
13 Webb	11		0- 0	0- 0	0	0	0	0	0	0	0
4 Rogers	5	0- 1	1- 2	1- 1	1	1	0	0	0	0	3
43 Hopgood	1		0- 0	0- 0	0	0	0	0	0	0	0
3 Kiser	1		0- 0	0- 0	0	0	0	0	0	0	0
5 Case	1		0- 0	0- 0	0	0	0	0	0	0	0
Team					1						
Totals		8-25	26-63	9-13	30	17	0	4	10	20	69

INDIANA 82

No.	Min	3FG	AFG	FT	R	A	BS	St	TO	PF	Pts
40 Cheaney, f	34	2- 3	10-12	10-12	8	4	1	1	2	2	32
34 Evans, f	16		0- 0	0- 1	3	4	0	1	1	1	0
24 Nover, c	40		7- 9	1- 1	8	1	0	0	2	2	15
20 G.Graham, g	35	1- 4	7-11	7- 7	1	3	1	3	3	2	22
22 Bailey, g	29	2- 4	2- 7	0- 0	1	2	0	0	1	1	6
33 P.Graham	19	1- 2	1- 3	0- 1	3	3	0	0	1	0	3
44 Henderson	11		0- 1	0- 0	3	1	1	1	1	0	0
30 Leary	10	1- 1	1- 2	0- 1	0	1	0	0	0	0	3
25 Knight	3		0- 0	0- 0	0	0	0	0	1	0	0
21 Reynolds	3		0- 0	1- 2	2	0	0	0	1	1	1
Team					1						
Totals		7-14	28-45	19-25	30	19	3	6	13	9	82

SCORE BY HALVES					3FG	AFG	FT
Louisville (22-9)			43	26— 69	.320	.413	.692
Indiana (31-3)			50	32— 82	.500	.622	.760

Technical fouls—Cheaney, Morton.
Officials—John Clougherty, Frank Scagliotta, Gerald Boudreaux.
Attendance—17,883.

Under the NCAA's anti-baiting rule, each was charged with a technical foul. That, with the previous call against Cheaney, gave him two personals on the same play. The Knight hook came out, though Cheaney had 14 points at the time and the Hoosiers obviously were in a point battle.

Cheaney had been part of a previous double-technical for a similar square-off with Brooks Taylor in the Illinois game at IU Feb. 17. It gave the soft-spoken Cheaney standing that no previous Knight era player had. He finished the season with more technical fouls (2) than his coach (1, against Western Michigan). "No!" Cheaney said when apprised of that. "I'd never in my life have imagined that.

"But I'll just say this: they must have worked. We won both games."

Both mellowed quickly. "It was just two young men expressing their emotions," Morton said.

"I was fouled. I was sorta hyper. It affected both of us. It sorta hyped me up a little bit. Calbert – maybe it made him a little mad. He came out and did a lot of good things."

Cheaney said, "We apologized after the game. It was the spirit of competition. You get emotional. It was just like playground ball."

What Cheaney did in the second half was like nothing most people in the arena had seen. Cheaney tried to describe how he felt when he was scoring in a dazzling array of ways – 15 points in just over five minutes, breaking the Hoosiers free of Louisville.

"You know in your mind you want the shot," Cheaney said. "Everything feels good – your release, your jump."

Your teammates…

"I got caught up watching him," Reynolds said. "It was unbelievable."

Bailey said, "We see that every day in practice. We expect Calbert to step up. We just try to get him the ball.

"Calbert's our all-American. He plays like an all-American every day, not just in games. When we see him working hard in practice, we know at game time he's going to be there for us."

During that special second-half stretch, Morton said, "I was thinking to myself, 'Somebody, *please* stop Calbert.'

"He was doing what he wanted to do. That's what great players do."

Greg Minor was the Cardinal assigned to Cheaney.

"Not many people get a chance to guard the No. 1 player in the nation," Minor said. "I felt fortunate."

There was more involved, of course, than just another Cheaney classic. "The Hoosiers look like every good Knight team always looks," Bob Ryan wrote in the Boston *Globe*. The aggressive, helping, man-to-man defense. The alert defense-to-offense transition. The kaleidoscopic motion offense. The seek-out-the-extra-pass offensive outlook. It could be the '76 team, the '81 team or the '87 team.

"Indiana has more left than just Calbert Cheaney. There is a guard named Greg Graham . . . Throw in the very underrated Matt Nover . . . and a platoon of solid players who have thoroughly digested The Game According to Knight. Indiana is proving that depth and a system can overcome just about anything, even the loss of a player like Alan Henderson."

In the Midwest Regional championship game, playing for a spot in the Final Four, Indiana ran into a team replicating the Hoosiers' 1992 turn-around. Kansas in the tournament bore no resemblance at all to the Kansas that staggered down the Big Eight stretch, just 6-5 after a 16-1 start that had them No. 1 in the land.

For the third time in three years, Kansas met and mastered Indiana – 83-77 this time, not drastically different from 74-69 when the same teams met in December at the Hoosier Dome, closer but no less definitive than 83-65 when a Jayhawk team bound for the '91 NCAA championship game punctuated a big season for Indiana at Charlotte.

At the Hoosier Dome, Indiana had led most of the way. Kansas did this time, using powerful big men Richard Scott, Eric Pauley and Greg Ostertag in two-man tandems that made the Hoosiers pay for running out of big bodies.

Alan Henderson played three minutes but ineffectively, his leg protected by the red brace and wrap that had given him stability but not the mobility and agility key to the real Alan Henderson's game. He had soared high to block a Clifford Rozier shot at one key point in the Hoosiers' victory over Louisville, but that became the only memorable moment for Henderson at St. Louis, an unsatisfying windup to a gallant try to beat the odds, and reality. He and his parents made the decision to delay the corrective surgery on his torn anterior cruciate ligament until he had completed semester work, including finals. He had the surgery in Indianapolis May 6, and days later launched into the

'Not many people get a chance to guard the No. 1 player in the nation. I felt fortunate.'

Louisville's Greg Minor

rehabilitation program that will determine how soon next fall he will be ready to be that real Alan Henderson again.

The Hoosiers had taken one last hit in the Louisville game. Brian Evans, at 6-8 a rebounding and defensive threat inside though more of a perimeter player on offense, felt his right thumb go numb after catching a Calbert Cheaney pass late in the Louisville game. Then, the pain began. Postgame x-rays showed a non-displaced hairline fracture.

Evans, left-handed, was fitted with a protective wrap, and he played – 27 minutes, 2-for-2 on 3-point shots with seven rebounds, a courageous effort on a day when every bump of the thumb stung.

He wasn't as effective at cutting off the high-low game the Kansas big men exploited from the opening minutes. Matt Nover could take one, but that Jayhawk – usually the 6-10 Pauley – would deploy just high enough to pull Nover out and look for the 6-7 Scott inside.

The guards who had been the difference in the first Kansas game had less spectacular days this time, though they did join the other starters in double figures (Walters with 21, Jordan 11, Scott's 16 leading the way).

Kansas led 38-34 at the half and widened it to 42-34 opening the second half. Then, Indiana made its rush. Cheaney's first basket of the second half tied the game, 46-46, and after Cheaney twice kept offensive rebounds alive, Bailey came out with one and put in a short jump shot for a 48-46 Indiana lead.

The Hoosiers were up 50-48 when Kansas capitalized on three straight Indiana turnovers for a 2-1/2-minute, 10-0 burst. Indiana got back within 76-73 on two baskets by Greg Graham. But, with 1:28 left and Indiana pressuring the Jayhawks, Walters broke open up the sidelines, took a deep pass, and dropped the ball off to Jordan for a layup that proved the backbreaker.

"We are a confident team, a poised team," Kansas coach Roy Williams said. "I think we maintained our poise when they were making that run at us.

"We did make a concentrated effort to get it inside, particularly early. Without Alan Henderson, who's just a great player – it's just a tragedy that he was hurt – we were stronger inside than they were."

Pauley also noted the absence of Henderson, "a big blow to them. They really only had one true inside guy, Matt Nover. I'd get the ball up high and look for Richard."

Scott said, "We just physically wore them down inside."

"Today," Knight said, "without any question Kansas was the better team. Their defense was exceptionally good, particularly on top. We had a tough time throughout the game getting into our offense, and that's the result of really good defensive play."

Cheaney declined to speculate on whether a healthy Henderson could have made the difference. "We'll never know," he said. "There's nothing we can say about that. The only way we could have known is if he were in there playing.

"Everybody's dream when you get into college basketball is to win a national championship. We came here with those aspirations. I take my hat off to Kansas. They played tougher than we did tonight. They just executed a lot better than we did."

NCAA tournament, Midwest Regional final
March 27, The Arena, St. Louis

KANSAS 83

No.	Min	3FG	AFG	FT	R	A	BS	St	TO	PF	Pts
32 Hancock, f	20		3- 4	6- 6	4	1	1	1	1	2	12
34 Scott, f	26		7-10	2- 4	2	0	0	0	2	1	16
51 Pauley, c	25		6-12	1- 1	4	3	2	1	3	2	13
23 Walters, g	29	1- 4	4- 8	3- 4	2	8	0	0	5	2	12
30 Jordan, g	37	2- 3	4- 7	1- 1	4	4	0	2	1	2	11
20 Woodberry	26	1- 2	2- 3	4- 4	2	4	0	3	2	4	9
33 Gurley	4		1- 1	0- 0	1	0	0	0	0	0	2
10 Rayford	3		1- 1	0- 0	0	2	0	1	0	0	2
00 Ostertag	15		3- 5	0- 0	6	0	2	0	0	1	6
12 Richey	14		0- 0	0- 0	2	1	0	0	1	1	0
21 Pearson	1	0- 1	0- 1	0- 0	0	0	0	0	0	1	0
Team					0						
Totals		**4-10**	**31-52**	**17-20**	**27**	**23**	**5**	**8**	**15**	**16**	**83**

INDIANA 77

No.	Min	3FG	AFG	FT	R	A	BS	St	TO	PF	Pts
40 Cheaney, f	40	0- 2	10-19	2- 2	9	1	0	0	1	3	22
33 P.Graham, f	11	0- 1	0- 3	0- 0	0	1	0	0	2	1	0
24 Nover, c	39		3- 5	3- 4	7	2	0	1	0	2	9
20 G.Graham, g	33	3- 4	8-14	4- 5	3	2	0	1	5	4	23
22 Bailey, g	27	0- 1	3- 7	1- 2	7	4	0	0	4	4	7
34 Evans	27	2- 2	4- 9	0- 0	7	1	0	3	1	3	10
30 Leary	12	0- 4	2- 7	2- 3	0	1	0	0	1	2	6
21 Reynolds	5	0- 1	0- 1	0- 0	0	1	0	0	1	1	0
44 Henderson	3		0- 1	0- 0	0	0	0	0	0	0	0
25 Knight	3		0- 0	0- 0	0	0	0	0	0	0	0
Team					3						
Totals		**5-15**	**30-66**	**12-16**	**36**	**13**	**0**	**5**	**15**	**20**	**77**

SCORE BY HALVES					3FG	AFG	FT
Kansas (29-6)			38	45— 83	.400	.596	.850
Indiana (31-4)			34	43— 77	.333	.455	.750

Officials—Dick Paparo, Bob Donato, Andre Pattillo.
Attendance—17,883.

Knight paid Kansas and Williams his highest tribute.

"Kansas was a very tough-minded team, a very deep team, with about 10 players who can play," he said.

"I really like and enjoy Roy Williams as a coach. I think he does a great job. I wish we could beat him some time. We haven't had any success with that in the three times that we've played against him...

"But they deserved to win the ballgame.

"We made some individual mistakes over the course of the game, we let some things happen in the post, and we didn't have the kind of patience we need. But that's what happens when you play against somebody that's good, that pressures you and that really comes out after you.

"I think the better team won the game. We don't like that, but that's the way it was."

He had even higher tributes for his own 31-4 team, especially for the seniors – Cheaney, Graham, Reynolds and Nover, at the end of a trail that had begun for the Cheaney class with that embarrassing first-day-of-practice scrimmage loss just 41 months before.

"The season was great for our kids," Knight said. "I'm incredibly pleased to have had a chance to have coached these seniors. It was a great thing to be able to have them here with us.

"I think they have left a real impression on Indiana basketball. They put a season together that we can really look back and try to get other teams to match.

"We really did about everything that was available to us in this season but get on to the next step. I'd give anything for these four seniors if I could have figured out a little better plan to get us there. We just weren't able to make it.

"But they were kids I think who won themselves or played themselves into a spot that really will be a great thing in the history of Indiana basketball."

On a rare open moment, Calbert Cheaney fires over Eric Pauley for two of his 22 against Kansas.

A state, a coach say goodbye

When Indiana's freshly crowned Big Ten champions ended their last practice at Assembly Hall before heading to Indianapolis to start their NCAA tournament quest, Bob Knight gathered them and talked very briefly, with one sharply focused theme: You're a very good basketball team. You know that. I know that. I'm proud of you. Let's see how far we can go with this.

As the Hoosiers, backs to Knight, left the court to shower and dress, Knight called out:

"I don't want this to be the last practice you ever have here."

More than one player instinctively shot a glance upward, or sideways, somewhere around their unique, enormous "classroom" in sudden realization that they really could be making this lockerroom walk for the last time.

It drove home the message of tournament fragility. It came back to Calbert Cheaney on the Monday afternoon after the loss to Kansas in St. Louis.

"I got done with class," Cheaney said, "and I thought, 'It's time to go to practice.'

"I honestly thought that.

"Then I realized, 'Wake up, Cal. It's over.' "

That was hard for a lot of Hoosiers to accept. Hundreds of thousands, apparently. That's the indication from TV viewership ratings which put Indiana basketball staggeringly high. Even more indicative than TV ratings is the extent of statewide devotion to the Hoosier basketball program. A major day in Indiana comes annually in late July or early August, when the official Indiana basketball schedule, complete with starting times and TV details, is released by the school and the Big Ten. Not just in Bloomington but also in communities reaching into each section of the state, Hoosiers routinely schedule governmental, professional, fraternal, business – even church – sessions around the nights when "IU's got a game." Not everybody watches, of course, but those who don't have learned they risk poor attendance, maybe even lack of a quorum, if they go ahead and schedule up against a Hoosier telecast.

It's a phenomenon that begins, without question, with Bob Knight. From the beginning, Knight's rigid discipline, his harsh Hoosier Schoolmaster demands for classroom attendance and academic production by his players, his unmatchable zest for winning all caught the attention and admiration of a state that always has been fierce and stubborn in its belief that its basketball is the best. Period.

At the start, there was suspicion of Knight. Here came a guy from Ohio, no less, who won his games out there at Army playing 52-50 games. Come *on*! That won't sell here. Not in Indiana.

Assembly Hall opened with the Knight era. Indiana christened it with three victories

The Indiana seniors' post-season state tour was a time of relaxation – sometimes in the bleachers – for Calbert Cheaney.

in five days, No. 3 over the first nationally renowned opponent: Kansas, a Final Four team and No. 4 in the polls the year before. The score was 59-56 and the attendance just 11,736. Game 4 blew away the stereotype of robotic, slow basketball, and stroked Hoosiers in their very sweetest spot. The score was Indiana 90, Kentucky 89 . . . double overtime, at Freedom Hall in Louisville . . . the kid coach, 30-year-old Bob Knight, against the curmudgeon who symbolized Kentucky basketball, Adolph Rupp . . . a heroic 47-point, 50-minute game for Steve Downing, on a bad knee . . . the stuff of legends, lasting legends.

The Hoosiers averaged 13,300 that year, a school record, of course. Their previous basketball home had a capacity of 9,200 and it rarely was reached. The team the year before Knight arrived had crowd-pleasing George McGinnis and averaged 8,500 in a 17-7 year. The year before that, closing out a period in which Indiana finished last in the Big Ten four out of five years, the attendance average was 4,500.

Knight's second Indiana team won the Big Ten championship and went to the Final Four. It averaged 14,031, No. 4 in the nation. From the next year on, for 20 straight years now, the basic home schedule has been a sellout.

But that first year . . .

A junior guard on Knight's first Indiana team was Cornelius "Bootsy" White, listed at 5-10 but probably closer to 5-8. Bootsy, from Hammond, was – still is – the only Knight player who didn't call him Coach. To Bootsy, Knight was Chief. "Gotcha, Chief."

The Hoosiers were in the process of reeling in league champion Minnesota at Assembly Hall in a game that wound up 61-42. Late in the game, the Hoosiers were operating at a super-slow, time-consuming pace, and the building was quiet enough that all the house could hear one exasperated fan of fast play scream:

"*Shoot* the ball, Bootsy."

White dribbled past the Indiana bench and, never taking his eyes from play, said out of the side of his mouth: "Don't worry, Chief, I don't hear 'em."

F rom that big Kentucky victory on, Knight had the state's attention. Then Hoosiers got to know him. *Boy*, ol' Bobby's got a temper. *Lord*, does he hate to lose. Did you see what he said the other day? He's not afraid of *any*-body.

And they got to know him as a man who loved to hunt and fish. A man who would answer personal letters. A man who would call or write or take the time to visit someone he had never met because he had heard somehow that he, or she, was in the hospital having a pretty tough time. A man who was mean-hard and kind-soft, all in one package. A Hoosier.

B.K., before Knight, Indiana had its sizable corps of rooters, but Purdue's was about as large, probably bigger and certainly noisier in the era of Rick Mount that had just ended. Notre Dame and Butler were statewide teams. Maybe biggest of all was the high school basketball tournament. In that big Hoosier basketball pie of interest, Indiana was just one slice. B.K.

The state tournament still is big. Purdue has maintained a consistency of success. Butler lost a state-loved figure when Tony Hinkle retired, and all basketball suffered a loss when Hinkle died last fall, at 92. Notre Dame's sphere of Indiana interest has shrunk, but the Irish have had great players and great moments over the Knight years.

That IU slice of the pie has spread wider and wider. In 1976, Knight's fifth Indiana team went undefeated. The watershed moment was when the first team Knight re-cruited and built capped college basketball's last undefeated season by winning his first national championship. The team returned from Philadelphia, in late-morning, on a Tuesday; a school day; a work day. Still, the crowd in the Indianapolis airport terminal was so huge space had to be wedged out for each Hoosier to get to the waiting team bus. With a police escort, the team bus wedged through massed fans to get to the highway. All the way down to Bloomington, people lined the road and waved from overpasses. And at Assembly Hall, thousands of students and townspeople waited.

The Indiana mystique had happened. Those impeccable, polite, unbeatable kids with INDIANA across their chest had shown the world where the best basketball *really* is played, Hoosiers felt. Bobby showed 'em.

That mystique has grown from there. And so, with that populace, has Knight – equal parts icon and iconoclast, each of those carrying special meaning to Hoosiers. They have loved him, shaken their heads over him at times, and most of all appreciated him for the common denominator between them and him: his and their basketball team that some years was better than in others but never changed in its essential makeup – good kids, who were in school to graduate, who played like hell.

Chris Reynolds drives for a layup on the seniors' tour.

The degree of fondness for those Indiana players never was shown better than in the days after the dreams of that vast following had died at St. Louis this year.

The four seniors on the team – Calbert Cheaney, Greg Graham, Matt Nover and Chris Reynolds – headed out on a seven-city swing lined up by the senior managers, a low-key farewell tour. None of the state's bigger towns was on it, except for Evansville and a night honoring Cheaney.

In Huntington, a town of 16,000 located 150 miles from the Bloomington campus, the evening newspaper, *The Herald-Press*, carried as its Tuesday, March 30, headline story spread across the top of Page 1: "I.U. seniors will play exhibition here." Pictures of the four ran with a story about the game to be played 15 days from then. The last two paragraphs concerned tickets – $7 for adults, $5 for children; "they can be purchased at the Huntington North Athletic Office beginning Thursday from 4 to 7 p.m."

The high school's athletic director, Joe Santa, arrived for work at 7 a.m. Thursday. Already, nine hours before the sale was to begin, 20 people were there, to start a ticket line. Santa had envisioned some people showing up that afternoon and the bulk of the sale probably coming the last three days before the game. The early arrivals showed him the first-day interest would be bigger than he expected.

By 8 a.m., it had built to the point where school administrators felt they had a decorum problem. "We had a school to run," Santa said. To get the would-be buyers out of the building till sale time, the old barber-shop approach was taken: take a numbered card and come back. By 9, seven hours early, about 70 cards had been issued. Selling started at 4, and 500 were there – not all from Huntington. People came in from communities 60 miles away, even over the state line in Ohio. "This is crazy," said a fan from Logansport, 52 miles away.

"The huge number of people took all involved by surprise," one of two Page 1 stories in the Friday *Herald-Press* said. "The last-minute details had to be decided on the fly, including number of tickets per person . . . " A limit of 20 per buyer was established. Teachers were given a hurry-up authorization to buy five before the sale began. Students could buy three.

In 45 minutes, 2,000 tickets were gone. At 6:24, the last available tickets in the 5,400-seat gym were sold. The buyers, Steve Ross and Jill Rogers of Huntington, had card No. 351. When No. 682 had been given out hours before, the card supply was gone but people kept coming, and lining up. It was not a happy mob that heard the news at 6:24 that they weren't going to get tickets.

Santa caught heavy flak. *The Herald-Press* came to his defense with an editorial:

"Hundreds of fans, many of whom waited hours in lines, went home disappointed – and mad. They vented their anger at Santa, the man in charge. Huntington County people take their basketball seriously . . .

"The fundamental miscalculation Joe Santa made was underestimating the drawing power of IU basketball. The 1992-93 edition of Bob Knight and the Boys is positively beloved everywhere in the state, with the possible exception of West Lafayette and its environs."

When the game was played, "everything just went great," Santa said. "The Indiana kids were super. The place was full. Everybody had a great time."

The seniors went on to big turnouts at Evansville, Richmond, Greencastle, Washington and Scottsburg. The windup game was planned at Bloomington North High. By then, additional games had been begged for and granted at Frankfort, Anderson and Chesterton, Nover's home town.

The Hoosiers won all the games – and all the crowds. They dunked with 360s, they made 3s from 10 to 15 feet behind the stripe, they sat on laps, they gave autographs and posed for pictures. They didn't spread the gospel, they demonstrated it.

At Washington, a town of 10,000 with a gym that seats 7,000, the place was almost full on a Sunday afternoon to see the Hoosiers against a team that included 7-foot Sascha Hupmann and guard Chaka Chandler from the strong Evansville program. On this day, everything clicked for the Hoosiers. At halftime, they led 74-44. The first half had been shortened to 15 minutes, by agreement. The second would go the usual 20. "Let's *really* turn it on," Reynolds suggested.

With 5:20 to go, the Hoosiers' point total was 151. Graham picked up a sideline microphone: "Does anyone here doubt that we can score 200?" His answer was laughter.

The final score was 203-97, and appropriately, the 3-point shot that nudged the Hoosiers over 200 was by Graham.

That day: Cheaney had 58 points, including ten 3s; Reynolds, who in his entire Hoosier career hit just four 3s and took only 19, hit eight 3s and matched Cheaney's 58 points; Graham hit twelve 3s and scored 43; Nover, 1-for-1 on 3s as a collegian (a late-game desperation shot against Duke in the 1991 NCAA Final Four), included six of them in a 37-point performance.

That's 196 points from the seniors. Jamal Meeks, who graduated a year ahead of them, scored the rest, including two 3s that gave the team 38 of those.

The tour "just reiterated that we've got the best fans in the country and the greatest support," Nover said. "We *knew* that, for four years, but, man, getting out to the different

In 45 minutes, 2,000 tickets were gone. At 6:24, the last available tickets in the 5,400-seat gym were sold.

cities and towns and seeing how people react to us was just amazing."

Reynolds said the seniors "knew we had great fan support, but I don't think it was until the second or third game that we realized there are so *many* IU fans out there. We just see the 17,000 at Assembly Hall, but there are so many people who just aren't able to go to games – for distance reasons, or they just can't get a ticket.

"It just meant so much to see all those people come out to see us play, even after we did not win the national championship.

"They still love us. That's awfully nice."

On its way to becoming a new Indiana tradition is Autograph Day, just after the season ends. It's an idea that had its roots in that long Knight walk home from the airport after the 1992 loss at Purdue. One decision, tentatively made earlier but firmed up with certainty that day of planning changes, was to scrub the annual basketball banquet. Since the day already had been set that year and Assembly Hall booked, and since a primary feature of past basketball banquets was a brief autograph opportunity for kids, the ultimate decision was to make the players available on that banquet date for two hours for anyone who wanted an autograph or picture.

A la the Huntington game, the signing session became a vastly bigger thing than anticipated. Assembly Hall's floor area was crammed with thousands of people, not just Bloomington kids for whom the late-afternoon scheduling hour was really planned but fans – young and adult, even senior – from throughout the state. It was at that session that a young couple from Zionsville put their young son and younger daughter on Damon Bailey's lap for a prized picture, and didn't mention till asked that the son's name was Damon, and the daughter's Bailey.

The second edition this year brought as many people out as the first did. It's an event that may have a Yogi Berra ending – Berra at least alleged to have said of a once-popular restaurant: "Nobody goes there anymore. It's too crowded." A two-hour time block is about all that can be asked of college kids who already have catching-up to do academically because of basketball travels. And, in two hours even at the frantic pace of an autograph every 10 seconds, which can't be maintained, a Calbert Cheaney could oblige only 720 people in two hours. A lot of people left, both times, feeling burned, because the estimate for each of the sessions was a turnout of at least 5,000.

A new Indiana team will start taking shape on Nov. 1, leading up to a new season's opening game at Butler on Saturday, Nov. 27.

The new one will include seven players with links to those two new banners that will go up – seniors Damon Bailey, Pat Graham and Todd Leary; juniors Alan Henderson and Pat Knight; sophomores Brian Evans and Todd Lindeman.

Neither they nor their coach will forget the four not

The Eastman Award was just one of 13 Player of the Year awards won by Calbert Cheaney, who swept every major post-season award.

coming back. Calbert Cheaney, Greg Graham, Chris Reynolds and Matt Nover go their separate directions taking away from Indiana, Nover said, "a lot more than just basketball . . . the things that we have been taught that will help us be successful in life. That's what I think we have learned more than anything: how to be successful, how to compete, how to go about things in a manner that shows professionalism and success. You see that in so many ex-players from IU, and you see it in Coach all the time.

"He's much more caring than a lot of people are aware of, much more of an understanding, a feeling person. People don't understand how much he cares about us, how much we mean to him."

Knight tried to let people know. In wrapping up the season on his television show the day after the Kansas game, Knight said:

"The greatest seasons are the ones where you win the national championship. And yet, as I look back on this season with the four seniors that we had – they've done some remarkable things.

"In the last three years, the 87 games that this group – and players before them such as Jamal Meeks, Eric Anderson and Lyndon Jones, and everybody on this year's team – won was an all-time high mark for a Big Ten team for a three-year period.

"These kids this year won 31 games, only the fourth time Indiana has won 30 games. They started out with a great win in the Pre-Season NIT. Then, for this team to go on and win the Big Ten as it did . . . only two teams have ever won more than 17 games in the Big Ten, and those were our two undefeated teams in 1975 and 1976. That's a great singular accomplishment.

"And this team wound up the season ranked No. 1 in the country. Obviously we would have wanted tremendously to go on and play in New Orleans, but that just wasn't to be.

"Matt Nover was an excellent player for us in his first three years, but this year – if Cheaney was the body and the soul of our team, Matt was the guts.

"Chris Reynolds hopes to go into law school.

"I think both Greg and Calbert will have careers in the NBA. Greg has matured and developed enormously as a player, and this has never been more in evidence than throughout the Big Ten season. Calbert's a great scorer . . . you've seen the tremendous number of moves, the variety of ways in which he can score, the critical baskets that he scored over the four years. But the pleasure in knowing Calbert Cheaney is in knowing him as a person. He's as good a kid as we've ever had, and that can be said of each of these four.

"We wrap up this chapter on a down note, but we put a season away where four seniors thrilled us all tremendously – with not only their play, but their demeanor, their presence, themselves."

Bob Knight, who knows his Big Ten history, touched on it several times in tribute primarily to his seniors but to all who were involved: the Hoosiers' last three years ranked with the best any Big Ten group ever put together.

Indiana won 87 games in that span, a league record. The Hoosiers' .852 Big Ten percentage was the best in a three-year period since 18-game scheduling began, third-best in the last 60-plus years.

Knight was involved with the only teams that had better marks: his 1974-76 Indiana teams that put back-to-back the only 18-0 league records in history, and the 1960-62 Ohio State teams on which he played.

BIG TEN'S 3-YEAR BESTS
SINCE NCAA TOURNAMENT (1939-1993)
Best of era (ranked by Big Ten percentage)

	Big Ten		All games		Ch	Co	FF	NC
1. Indiana, 1974-76	48- 2	.960	86- 6	.935	3	0	1	1
2. Ohio State, 1960-62	40- 2	.952	78- 6	.929	3	0	3	••0
3. Indiana, 1991-93	46- 8	.852	87-16	.845	1	1	1	0
4. Illinois, 1951-53	39- 7	.848	62-13	.827	2	0	2	0
5. Ohio State, 1944-46	30- 6	.833	45-17	.726	2	0	3	0
Iowa, 1954-56	35- 7	.833	56-17	.767	2	0	2	•0
Michigan, 1963-65	35- 7	.833	65-17	.793	2	1	2	•0
Purdue, 1969-71	35- 7	.833	59-18	.766	1	0	1	•0
9. Indiana, 1952-54	38- 8	.819	59-13	.819	2	0	1	1
10. Purdue, 1986-88	42-12	.778	76-19	.800	1	1	0	0

Overlapping years

	Big Ten		All games		Ch	Co	FF	NC
Ohio State, 1961-63	38- 4	.905	73- 7	.913	2	1	2	2•0
Indiana, 1973-75	41- 5	.891	76-12	.864	2	1	1	0
Ohio State, 1962-64	35- 7	.833	62-14	.816	1	2	1	•0

KEY: Ch, Big Ten championships; Co, co-championships; FF, Final Four trips; NC, national championship; •, NCAA tournament runnerup.

BEFORE NCAA TOURNAMENT
Best of era (ranked by Big Ten percentage)

	Big Ten		All games		Ch	Co
1. Wisconsin, 1912-14	35- 1	.978	44- 1	.978	3	0
2. Chicago, 1907-09	25- 3	.893	55- 4	.932	1	2
3. Purdue, 1928-30	29- 5	.853	41- 8	.837	1	1
4. Purdue, 1934-36	30- 6	.833	50-10	.833	1	2

Overlapping years

	Big Ten		All games		Ch	Co
Wisconsin, 1914-16	31- 5	.861	48- 5	.906	2	0
Chicago, 1908-10	28- 4	.875	42- 5	.894	2	1
Purdue, 1936-38	29- 7	.806	49-11	.817	1	1

CALBERT CHEANEY'S INDIANA CAREER

CAREER HIGHS

Points: 36, Seton Hall, 1992-93
Field goals: 14, Seton Hall, 1992-93
Northwestern, 1992-93
Steals: 4, Indiana State, 1991-92
Minnesota, 1992-93
Rebounds: 14, Coastal Carolina, 1990-91
Assists: 6, Northwestern, 1989-90
Notre Dame, 1992-93
3-point field goals: 5, Kentucky, 1992-93
Free throws: 14, Illinois, 1992-93

1989-90

Opponent	Min	3FG	AFG	FT	R	A	BS	St	TO	PF	Pts	Total
Miami (Ohio), h, W 77-66	24	0- 0	9- 11	2- 4	5	1	0	1	3	2	20	20
Kent State, h, W 79-68	36	0- 0	7- 10	4- 5	5	2	0	1	1	1	18	38
Kentucky, n, W 71-69	28	2- 3	5- 12	0- 0	4	2	0	0	2	4	12	50
Notre Dame, h, W 81-72	31	0- 0	8- 10	4- 5	3	1	0	1	2	2	20	70
South Alabama, h, W 96-67	32	0- 0	9- 15	2- 2	6	0	0	1	2	1	20	90
Long Beach St., h, W 92-75	36	0- 0	6- 10	4- 5	9	3	0	2	4	1	16	106
Texas-El Paso, a, W 69-66	22	0- 1	9- 13	4- 5	3	2	0	1	2	4	22	128
Iowa State, h, W 115-66	20	2- 3	6- 9	4- 4	6	0	0	0	0	2	18	146
Wichita State, n, W 75-54	29	1- 2	7- 15	2- 2	7	2	2	2	1	3	17	163
Texas A&M, n, W 94-66	32	1- 2	8- 11	4- 5	5	1	0	1	1	3	21	184
Ohio State, a, L 67-69	38	2- 2	8- 15	0- 0	3	0	0	2	4	2	18	202
Michigan, h, W 69-67	38	0- 0	7- 16	4- 7	5	0	2	0	2	1	18	220
Northwestern, a, W 77-63	39	1- 2	5- 10	1- 2	1	1	1	4	1	4	12	232
Purdue, h, L 79-81	•26	0- 0	3- 6	3- 4	1	2	1	1	1	5	9	241
Iowa, a, W 83-79	20	1- 3	3- 6	3- 5	2	1	0	0	1	4	10	251
Michigan State, h, L 57-75	32	1- 2	4- 8	0- 2	6	1	0	1	0	2	9	260
Minnesota, a, L 89-108	36	1- 3	10- 14	3- 3	6	3	0	0	3	4	24	284
Wisconsin, h, W 85-61	26	1- 2	7- 10	5- 7	6	1	0	1	2	4	20	304
Illinois, a, L 65-70	35	1- 2	6- 13	4- 4	6	4	0	1	2	4	17	321
Michigan, a, L 71-79	32	0- 0	5- 10	1- 1	4	3	1	0	1	4	11	332
Northwestern, h, W 98-75	26	0- 1	5- 7	5- 6	4	6	1	0	2	3	15	347
Iowa, h, W 118-71	16	1- 2	5- 8	0- 1	2	1	0	2	0	2	11	358
Purdue, a, L 49-72	31	1- 1	5- 8	1- 2	5	3	0	1	5	2	12	370
Michigan State, a, L 66-72	40	4- 6	12- 17	4- 4	5	1	0	0	2	3	32	402
Minnesota, h, L 70-75	40	2- 3	8- 17	0- 0	3	4	2	0	1	3	18	420
Wisconsin, a, W 70-68	40	0- 2	7- 13	1- 3	2	2	1	0	2	2	15	435
Ohio State, h, W 77-66	40	2- 2	9- 18	2- 2	7	1	2	0	2	0	22	457
Illinois, h, L 63-69	32	1- 7	8- 18	4- 4	4	0	2	0	1	3	21	478
California, n, L 63-65	39	0- 0	8- 18	1- 2	8	0	1	1	1	3	17	495
Totals	**926**	**25- 51**	**199-348**	**72- 96**	**133**	**48**	**16**	**24**	**51**	**78**	**495**	

1990-91

Opponent	Min	3FG	AFG	FT	R	A	BS	St	TO	PF	Pts	Total
Northeastern, n, W 100-78	25	2- 4	12- 18	0- 0	4	1	1	0	3	3	26	521
Santa Clara, n, W 73-69	28	1- 4	10- 20	2- 3	5	3	1	0	2	2	23	544
Syracuse, n, L 74-77	34	0- 6	5- 14	2- 3	4	4	0	0	2	4	12	556
Notre Dame, a, W 70-67	33	1- 3	6- 14	2- 2	5	1	0	1	1	5	15	571
Louisville, n, W 72-52	27	1- 2	9- 14	0- 1	6	0	0	0	3	4	19	590
Vanderbilt, a, W 84-73	29	2- 2	11- 13	6- 7	8	1	1	2	2	2	30	620
Niagara, h, W 101-64	17	2- 3	8- 11	1- 3	5	2	0	2	0	1	19	639
San Diego, h, W 91-64	33	1- 2	11- 18	2- 2	4	2	2	0	5	3	25	664
Western Mich., h, W 97-68	21	1- 1	7- 10	3- 4	2	3	0	2	2	2	18	682
Kentucky, h, W 87-84	29	1- 1	9- 17	4- 7	9	0	1	0	2	4	23	705
Iowa State, a, W 87-76	28	1- 3	11- 16	6- 7	5	3	1	1	1	3	29	734
Marshall, n, W 91-67	27	3- 5	12- 17	0- 1	5	0	1	2	2	3	27	761
Ohio, n, W 102-64	25	3- 5	8- 12	2- 3	3	1	0	1	1	2	21	782
Illinois, h, W 109-74	29	1- 3	13- 18	3- 3	3	2	0	1	3	1	30	812
Northwestern, h, W 99-58	17	1- 2	7- 10	0- 0	5	0	0	0	3	0	15	827
Purdue, a, W 65-62	29	2- 4	6- 13	0- 0	5	0	0	1	4	4	14	841
Iowa, a, W 99-79	29	2- 6	11- 19	6- 6	6	2	0	2	3	1	30	871
Ohio State, h, L 85-93	31	1- 4	10- 20	7- 7	4	0	0	1	1	4	28	899
Michigan, a, W 70-60	34	0- 0	7- 14	3- 4	12	2	1	1	6	0	17	916
Michigan State, h, W 97-63	23	0- 0	7- 11	3- 4	1	0	0	0	2	3	17	933
Wisconsin, h, W 73-57	25	0- 0	4- 5	6- 6	3	0	0	1	1	3	14	947
Minnesota, a, W 77-66	38	0- 0	6- 18	10- 10	5	0	0	0	3	3	22	969
Northwestern, a, W 105-74	30	0- 0	9- 16	3- 5	9	3	0	0	5	3	21	990
Purdue, h, W 81-63	39	1- 1	6- 13	5- 6	6	3	1	1	1	3	18	1018
Ohio State, a, L 95-97	••34	2- 2	10- 16	4- 4	2	2	0	0	1	5	26	1044
Iowa, h, L 79-80	•43	1- 3	9- 13	7- 13	3	1	1	1	2	4	26	1070
Michigan, h, W 112-79	29	1- 3	12- 17	5- 6	5	2	1	0	1	4	30	1100
Michigan State, a, W 62-56	38	1- 2	6- 11	5- 6	9	2	0	0	2	2	18	1118
Wisconsin, a, W 74-61	38	2- 3	10- 15	8- 8	4	1	0	1	3	4	30	1148
Minnesota, h, W 75-59	29	2- 5	7- 15	0- 0	7	0	0	0	1	3	16	1164
Illinois, a, W 70-58	25	1- 2	4- 12	2- 3	5	0	0	1	3	3	11	1175
Coastal Carolina, n, W 79-69	32	1- 2	7- 15	2- 2	14	2	0	1	2	2	17	1192
Florida State, n, W 82-60	37	2- 3	11- 14	0- 0	10	3	0	1	1	4	24	1216
Kansas, n, L 65-83	36	3- 6	8- 14	4- 5	6	1	1	1	0	4	23	1229
Totals	**1020**	**43- 91**	**289-485**	**113-141**	**188**	**47**	**13**	**24**	**77**	**97**	**734**	

1991-92

Opponent	Min	3FG	AFG	FT	R	A	BS	St	TO	PF	Pts	Total
UCLA, n, L 72-87	24	1- 1	2- 9	3- 3	2	4	0	0	5	4	8	1237
Butler, h, W 97-73	25	1- 3	9- 16	0- 0	5	4	0	0	0	4	19	1256
Notre Dame, h, W 78-46	30	2- 2	6- 14	5- 7	5	0	0	1	0	1	19	1275
Kentucky, n, L 74-76	37	0- 1	8- 15	0- 0	4	4	0	0	3	2	16	1291
Vanderbilt, h, W 88-51	8	1- 2	2- 3	0- 0	2	1	0	0	2	2	5	1296
Boston U., h, W 88-47	14	1- 3	3- 5	3- 4	6	1	0	0	0	1	10	1306
Central Mich., h, W 99-52	23	0- 1	7- 10	2- 3	6	2	2	3	3	1	16	1322
St. John's, a, W 82-77	22	3- 3	9- 12	4- 6	4	0	0	0	2	4	25	1347
Texas Tech, n, W 86-69	32	2- 5	9- 15	0- 0	1	2	1	2	1	2	20	1367
Indiana State, n, W 94-44	21	2- 5	2- 11	3- 4	4	1	1	4	2	2	9	1376
Cincinnati, a, W 81-60	30	1- 5	5- 14	6- 6	7	3	0	0	3	3	17	1393
Minnesota, h, W 96-50	25	1- 2	5- 8	4- 6	1	0	0	0	0	3	15	1408
Wisconsin, a, W 79-63	40	0- 3	6- 17	4- 5	9	2	0	2	3	3	16	1434
Ohio State, h, W 91-83	25	0- 0	6- 9	4- 4	6	0	0	1	2	4	16	1450
Northwestern, a, W 96-62	33	2- 3	10- 18	4- 8	7	1	1	3	1	0	26	1466
Michigan, h, W 89-74	39	0- 2	7- 13	8- 11	4	3	0	1	2	3	22	1488
Purdue, h, W 106-65	25	1- 1	10- 14	2- 2	6	0	0	1	3	2	23	1511
Michigan State, a, L 60-76	36	0- 2	8- 19	1- 1	3	0	0	2	1	1	17	1538
Illinois, a, W 76-65	36	0- 0	7- 10	9- 11	8	0	0	2	2	3	23	1561
Iowa, h, W 81-66	38	0- 2	7- 17	3- 4	13	0	0	1	4	2	17	1568
Minnesota, a, L 67-71	37	3- 5	9- 17	5- 6	8	2	0	1	4	5	26	1594
Northwestern, h, W 91-60	26	1- 4	6- 11	4- 4	2	1	0	0	0	0	17	1611
Michigan State, h, W 103-73	24	1- 1	6- 8	0- 0	4	1	0	1	5	2	13	1624
Ohio State, a, W 86-80	38	4- 4	11- 18	2- 2	6	2	0	0	1	3	28	1652
Illinois, h, W 76-70	32	1- 3	10- 19	0- 0	2	0	0	0	1	4	21	1673
Iowa, a, W 64-60	28	1- 4	13- 17	2- 3	2	2	0	3	1	4	29	1702
Michigan, a, L 60-68	32	0- 1	3- 13	4- 6	2	2	0	1	2	3	10	1712
Wisconsin, h, W 66-41	26	0- 3	1- 10	2- 2	2	2	1	3	0	0	4	1716
Purdue, a, L 59-61	40	0- 1	6- 10	8- 9	6	0	0	1	2	3	20	1736
Eastern Illinois, N, W 94-55	16	1- 1	5- 6	0- 0	1	1	0	1	1	3	11	1747
Louisiana State, n, W 89-79	38	1- 5	10- 18	9- 9	8	2	0	0	3	1	30	1777
Florida State, n, W 85-74	34	1- 3	6- 11	4- 4	11	4	0	1	0	2	17	1794
UCLA, n, W 106-79	29	0- 2	9- 15	5- 6	2	0	0	1	3	2	23	1817
Duke, n, L 78-81	28	1- 3	4- 13	2- 4	7	1	0	0	2	5	11	1828
Totals	**991**	**33- 86**	**227-435**	**112-140**	**166**	**48**	**6**	**36**	**64**	**84**	**599**	

1992-93

Opponent	Min	3FG	AFG	FT	R	A	BS	St	TO	PF	Pts	Total
Murray State, h, W 103-80	26	1- 3	5- 12	2- 2	5	2	0	0	3	1	13	1841
Tulane, h, W 102-92	26	1- 2	9- 14	2- 2	7	4	1	0	3	2	21	1862
Florida State, n, W 81-78	•42	1- 3	12- 22	9- 10	8	1	0	2	5	3	34	1896
Seton Hall, n, W 78-74	39	2- 4	14- 27	6- 10	4	3	0	1	3	2	36	1932
Kansas, n, L 69-74	35	2- 3	11- 19	2- 4	9	0	0	0	4	4	26	1958
Notre Dame, a, W 75-70	36	2- 4	6- 10	5- 8	3	6	0	2	4	3	19	1977
Austin Peay, h, W 107-61	20	3- 4	6- 11	1- 1	1	3	0	2	0	1	16	1993
Western Mich., h, W 97-58	28	2- 4	9- 14	2- 2	7	3	0	2	3	4	22	2015
Cincinnati, h, W 79-64	37	0- 3	6- 16	5- 6	10	4	0	1	1	1	17	2032
St. John's, h, W 105-80	27	1- 2	10- 15	2- 3	6	1	0	0	1	1	23	2055
Butler, n, W 90-48	24	1- 2	8- 14	0- 0	5	2	0	0	1	2	17	2072
Colorado, n, W 85-65	31	0- 5	9- 23	2- 2	5	2	0	1	2	2	20	2092
Kentucky, n, L 78-81	38	5- 6	12- 19	0- 0	8	5	0	0	4	3	29	2121
Iowa, h, W 75-67	29	1- 4	6- 13	1- 3	4	2	0	0	1	4	14	2135
Penn State, h, W 105-57	30	0- 5	7- 13	0- 0	7	4	0	0	1	2	14	2149
Michigan, a, W 76-75	39	1- 5	9- 19	1- 2	3	3	0	0	4	2	20	2169
Illinois, a, W 83-79	33	0- 2	8- 14	14- 16	2	1	0	1	4	3	30	2199
Purdue, a, W 74-65	39	2- 3	11- 15	9- 10	10	4	0	2	2	2	33	2232
Ohio State, h, W 96-69	31	1- 4	10- 22	6- 6	11	2	1	1	4	2	27	2259
Minnesota, h, W 61-57	39	0- 1	2- 9	7- 8	5	2	0	0	3	1	11	2270
Northwestern, a, W 93-71	32	0- 2	7- 15	8- 9	5	0	1	2	2	2	22	2292
Iowa, a, W 73-66	38	3- 3	12- 15	0- 0	9	3	0	2	2	2	27	2319
Penn State, a, W 88-84	••50	2- 5	11- 23	0- 0	8	3	0	0	4	2	24	2343
Michigan, h, W 93-92	36	1- 2	7- 17	5- 7	9	4	0	0	2	2	20	2363
Illinois, h, W 93-72	34	4- 5	10- 20	5- 7	9	0	0	3	1	3	29	2392
Purdue, h, W 93-78	25	1- 2	6- 8	1- 2	2	3	1	1	1	5	14	2406
Ohio State, a, L 77-81	•43	0- 1	5- 12	2- 2	9	0	0	1	3	0	12	2418
Minnesota, a, W 86-75	32	2- 3	5- 9	3- 4	5	2	0	4	3	3	15	2433
Northwestern, h, W 98-69	34	3- 4	14- 19	4- 6	6	1	2	1	3	3	35	2468
Michigan State, h, W 99-68	34	1- 1	7- 13	2- 2	4	4	1	0	2	0	17	2485
Wisconsin, a, W 87-80	40	1- 3	8- 15	3- 3	4	4	0	2	3	1	22	2507
Wright State, n, W 94-54	21	1- 3	12- 17	4- 6	8	0	0	1	1	2	29	2536
Xavier, n, W 73-70	39	0- 1	8- 17	7- 9	8	1	2	0	2	1	23	2559
Louisville, n, W 82-69	34	2- 3	10- 12	10- 12	8	4	1	1	2	2	32	2591
Kansas, n, L, 77-83	40	0- 2	10- 19	2- 2	9	1	0	0	1	3	22	2613
Totals	**1181**	**47-110**	**303-552**	**132-166**	**223**	**84**	**10**	**33**	**85**	**76**	**785**	

•Overtime

YEAR-BY-YEAR TOTALS

	G	S	Min	Hi	40	FG	Pct.	3FG	Pct.	FT	Pct.	Reb	RPG	Hi	A	Bl	St	TO	PF-FO	Pts	PPG	Hi
1992-93	35	35	1181	50	3	303- 552	.549	47-110	.427	132-166	.795	223	6.4	13	84	10	33	85	76- 1	785	22.4	36
1991-92	34	32	991	40	2	227- 435	.522	33- 86	.384	112-140	.800	166	4.9	13	48	6	36	64	84- 2	599	17.6	30
1990-91	34	34	1020	40	0	289- 485	.596	43- 91	.473	113-141	.801	188	5.5	14	47	13	24	77	97- 2	734	21.6	30
1989-90	29	29	928	40	4	199- 348	.572	25- 51	.490	72- 96	.750	133	4.6	9	48	16	24	51	78- 1	495	17.1	32
Career	**132**	**130**	**4120**	**50**	**9**	**1018-1820**	**.559**	**148-338**	**.438**	**429-543**	**.790**	**710**	**5.2**	**14**	**227**	**45**	**117**	**277**	**335- 6**	**2613**	**19.8**	**36**

1992-93 INDIANA BASKETBALL STATISTICS
Overall: Won 31, Lost 4

	G	S	M	Hi	40	FG	Pct.	3FG	Pct.	FT	Pct.	OR	DR	Reb	RPG	Hi	A	Bl	St	TO	PF-FO	Pts	PPG	Hi
Calbert Cheaney	35	35	1181	50	3	303-552	.549	47-110	.427	132-166	.795	75	148	223	6.4	11	84	10	33	85	76-1	785	22.4	36
Greg Graham	35	32	1116	42	1	180-327	.551	57-111	.514	160-194	.825	39	73	112	3.2	7	102	8	47	66	71-1	577	16.5	32
Matt Nover	35	35	1013	40	1	147-234	.628	0-0	.000	92-160	.575	72	135	207	5.9	10	26	24	11	69	88-3	386	11.0	29
Damon Bailey	35	24	932	45	0	117-255	.459	38-91	.418	83-114	.728	38	79	117	3.3	7	144	7	20	58	79-0	355	10.1	28
Alan Henderson	30	25	737	40	0	130-267	.487	1-6	.167	72-113	.637	90	153	243	8.1	19	27	43	35	45	74-1	333	11.1	28
Brian Evans	35	4	615	35	0	62-146	.425	23-65	.354	37-54	.685	32	106	138	3.9	9	46	5	18	27	50-0	184	5.3	20
Todd Leary	35	4	422	28	0	57-122	.467	22-57	.386	32-36	.889	5	29	34	1.0	3	43	1	12	23	30-0	168	4.8	14
Chris Reynolds	35	13	640	36	0	35-64	.547	0-2	.000	43-71	.606	12	57	69	2.0	6	102	1	29	39	55-1	113	3.2	16
Pat Graham	13	3	205	27	0	31-61	.508	9-21	.429	13-18	.722	2	15	17	1.3	4	18	0	7	15	16-0	84	6.5	14
Pat Knight	32	0	196	23	0	14-30	.467	0-0	.000	4-9	.444	1	16	17	0.5	4	27	0	3	17	10-0	32	1.0	6
Malcolm Sims	8	0	41	15	0	0-4	.000	0-0	.000	11-12	.917	0	3	3	0.4	2	1	0	3	6	8-0	11	1.4	4
Indiana	35		1076-2062			.522		197-464	.425	679-947	.717	366	814	1282	36.6	52	620	99	218	450	557-7	3028	86.5	107
Opponents	35		851-2176			.437		192-533	.360	412-588	.701	382	680	1178	33.7	56	468	89	198	541	783-37	2506	71.6	92

Big Ten: Won 17, Lost 1

	G	S	M	Hi	40	FG	Pct.	3FG	Pct.	FT	Pct.	OR	DR	Reb	RPG	Hi	A	Bl	St	TO	PF-FO	Pts	PPG	Hi
Calbert Cheaney	18	18	638	50	2	146-271	.539	23-56	.411	71-87	.816	35	77	112	6.2	11	42	6	20	45	39-1	386	21.4	35
Greg Graham	18	16	601	42	1	101-172	.587	38-71	.535	92-110	.836	19	32	51	2.8	5	55	4	27	25	32-0	332	18.4	32
Damon Bailey	18	13	509	45	0	61-135	.452	24-54	.445	56-74	.757	21	42	63	3.5	7	75	2	10	33	39-0	202	11.2	28
Alan Henderson	13	12	331	36	0	55-123	.447	0-3	.000	28-42	.667	35	51	86	6.6	17	6	18	16	17	33-1	138	10.6	22
Matt Nover	18	18	540	40	1	65-104	.625	0-0	.000	40-66	.606	40	65	105	5.8	10	11	12	3	38	49-3	170	9.4	20
Brian Evans	18	2	343	35	0	42-96	.438	15-44	.341	24-38	.632	15	58	73	4.1	8	27	3	9	15	34-0	123	6.8	20
Todd Leary	18	2	247	28	0	34-72	.472	14-32	.438	21-21	1.000	1	20	21	1.2	3	31	1	9	5	20-0	103	5.7	12
Chris Reynolds	18	7	297	36	0	14-27	.519	0-0	.000	16-25	.640	6	25	31	1.7	6	46	1	13	16	29-1	44	2.4	8
Pat Graham	6	2	87	27	0	15-30	.500	4-10	.400	1-3	.333	0	7	7	1.2	3	7	0	2	6	10-0	35	5.8	11
Pat Knight	17	0	82	23	0	7-14	.500	0-0	.000	3-6	.500	0	6	6	0.4	2	12	0	2	7	5-0	17	1.0	4
Indiana	18		540-1044			.517		118-270	.437	352-472	.746	172	383	604	33.6	44	312	47	111	207	290-6	1550	86.1	105
Opponents	18		497-1075			.462		85-230	.370	226-316	.715	183	358	595	33.1	39	255	54	95	265	398-17	1305	72.5	92

NCAA Tournament: Won 3, Lost 1

	G	S	M	Hi	40	FG	Pct.	3FG	Pct.	FT	Pct.	OR	DR	Reb	RPG	Hi	A	Bl	St	TO	PF-FO	Pts	PPG	Hi
Calbert Cheaney	4	4	134	40	1	40-65	.615	3-9	.333	23-29	.793	10	23	33	8.3	9	7	3	2	6	8-0	106	26.5	32
Greg Graham	4	4	131	35	0	24-42	.571	7-15	.467	18-19	.947	6	5	11	2.8	5	9	3	6	13	11-0	73	18.3	23
Matt Nover	4	4	140	40	1	20-29	.690	0-0	.000	7-10	.700	6	22	28	7.0	8	3	2	2	5	10-0	47	11.8	17
Damon Bailey	4	4	109	29	0	9-28	.321	2-9	.222	8-12	.667	5	8	13	3.3	7	18	0	4	8	9-0	28	7.0	11
Pat Graham	4	1	75	26	0	8-16	.500	5-8	.833	5-6	.833	2	7	9	4.5	4	8	0	2	5	4-0	25	6.3	12
Brian Evans	4	2	85	27	0	8-17	.471	4-7	.571	0-2	.000	6	17	23	5.8	9	9	1	5	2	6-0	20	5.0	13
Todd Leary	4	0	43	12	0	7-15	.467	3-9	.333	2-4	.500	0	2	2	0.5	2	4	0	0	3	2-0	19	4.8	8
Alan Henderson	4	0	29	11	0	2-10	.200	0-0	.000	0-0	.000	6	2	8	2.0	3	1	1	1	2	1-0	4	1.0	4
Pat Knight	3	0	11	5	0	2-2	1.000	0-0	.000	0-0	.000	0	0	0	0.0	1	0	0	1	0	0-0	4	1.3	4
Chris Reynolds	4	1	43	19	0	1-6	.167	0-1	.000	1-5	.200	1	9	10	2.5	6	9	0	2	3	2-0	3	0.8	2
Indiana	4		121-230			.526		23-56	.411	64-87	.736	42	95	148	37.0	50	68	10	24	48	53-0	329	82.3	97
Opponents	4		106-248			.427		22-68	.324	42-55	.764	42	77	126	31.5	39	63	9	24	48	77-2	276	69.0	83

IU'S 1,000-POINT CLUB

	Fr.	So.	Jr.	Sr.	Total
1. Calbert Cheaney, 1990-93	495	734	599	785	**2,613**
2. Steve Alford, 1984-87	479	580	630	749	**2,438**
3. Don Schlundt, 1952-55	376	661	583	572	**2,192**
4. Mike Woodson, 1977-80	500	577	714	270	**2,061**
5. Kent Benson, 1974-77	250	480	554	456	**1,740**
6. Eric Anderson, 1989-92	404	473	466	372	**1,715**
7. Scott May, 1974-76		351	491	751	**1,593**
8. Greg Graham, 1990-93	281	296	436	577	**1,590**
9. Randy Wittman, 1979-83	241	392	347	569	**1,549**
10. Archie Dees, 1956-58		383	550	613	**1,546**
11. Walt Bellamy, 1959-61		382	537	522	**1,441**
12. Ray Tolbert, 1978-81	292	407	300	428	**1,427**
13. Jimmy Rayl, 1961-63		79	714	608	**1,401**
14. Uwe Blab, 1982-85	179	283	366	529	**1,357**
15. Ted Kitchel, 1979-83	39	314	568	415	**1,336**
16. Tom Bolyard, 1961-63		371	447	481	**1,299**
17. Joby Wright, 1969-72		352	422	498	**1,272**
18. Steve Green, 1973-75		282	467	516	**1,265**
19. Tom VanArsdale, 1963-65		299	512	441	**1,252**
20. Dick VanArsdale, 1963-65		292	535	413	**1,240**
21. Steve Downing, 1971-73		220	437	563	**1,220**
22. Quinn Buckner, 1973-76	301	229	379	286	**1,195**
23. Damon Bailey, 1991-	375	422	355		**1,152**
24. Vern Payne, 1966-68		340	407	354	**1,101**
25. Joe Cooke, 1968-70		308	523	268	**1,099**
26. Bob Leonard, 1952-54		319	424	355	**1,098**
27. Daryl Thomas, 1984-87	69	115	377	534	**1,095**
28. Rick Calloway, 1986-88	403	364	306		**1,073**
29. Jay Edwards, 1988-89	358	680			**1,038**
30. Butch Joyner, 1966-68		298	481	251	**1,030**

INDIANA'S TOP TANDEMS

1. Calbert Cheaney-Greg Graham, 1993	1,362
2. Scott May-Kent Benson, 1976	1,305
3. Steve Alford-Daryl Thomas, 1981	1,303
4. Calbert Cheaney-Eric Anderson, 1990	1,200
5. Jimmy Rayl-Tom Bolyard, 1962●	1,161
6. George McGinnis-Joby Wright, 1971	1,141
7. Mike Woodson-Ray Tolbert, 1979	1,121
8. Jay Edwards-Joe Hillman, 1989	1,110
9. Steve Alford-Uwe Blab, 1985	1,109
10. Jimmy Rayl-Tom Bolyard, 1963	1,089
11. Don Schlundt-Bob Leonard, 1953	1,085
12. Dick-Tom Van Arsdale, 1964	1,047
13. Calbert Cheaney-Greg Graham, 1992	1,035
14. Mike Woodson-Wayne Radford, 1978	1,030
15. Steve Green-Scott May, 1975	1,007
Steve Alford-Daryl Thomas, 1986	1,007

●Best combined points per game, 48.4

BIG TEN LEADERS

	Points
1. Calbert Cheaney, Indiana, 1990-93	2,613
2. Glen Rice, Michigan, 1986-89	2,442
3. Mike McGee, Michigan, 1978-81	2,439
4. Steve Alford, Indiana, 1984-87	2,438
5. Rick Mount, Purdue, 1968-70	2,323
6. Steve Smith, Michigan State, 1988-91	2,263
7. Gary Grant, Michigan, 1985-88	2,222
8. Don Schlundt, Indiana, 1952-55	2,192
9. Joe Barry Carroll, Purdue, 1977-80	2,175
10. Cazzie Russell, Michigan, 1964-66	2,164

IU LEADERS

FRESHMAN YEAR
1. Mike Woodson, 1977	500
2. Calbert Cheaney, 1990	495
3. Steve Alford, 1984	479
4. Eric Anderson, 1989	404
5. Rick Calloway, 1986	403

SOPHOMORE YEAR
1. Calbert Cheaney, 1990	734
2. George McGinnis, 1971	719
3. Jay Edwards, 1989	680
4. Don Schlundt, 1953	661
5. Steve Alford, 1985	580

FIRST TWO YEARS
Freshman-Sophomore
1. Calbert Cheaney, 1989-90	1,229
2. Mike Woodson, 1977-78	1,077
3. Steve Alford, 1984-85	1,059
4. Don Schlundt, 1952-53	1,038
Jay Edwards, 1988-89	1,038

Ineligible as freshman
1. Archie Dees, 1956-57	933
2. Walt Bellamy, 1959-60	919
3. Scott May, 1974-75	842
4. Joe Cooke, 1968-69	831
5. Dick Van Arsdale, 1963-64	827
6. Tom Bolyard, 1961-62	818
5. Tom Van Arsdale, 1963-64	811

JUNIOR YEAR
1. Jimmy Rayl, 1962	714
Mike Woodson, 1979	714
3. Steve Alford, 1986	630
4. Calbert Cheaney, 1992	599
5. Don Schlundt, 1954	583

FIRST THREE YEARS
Freshman-Junior
1. Calbert Cheaney, 1990-91	1,828
2. Mike Woodson, 1977-79	1,791
3. Steve Alford, 1984-86	1,689
4. Don Schlundt, 1952-54	1,621
5. Eric Anderson, 1989-91	1,343